The ILLUSTRATED *History of*
BRITISH COLUMBIA

TERRY REKSTEN

The ILLUSTRATED *History of* BRITISH COLUMBIA

Douglas & McIntyre

VANCOUVER / TORONTO

Douglas & McIntyre
2323 Quebec Street, Suite 201
Vancouver, British Columbia
V5T 4S7

National Library of Canada Cataloguing in Publication Data
Reksten, Terry, 1942-
      The illustrated history of British Columbia
      Includes bibliographical references and index.
      ISBN 1-55054-859-x
1. British Columbia—History. 2. British Columbia—History—Pictorial
works. I. Title.
FC3811.R45 2001   971.1   C2001-910497-9
F1088.R45 2001

Editing by Saeko Usukawa
Design by George Vaitkunas
Jacket front: (top to bottom, all are details): women's field hockey team,
Victoria, c. 1910 / coal miners at Ladysmith, c. 1910 / Native women and
children, c. 1901 / children in Victoria Oriental Home, 1913 / Swedish
lumber workers, Crowsnest Pass, 1906
Jacket back: (top to bottom, all are details): Sikh Temple Congregation,
Vancouver, 1936 / Native men and boys, Alert Bay, c. 1926 / nurses
at Nanaimo, 1906 / VPL 11750, Asahi Baseball Club, seniors, 1929 /
members of Nanaimo Bicycle Club, 1891
Printed and bound in Canada by Friesens
Printed on acid-free paper

The publisher gratefully acknowledges the financial support of the
Canada Council for the Arts, the British Columbia Ministry of Tourism,
Small Business and Culture, and the Government of Canada through
the Book Publishing Industry Development Program (BPIDP) for our
publishing activities.

Front endpapers: The Haida village of Skidegate, 1890s.
Back endpapers: Vancouver's West End, 1971.
Title page: Men women and children at a logging camp, 1890s.

Contents

THE ILLUSTRATED HISTORY OF BRITISH COLUMBIA EDITORIAL ADVISORY BOARD

Madeleine Aalto, Director, Vancouver Public Library

The Honourable Thomas Berger, Q.C., lawyer and author

Neil Reynolds, Editor, The Vancouver Sun

James Delgado, historian and Executive Director, Vancouver Maritime Museum

Ian Gill, journalist and environmentalist, President, Ecotrust Canada

Verna Kirkness, Associate Professor Emerita, University of British Columbia, and Founding Director of the First Nations House of Learning at the University of British Columbia

Ian MacPherson, Dean of Humanities and Professor of History, University of Victoria

David Mitchell, historian, Vice-President and Chief Development Officer, Simon Fraser University

Peter Newman, journalist and author

Doris Shadbolt, art historian and critic

Jim Munro, bookseller

Sponsors

ACKNOWLEDGEMENTS

I OWE THANKS TO A GREAT MANY PEOPLE for their help in preparing this book. I am grateful to Chris Hanna for his research assistance (and insightful criticism); to Brad Morrison for permitting me access to his vast library; and to James Hoffman, Bruce Watson, Ken Favrholdt, Daniel P. Marshall and Keith Wood for sharing their research. For their help in a variety of ways, I would like to thank Rosemary Crawford, Charlene Rees, Ron Armstrong, Branwen Patenaude, Heather Welch and the late Paddy Mackie. In addition, I would like thank the members of the editorial board on this book.

At the British Columbia Archives, I received unstinting assistance, as I did at a number of other museums and archives throughout the province, including: Chase and District Museum and Archives Society, Chilliwack Museum and Historical Society, Cowichan Historical Society, Cumberland Museum and Archives, Enderby and District Museum Society, Fraser–Fort George Regional Museum, Kamloops Museum and Archives, Lillooet Museum, Maritime Museum of British Columbia, New Westminster Public Library, City of Penticton Museum, The Province, Quesnel and District Museum and Archives, Revelstoke Museum and Archives, Revelstoke Railway Museum, Secwepemc Museum and Heritage Park, Sisters of St. Ann Archives, Trail Historical Society, United Church of Canada B.C. Conference Archives, University of British Columbia Library Special Collections and University Archives Division, Valemount and Area Museum, City of Vancouver Archives, Vancouver Maritime Museum, Vancouver Museum, Vancouver Public Library, The Vancouver Sun, Greater Vernon Museum and Archives, City of Victoria Archives and Historic Yale Museum.

My husband, Don, provided unfailing encouragement, help and technical support.

I am especially grateful to Scott McIntyre, whose idea this illustrated history was, for giving me the opportunity to work on it. I would also like to give special thanks to the sponsors—the British Columbia Archives, BC Hydro, the Insurance Corporation of British Columbia, the Savings and Credit Unions of British Columbia and Telus—for their generous support in helping to make the writing and production of this book possible.

PART ONE

THE LURE OF WILDERNESS AND FUR

PREHISTORIC TIMES TO 1857

CHAPTER I

THE BEGINNING

IN JANUARY 1700, Japanese record keepers reported the arrival of a huge tsunami that had swept westward across the Pacific to crash ashore on the island of Honshu. Meanwhile, on the west coast of Vancouver Island, the Nuu-chah-nulth people added a chilling account of a great earthquake and its rebound wave to their spoken history. Two hundred and sixty-four years later, Chief Louis Clamhouse was able to recount the event: "The Pachena Bay people were lost. I think it was at night that the land shook. They simply had no time to get hold of canoes; no time to get awake. They sank all at once, were all drowned; not one survived. It is said that no one ever knew what happened. I think a big wave washed into the beach. Everything then drifted away, everything was lost and gone."

As destructive as it was, the great earthquake of 1700 was only a minor demonstration of the forces that created the land that became British Columbia. About 200 million years ago, the western edge of the

Previous page: Dancer wearing mask of a supernatural bird for the Hamatsa ceremony of the Kwakwa̱ka̱'wakw.

This page: Petroglyphs are rock carvings that depict humans, animals and mythic beings, and may represent the interaction between people and spirits. They may also be representations of historic events as they were interpreted at the time. Most petroglyphs are found near the coast, and some may date back to prehistoric times.

continent of North America ended near present-day Calgary; British Columbia existed only as a shelf extending under the sea to today's Okanagan, Quesnel and Cassiar regions. Over millions of years, terranes— chains of islands that had been formed when magma bubbled through cracks in the earth's crust and were then transported by shifting plates— collided with and overrode the continental shelf. Upward pressure from the Pacific Plate as it plunged below the continent formed mountain ranges.

Then, about 2 million years ago, the climate cooled and glaciers formed. During periods of warming, some of which lasted up to sixty thousand years, the glaciers retreated. But, during colder times, an ice sheet more than 1.6 km thick lay heavy over the land. With so much water trapped in the ice, sea levels fell. Asia and North America were connected by land rather than being separated by the Bering Strait. And Hecate Strait, which lies between the British Columbia mainland and the Queen Charlotte Islands (Haida Gwaii), was mostly dry. As the ice advanced and retreated, it sculpted mountains, scoured out valleys, and created rivers and lakes.

No one knows when the first people arrived. One theory supposes that, perhaps twenty thousand years ago, nomadic hunters began to drift across the land bridge that connected Siberia and Alaska, and that they then travelled south through an ice-free corridor east of the Rocky Mountains to the American plains. Spear tips discarded 10,500 years ago and discovered at Charlie Lake Cave, near Fort St. John, support this theory.

Current thinking suggests that Haida Gwaii and portions of the coast escaped glaciation and that people not only passed through these relatively ice-free areas as they migrated south but also managed to survive, clinging to the continent's western edge, while the rest of the land remained bound by ice. Recently, on Haida Gwaii, artifacts were found under the sea, but at a level at which a coastal village could have existed during the last Ice Age.

On the other hand, First Nations traditionalists believe that "our people have always lived here"; that they have been here since creation, since Raven dropped a clamshell on the beach and out crawled the first humans, since the "Old One" changed the Earth to make it more welcoming to people.

Early aboriginal artifacts found at an archaeological dig on Kuper Island, part of the territory of the Penelakut, a Coast Salish group.

Whatever the case, when the current warming period began about twelve thousand years ago, people advanced across the land. The oldest human remains discovered in British Columbia, near Kamloops, are those of a young man who was trapped in a mudslide that held fast to his skeleton for eight thousand years.

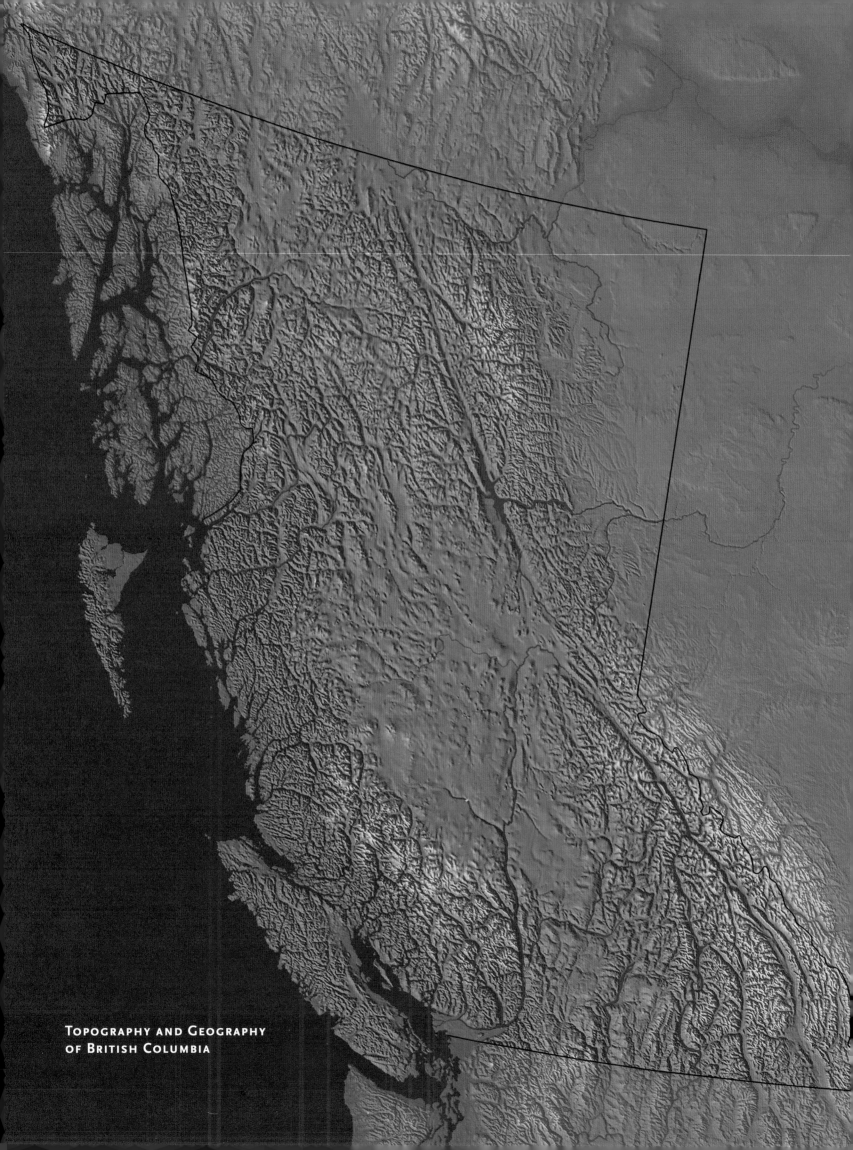

TOPOGRAPHY AND GEOGRAPHY
OF BRITISH COLUMBIA

Whenever they came, the people found a land of great diversity. A "sea of mountains" with a broad Interior plateau. A land of dripping rain forests and dusty deserts. A land where the annual rainfall can be as much as 813 cm (Henderson Lake on Vancouver Island) and as little as 20 cm (Ashcroft). A land where temperatures can plummet to -58.9°C (Smith River near the Yukon border) and climb to 44.4°C (Lytton and Lillooet). They also found a land of stunning biological diversity. Of the 196 species of mammals found in Canada, 143 make their home in British Columbia. Of the 3,218 plant species, 2,500 are native to the province.

It has been estimated that nearly half of all First Nations people in Canada lived in British Columbia, and when Europeans began arriving in the late eighteenth century, they encountered people wherever they went— people who had been here for a very long time, long enough to develop distinct cultures and languages.

On Haida Gwaii, the Haida spoke a language unique to themselves. On the west coast of Vancouver Island, the Nuu-chah-nulth hunted whales, an occupation they shared with few other groups on the Pacific coast. On the central and northern coast, the Kwakwaka'wakw and the Nuxalk decorated their housefronts with symbols representing their clan lineage. On the south coast, the Halkomelem left their house exteriors unadorned, and neither did they erect the freestanding totem poles that were a feature of more northern villages.

A Halkomelem village (photographed in the 1860s), shows the shed-roofed, unadorned cedar plank houses common to the Coast Salish people.

The houses were about 11.5 m wide, 24.5 m long and 3 m high, and each sheltered a number of families.

Top: The Haida village of Skidegate (photographed in the 1880s) was described by visitors as a "forest of totem poles." The gable-roofed Haida houses were large and substantial. Many were designed so that roof and wall planks could be removed and used at summer villages.

Bottom: The figure on the right (on this otherwise traditionally painted housefront) bears witness to the fact that by the time this photograph was taken in 1881, the Nuxalk people had been exposed to European influences for almost a century.

Some coastal people, like the Mowachaht, who spent the winter at the head of Tahsis Inlet and moved to the more exposed Friendly Cove in the summer, made short annual migrations coinciding with the fishing season, but most lived in permanent villages of large, cedar-plank houses. The people of the Interior—the Secwepemc, Nlaka'pamux and Stl'atl'imx who lived on the Interior plateau, and the Dakelh who lived farther north—spent the summer on the move, hunting game and gathering seasonal berries and herbs. Their summer homes were easily portable, teepee-like structures: the cone-shaped frameworks of light poles were cloaked with

Totem poles, each carved from a single cedar log, document the owners' territorial rights and other property, as well as status, lineage, family history and associated myths and crests.

After the 1890s, there was a temporary decline in the carving of totem poles, attributed to the influence of missionaries; to the Canadian government's 1884 banning of the potlatch, the ceremony at which guests were given gifts in payment for witnessing the raising of a new pole; and to the severe decline in the Native population due to diseases introduced by Europeans.

In the middle of the twentieth century, the number of poles being raised began to increase with the resurgence of Native cultures.

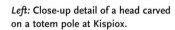

Left: Close-up detail of a head carved on a totem pole at Kispiox.

Bottom: A carved housepost (photographed in 1881) in the Haida village of Skidegate.

Right: A freestanding totem pole at Salmon River in front of a painted housefront (photographed in the 1900s).

BRITISH COLUMBIA's first peoples did not develop a written language, but they created a rich oral tradition. Narratives, many of them long and detailed, were passed from generation to generation. Some recount the exploits of animals or ancestral and mythic beings—like Raven, Whale, Eagle, Bear and Coyote—and of the Transformers, spirits who could assume any form they chose and who had come to Earth to make the world safe for humans. Some stories were intended to amuse, others to educate and still others to provide moral guidance by detailing the unhappy results of bad behaviour.

Some narratives account for observable features of the natural world. A story from the coast explains the pointed ears of the deer. "When he heard that the Transformer was coming around, Deer was angry and planned to kill him. So he sat outside and sharpened his knife, saying, 'I am going to cut the Transformer's head off.' Deer's knife was very sharp; it was made of mussel shell. A man came up and asked Deer, 'What are you sharpening?' 'A knife,' Deer replied. 'And why are you sharpening it?' the man continued. 'I am going to cut off

the Transformer's head when he comes around here,' was Deer's answer. 'That is a nice knife. May I see it?' the man asked. And Deer, not knowing this man was the Transformer, gave him the knife. 'This will make nice ears for you,' said the Transformer as he stuck the mussel-shell knife into Deer's head. That is why deer have pointed ears today—their ears are shaped like a mussel shell."

Some narratives seem to recall historical events, such as one Haida legend that might be describing the end of the last Ice Age. A boy named Scannah-gan-nuncus ventured up the Honna River (near Skidegate). "While resting by the river, he heard a dreadful noise up stream, coming toward him . . . he went to see what was crushing the stones and breaking the trees . . . he found that a large body of ice was coming down, pushing everything before it."

In a Nuxalk story, a man dreamed of a coming flood and prepared for its arrival by making an anchor and a long rope of cedar bark. "The Flood came. The man . . . tied his canoe's anchor to the top of a high mountain (Estero Peak, Bute Inlet). The entire area was covered in water and only this peak was still above the surface.

Two generations in their ceremonial regalia of Chilkat blankets and carved frontlets on their heads, at Hazelton (photographed in 1909).

Although other people had canoes, only this one man had prepared an anchor and a rope that was long enough. The people in the other canoes asked the man if they could tie their canoes to his, but only those who had offered

him wives or goods were allowed to tie up. Finally, the Floodwaters went down. The only people who survived were those who were allowed to tie up to the man's canoe—the Homalco people are descended from them."

A similar story is told by the Nlaka'pamux people: "There was once a great flood which covered the whole country excepting the tops of the highest mountains. All the people were drowned except Coyote, who turned himself into a piece of wood . . . When the waters subsided, Coyote was left high a dry. He then resumed his natural form, and looked around. He found that he was in the Thompson River country. He took trees for wives, and the Indians are said to be his descendants. Before the flood, there were no lakes or streams in the mountains and consequently no fish. When the water receded, it left lakes in the hollow of mountains, and streams began to run from them. That is the reason we now find lakes in the mountains, and fish in them."

Israel Sgat'iin, a Nisga'a chief from the Nass River, with objects that symbolize his rank (photographed in the 1890s)

A young Kwakwa̱ka'wakw woman (photographed in the 1910s), wearing large earrings of abalone shell.

reed mats through which cooling breezes could easily pass. When winter temperatures plunged, they moved into more permanent, semi-subterranean dwellings, known as *kekuli*: circular pits roofed with bark, dried grasses and earth laid over a wooden framework.

Salmon was a particularly valuable foodstuff because it could be smoked or air-dried and preserved for winter. On the lower Fraser River, Stó:lō families had defined fishing places, as did the Cowichan of Vancouver Island, who migrated to the mainland for the annual salmon runs. In the Interior, the Secwepemc, the Nlaka'pamux, the Stl'atl'imx and the Dakelh moved to their traditional fishing places on the upper Fraser, the Thompson and the Nechako Rivers.

British Columbia's first peoples spoke more than thirty languages, some as different from another as English is from Cantonese. But that did not prevent them from trading. Before Europeans arrived, ancient trade routes criss-crossed the country. Oolichan oil, prized for its high fat content, made its way from the coast to the Interior along the Nuxalk-Carrier "grease trail," the well-travelled path that Alexander Mackenzie would follow to the coast in 1793. Hides and skins from the prairies travelled west along "leather trails" through the Rockies.

Had they not been such enthusiastic traders, the people might have been more cautious and less welcoming when the first Europeans arrived. But, in the end, it would not have mattered. Once British Columbia was recognized as a source of profit, there was no turning back. Change would come and the speed of that change would be overwhelming.

The semi-subterranean winter houses used by the people of the Interior took advantage of the insulating properties of the ground. The notched log emerging from the roof entrance served as a ladder.

CHAPTER 2

THE PRIZE *of* RIVAL POWERS

THE FIRST EUROPEAN to see the land that would become known as British Columbia may have been an Elizabethan pirate on a secret mission for the queen or he may have been a Greek mariner in the employ of the Spanish. Both men were searching for the Pacific entrance of the mythical waterway, known to the Spanish as the Strait of Anian and to the British as the Northwest Passage, that was believed to connect the Atlantic and Pacific Oceans. Any European nation that controlled a water route allowing mariners to reach the Pacific without having to undertake the long voyage around the Cape of Good Hope or the treacherous passage around Cape Horn would dominate trade to the Orient. To the British and the Spanish, the Northwest Passage was a prize worth pursuing.

In 1577, Francis Drake sailed from England aboard the *Golden Hinde*. Officially, the purpose of his voyage was the plunder of Spanish treasure ships off the coasts of Chile and Peru. But Drake may also have carried with him secret instructions from Elizabeth I to follow the coast north, beyond Spanish territory, in search of the Northwest Passage. Circumstantial evidence suggests that he reached the Queen Charlotte Islands and the mouth of the Stikine River; and then, turning south, he sailed through Johnstone Strait and along the east coast of Vancouver Island. According to one contemporary, Drake had sailed to "the backside of Canada, further than any Christian hitherto hath pierced."

Recent research (undertaken by Samuel Bawlf) suggests that in 1579, Sir Francis Drake selected Comox as the site of Nova Albion, the proposed colony that would defend British control of the Northwest Passage.

In Venice, almost twenty years later, an English merchant named Michael Lok encountered Apostolos Valerianos, an old Greek seaman with an amazing story to tell. Valerianos said that he had worked as a ship's pilot for the Spanish in Mexico, where he had been known as Juan de Fuca. In 1592, he had been sent north to search for the Strait of Anian and had found, near latitude 48°N, a wide inlet that led to "a very much broader Sea." Convinced that he had "done the thing he was sent to do," Valerianos expected to be rewarded for his service but received nothing. That was why he was prepared to share the secret of his discovery with the Englishman.

Lok was convinced that Valerianos had discovered the Northwest Passage and, in 1625, published an account of the Greek's voyage. Skeptics dismissed it as a tall tale. But when interest in the North Pacific began to grow, mariners carried with them the details of Valerianos's story, just in case "the pretended strait of Juan de Fuca" actually existed.

ALMOST TWO HUNDRED YEARS after the voyages of Sir Francis Drake and Apostolos Valerianos, the Spanish ambassador in St. Petersburg began to hear rumours that Russian merchants were making fortunes from furs acquired on the Aleutian Islands. The potential for profit renewed Spanish interest in the Northwest Coast. Early in 1774, Juan Pérez was dispatched from Mexico on the frigate *Santiago*, with instructions to sail north to latitude 60°N, where he was to take possession of the land in the name of the King of Spain.

On 15 July, with his supply of fresh water running low, Pérez turned east toward land. For three days, he sailed through fog and rain, and then on 18 July, he sighted the Queen Charlotte Islands. Two days later, as the *Santiago* moved slowly along the coast, a canoe put out from shore. Fray Juan Crespi, a priest who had been sent along to lift "the shadows of idolatry" from any people he might meet and who had spent most of the voyage in his bunk plagued by seasickness, dragged himself on deck to witness the arrival. "While they were still some distance, we heard them singing," he noted. "We saw that there were eight men and a boy in the canoe, seven of them rowing, while the eighth, who was painted, was standing up in the attitude of dancing, and throwing feathers on the water." The Haida

"These people are very fat, of good appearance, red and white in colour, with long hair, and they cover themselves with skins of beaver and sea lions. All or most of them wear rush hats, well woven, with a pointed crown. They are not at all noisy, and seemed to us mild and good-tempered."
—Fray Juan Crespi

According to European accounts, the Haida (sketched here in 1793) welcomed the opportunity to trade.

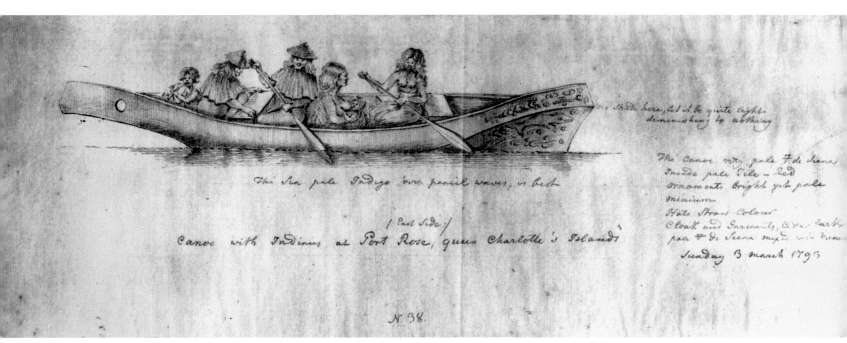

In 1776, Captain James Cook was forty-eight years old and considered himself retired, having completed two great voyages of exploration and discovery, during which he had sailed around the world twice, once in each direction.

But he found the Admiralty commission to explore the North Pacific in search of the Northwest Passage impossible to resist.

"It is in this very latitude we are now in, where geographers have placed the pretended strait of Juan de Fuca. But we saw nothing like it; nor is there the least probability that ever any such thing existed."

—Captain James Cook

Cook's anchorage, now known as Resolution Cove, was on Bligh Island, named by Cook after one of his junior officers, twenty-four-year-old William Bligh. Later, Bligh provoked one of the most famous events in naval history. He was captain of the *Bounty*, outbound from Tahiti, when mutineers took over his ship and set Bligh and eighteen loyal crewmen adrift in a 23-foot open boat. With no charts and scanty provisions, Bligh completed a voyage of 3,618 miles to reach land.

gestured to the Spaniards to come ashore. But Pérez could not find an anchorage, and the *Santiago* sailed on.

The following day, as the *Santiago* lay becalmed off Langara Island, twenty-two canoes surrounded the ship. Fray Crespi wrote: "A fair was opened at once between them and our people, for we understood that they came to trade with our folks and exchange their little trinkets for ours."

After two days battling strong currents and contrary winds, Pérez turned the *Santiago* about and made sail for Mexico. On 8 August, he was off the west coast of Vancouver Island in the vicinity of Nootka Sound. Two canoes carrying seven men left the shore. "Before reaching the frigate they began to shout and make gestures that we should go away," Fray Crespi reported. But Pérez, desperate for fresh drinking water, dropped anchor.

The following day, a hundred Nuu-chah-nulth in fifteen canoes drew near the *Santiago*, and a cautious trade began. Pérez was about to launch the longboat, when a sharp wind blew up. With her anchor beginning to drag, the *Santiago* was forced to set sail for the safety of the open sea without any of her crew having stepped ashore. The first recorded contacts between Europeans and the people of the coast had been fleeting but not unfriendly.

IN JULY 1776, Captain James Cook left England on his third great voyage of exploration, carrying with him instructions to search for the Northwest Passage. The 110-foot HMS *Resolution*, with 113 officers and crew, and the smaller *Discovery* and her crew of 81, sailed around the Cape of Good Hope and spent the following year in the South Pacific, visiting New Zealand and Tahiti and discovering the Sandwich (Hawaiian) Islands. By 7 March 1778, Cook was off the coast of California, pressing north through fog, gales, rain and sleet. On 22 March, he sighted and named Cape Flattery but missed Juan de Fuca Strait, partly because the weather was foul and partly because he did not believe in its existence.

Cook knew none of the details of Pérez's voyage, for the Spanish chose to keep their explorations quiet. But a week later, by accident of wind and current, Cook's ships were off the west coast of Vancouver Island at the same spot Pérez had visited four years earlier. Sailing through the narrow entrance to Nootka Sound, Cook was met by a fleet of canoes. The Mowachaht directed him to an anchorage near Yuquot, their village at

Homme de Noolka.

"So the chief told them to go out there and try
to understand what those people wanted . . .
And they started making signs and they were talking Indian
and they were saying: 'Nu·tka·ʔičim. Nu·tka·ʔičim.'
That means, you go around the harbour. So Captain Cook
said, 'Oh, they're telling us the name of this place is Nootka.'
That's how Nootka got its name. But the Indian name
is altogether different. It's Yuquot that Indian village."
—Nuu-chah-nulth elder Winifred David

"Our friends the natives attended us till we were almost
out of the sound, some on board the ships, and others
in their canoes. One of their chiefs, who had some time before
attached himself to me, was amongst the last who left us.
Having before he went bestowed on him a small present,
I received a beaver-skin [sea otter] of much greater value.
This called upon me to make some addition to my present,
which pleased him so much that he insisted on my
acceptance of the beaver-skin cloak which he then wore,
and of which I knew he was particularly fond."
—Captain James Cook

Friendly Cove, but Cook chose to keep his distance, sailing deeper into the sound until he found "a pretty snug cove."

Soon *Resolution* and *Discovery* were surrounded by thirty or forty canoes, and a brisk trade commenced. That evening, five or six canoes remained hovering close to the ships. Suddenly, the Mowachaht began to sing. The sailors responded with a few tunes on two French horns. After listening intently, the Mowachaht answered with another song, to which the seamen replied with a tune on the fife and drum.

Both the British and the Mowachaht were eager traders. In exchange for "knives, chisels, pieces of iron and tin, nails, looking-glasses, buttons, and any kind of metal," the people of Yuquot offered "skins of various animals." The seamen, knowing Cook's orders called for them to sail far to the north, prepared for colder climes by buying hundreds of sea otter pelts.

Cook had planned to stay only long enough to take on fresh water and to prepare spruce beer, a strange brew that was helpful in preventing scurvy (a disease producing spongy gums, loose teeth and bleeding under the skin, to which sailors were prone because their diet was deficient in vitamin C). But, impressed by the warmth of his welcome and alarmed by the deteriorating condition of his ships, he decided to dally while the men made necessary repairs.

Almost a month passed before Cook's ships weighed anchor. The British took leave of Nootka Sound with some regret, and their feelings were shared by their hosts, who "importuned" them to pay another visit and "by way of encouragement, promised to lay in a good stock of skins."

Captain Cook did not return to Nootka. While overwintering in Hawaii, he and four of his men were attacked and killed on the beach at Kealakekua Bay. After Cook's remains were buried at sea, the expedition pressed on under the command of Lieutenant James King.

In 1779, after a summer on the Northwest Coast, King was on his way back to England when he stopped at a Russian settlement on the Kamchatka peninsula. There, he and his men received a pleasant surprise. Russian merchants were prepared to pay them fabulous prices for the sea otter skins they no longer needed.

In 1784, when the journals kept by Captain Cook and Lieutenant King were published, attention soon was riveted on King's account of the prices paid for sea otter furs. For merchants and seamen, the journals were like a gift from a benevolent providence: unlike the Russians and the Spanish, who preferred to operate in some secrecy, the British had not only located a rich new source of profit but also described in detail where it was to be found.

First off the mark was Englishman James Hanna, who set out from Macao in April 1785, reached Nootka in August and left with 560 sea otter pelts. The following year, another Englishman, James Strange, arrived at Nootka and sailed away with "every rag of Furr within the Sound."

Of the six ships calling at Nootka during the summer of 1787, the *Imperial Eagle* stood out: her captain sighted and named the fabled "Strait of Juan de Fuca," and aboard her was the first European woman to see British Columbia. A convent-educated young Englishwoman with a "cloud of golden hair to her feet," Frances Barkley had married Captain Charles Barkley in October 1786. A month later, she was aboard her husband's ship, embarking on a voyage that would last for almost three years. Soon after the *Imperial Eagle* dropped anchor in Friendly Cove, a single canoe came alongside. "A man, in every respect like an Indian . . . clothed in a greasy sea-otter skin, came on board." To the "utter astonishment" of the Barkleys, he introduced himself as Dr. John Mackay.

Sea otters were prized for their soft, thick fur. Mature sea otters reach a length of 5 feet and weigh as much as 80 pounds.

"In the afternoon, we arrived off a large opening extending to the eastward, the entrance of which appeared to be about four leagues in width, and remained about that width as far as the eye could see, with a clear easterly horizon, which my husband immediately recognized as the long-lost Strait of Juan de Fuca, and to which he gave the name of the original discoverer, my husband placing it on his chart."

—Frances Barkley

A hapless young Irishman, Mackay had shipped to Nootka as the surgeon's mate on Captain Strange's expedition of 1786. He had agreed to stay behind to learn all he could about the residents of the sound in preparation for Strange's return the following summer. Supplied with salt beef, ship's biscuits, salt, tea, sugar, tobacco, two goats and a variety of seeds, he had been placed under the protection of Maquinna, a Mowachaht chief. Maquinna promised to provide Mackay with a wife and assured Captain Strange that he would find the young man "fat as a whale" on his return.

But Mackay proved that his reputation as a "very ignorant young fellow" gifted with "natural stupidity" was well deserved. Early in his residency, he meekly agreed to dismantle his musket to show how it worked. "The screws and Springs were handed from one to the other," Mackay admitted. "They were soon carried out of sight and it was impossible to retrieve them."

Having managed to disarm himself, Mackay committed an unfortunate faux pas when he stepped over the cradle holding Maquinna's child. Outraged by the Irishman's disrespect, Maquinna beat him, banished him from the house and, from then on, treated him as an outcast. Mackay's goats died. His garden failed. His health declined. The first European to reside on Vancouver Island, Mackay spent a miserable winter, longing for the arrival of a ship that would bring him deliverance.

A year after the Barkleys' visit, John Meares, a former lieutenant in the Royal Navy, arrived at Nootka with plans to establish a land-based fur trade. After negotiating with Maquinna for "a spot of ground," he began construction of a fortified building and a small boat to be used for coastal trade. In September, *North West America*, "the first bottom ever built and launched in this part of the globe," was set afloat at Nootka Sound. Then, Meares

Top: The publication of the journals of Captain James Cook and Lieutenant James King transformed life at Friendly Cove. In 1788, eight trading vessels entered Nootka Sound. By 1791, the number had risen to twelve, by 1792 to twenty-one.

Bottom: In 1788, John Meares became the first European to purchase land on Vancouver Island.

The arrest of the English traders at Nootka Sound was depicted in a manner calculated to inflame anti-Spanish passions.

returned to China, where he joined with other English merchants to organize a new, more ambitious expedition. The following summer, Meares dispatched from China the *Argonaut*, commanded by James Colnett and carrying everything necessary to establish a permanent settlement, including twenty-nine Chinese workmen: carpenters, blacksmiths, masons, tailors, shoemakers and a cook.

Colnett was astonished to discover that the Spanish had taken possession of Friendly Cove and furious when he was ordered away. Neither Esteban José Martínez, the Spanish commander, nor James Colnett, was a temperate man. At the height of one angry shouting match, Martínez arrested Colnett, boarded the *Argonaut*, hauled down the British ensign and raised the Spanish flag. The *Argonaut* was being prepared to carry Colnett and his men to Mexico and a Spanish prison when another of Meares's ships sailed into the sound and was promptly captured.

John Meares was in China when he heard the news. He hurried to London, arriving there in April 1790, to launch a campaign calculated to inflame public opinion and produce political action. His ships had been seized. Englishmen had been thrown into irons and were, even now, languishing in a Mexican jail.

On 5 May 1790, the British Parliament voted £1 million to prepare for war with Spain. The Spanish preferred to negotiate. On 28 October 1790,

By 1803, when the American ship *Boston* sailed into Nootka Sound to take on fresh water and wood for spars, the friendly relations that marked the first years of the fur trade had become a distant memory. As competition for furs increased, supplies declined and tensions rose. Some traders resorted to threats of violence to force the Haida and the Nuu-chah-nulth to part with furs on favourable terms. At the same time, they regarded Native petty pilfering as a serious crime deserving stern punishment.

By all accounts, Maquinna was an imposing figure. Alexander Walker, who encountered him in 1785, described "a stout handsome young Man, with a fine manly countenance . . . He was the most intelligent Person we met with, and sufficiently shrewd."

In 1789, when Captain John Kendrick, a Boston-based trader, became irritated by the theft of linen hanging on his washing line, he ordered two Haida chiefs thrown into irons and kept prisoner on the deck until the items were returned. Two years later, when Kendrick sailed back to the Queen Charlotte Islands, the Haida swarmed aboard his ship. After a brief battle, fifty Haida lay dead.

Accounts of that battle and a series of other confrontations echoed up and down the coast. When the *Boston* sailed into Nootka Sound, she encountered people who were full of mistrust. At first the visit went well, but then the *Boston*'s captain made a remark that Maquinna, a Mowachaht chief, interpreted as

a personal insult. Maquinna and his men attacked the ship.

John Jewitt, a nineteen-year-old Englishman who had signed on as blacksmith and armourer, was struck by an axe blow that split open his forehead. When he regained consciousness, the deck was awash with blood. Maquinna offered to spare Jewitt if he would agree to be his slave for life. "I was careful to answer, yes," the blacksmith admitted.

The *Boston*'s sail-maker, John Thompson, had also escaped death. Over the months that followed, Maquinna took advantage of the talents of the two useful men he had spared. Jewitt was ordered to make blades for his whaling harpoons, and Thompson was told to make sails for his canoe.

Jewitt, who kept a journal throughout his captivity, made the best of things. He learned the Mowachaht's language, studied their customs and did everything he could to ingratiate himself to Maquinna and the lesser chiefs. "I scarcely ever failed experiencing kind treatment from them," Jewitt reported. He came to believe that the attack on the *Boston* had been a consequence of "the imprudent conduct of some of the captains and crews" who had been guilty of "exasperating them by insulting,

A portrait of John Jewitt in his later years.

plundering and even killing them on slight grounds."

Jewitt was rescued in 1805 and eventually reached Boston in 1807. Deciding to capitalize on his misfortune, he published his journal and peddled it from town to town. In 1815, his journal was rewritten as a story, and once again Jewitt took his show on the road, selling the *Narrative of the Adventures and Sufferings of John R. Jewitt* for a

dollar a copy. Two years later, his story was turned into a melodrama, *The Armourer's Escape*, with Jewitt himself playing the title role.

This interior view of a house at Nootka Sound (probably Maquinna's) shows people sitting on plank sleeping platforms (on the left). Behind them are piled bentwood storage boxes, and above them hang dried fish and bladders filled with whale oil.

In June 1790, at the height of the Nootka Sound crisis, the play *Nootka Sound; or, Britain Prepar'd* was presented in London at the Theatre Royal, Covent Garden. (This performance was an actors' benefit.) After James Hoffman discovered the original script in London, the play was staged in Kamloops at the University College of the Cariboo, 209 years after its debut.

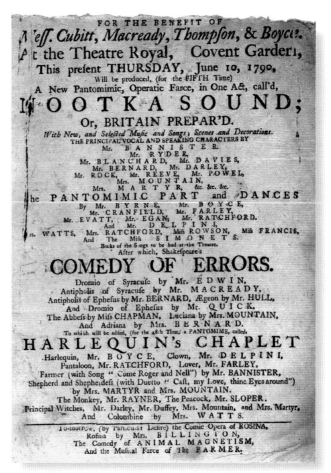

FOR THE BENEFIT OF

Mess. Cubitt, Macready, Thompson, & Boyce.

At the Theatre Royal, Covent Garden,

This present THURSDAY, June 10, 1790.

Will be produced, (for the FIFTH Time)

A New Pantomimic, Operatic Farce, in One Act, call'd,

NOOTKA SOUND;

Or, BRITAIN PREPAR'D.

With New, and Selected Music and Songs, Scenes and Decorations.
THE PRINCIPAL VOCAL AND SPEAKING CHARACTERS BY
Mr. BANNISTER.
Mr. RYDER,
Mr. BLANCHARD, Mr. DAVIES,
Mr. BERNARD, Mr. DARLEY,
Mr. ROCK, Mr. REEVE, Mr. POWEL,
Mrs. MOUNTAIN,
Mrs. MARTYR, &c. &c. &c.

The PANTOMIMIC PART and DANCES
By Mr. BYRNE, Mr. BOYCE,
Mr. CRANFIELD, Mr. FARLEY,
Mr. EVATT, Mr. EGAN, Mr. RATCHFORD.
And Mr. DELPINI,
Mrs. WATTS, Mrs. RATCHFORD, Miss ROWSON, Miss FRANCIS,
And The Miss SIMONETS.
Books of the Songs to be had at the Theatre.
After which, Shakespeare's

COMEDY OF ERRORS.

Dromio of Syracuse by Mr. EDWIN,
Antipholis of Syracuse by Mr. MACREADY,
Antipholis of Ephesus by Mr. BERNARD, Ægeon by Mr. HULL,
And Dromio of Ephesus by Mr. QUICK,
The Abbess by Miss CHAPMAN, Luciana by Mrs. MOUNTAIN,
And Adriana by Mrs. BERNARD.
To which will be added, (for the 48th Time) a PANTOMIME, called,

HARLEQUIN's CHAPLET

Harlequin, Mr. BOYCE, Clown, Mr. DELPINI,
Pantaloon, Mr. RATCHFORD, Lover, Mr. FARLEY,
Farmer (with Song " Come Roger and Nell") by Mr. BANNISTER,
Shepherd and Shepherdess (with Duetto " Cast, my Love, thine Eyes around")
by Mrs. MARTYR and Mrs. MOUNTAIN.
The Monkey, Mr. RAYNER, The Peacock, Mr. SLOPER.
Principal Witches, Mr. Darley, Mr. Duffey, Mrs. Mountain, and Mrs. Martyr,
And Colombine by Mrs. WATTS.

To-morrow, (by Particular Desire) the Comic Opera of ROSINA,
Rosina by Mrs. BILLINGTON,
The Comedy of ANIMAL MAGNETISM,
And the Musical Farce of The FARMER.

When he set sail for the west coast, thirty-two-year-old George Vancouver was an experienced mariner. He had gone to sea when he was fourteen, sailed with Captain James Cook on his second great voyage of discovery, and joined him again in 1776, as a nineteen-year-old midshipman, on the voyage that took him to Nootka Sound.

the Nootka Sound Convention was signed. Discussions leading to a final demarcation line between Spanish and British possessions would continue. Meanwhile, traders from both countries would enjoy unimpeded access to the Northwest Coast; Meares would be compensated for his losses and his ships handed back at Nootka Sound. A British expedition that had already been planned to perform a thorough survey of the coast now added diplomacy to its orders.

In command of the expedition was Captain George Vancouver. On 29 April 1792, a year after leaving home, Vancouver's ships, HMS *Discovery* (named after Cook's vessel) and HMS *Chatham*, rounded Cape Flattery and entered Juan de Fuca Strait. In June, they dropped anchor in Birch Bay. From there, the surveying was accomplished in small open boats. On 13 June, Captain Vancouver, aboard *Discovery*'s yawl, and Lieutenant Peter Puget, in command of the launch, pulled ashore at Point Grey. They spent the following week exploring Burrard Inlet, Howe Sound and Jervis Inlet, all of which Vancouver named after naval officers. On his way back to *Discovery*, Vancouver was stunned to see two Spanish vessels anchored in English Bay.

Vancouver had not the slightest idea that the Spanish had been exploring the area for two years. But already Manuel Quimper had explored the coast as far north as Prince William Sound, and Salvador Fidalgo had sailed the length of Juan de Fuca Strait. On 22 June 1792, when Vancouver encountered the *Sutil* commanded by Dionisio Alcalá Galiano and the *Mexicana* under Cayetano Valdés, the Spanish had already explored and charted the area Vancouver believed he had just discovered.

As Vancouver entered Nootka Sound for his appointed meeting with the Spanish, he gave the Spanish flag a thirteen-volley salute from his ship's guns, to which Nootka's commander, Juan Francisco de la Bodega y

Quadra, responded in kind, setting the convivial tone that typified the meetings of the two men. Quadra was devoted to gracious living and loved to entertain. "A dinner of five courses, consisting of a superfluity of the best provisions, was served with great elegance," Vancouver reported.

Quadra and Vancouver discovered that they interpreted the terms of the Nootka Convention very differently. Agreeing to disagree, the two decided to refer the dispute to their home governments and continued to enjoy one another's company. Their mutual regard was commemorated by Vancouver's decision to name the island "Quadra and Vancouver's Island."

In September, they paid a complimentary visit to Maquinna, who had recently moved to his winter quarters. The sun was shining as they rowed up Tahsis Inlet "with drums beating & Fifes playing to the no small entertainment of the Natives." At the village, they were treated to an extraordinary piece of theatre. A number of men appeared "dressed, armed and masked in imitation of various characters of different Countries, some represented Europeans armed with Muskets & Bayonets, others were dressed as Chinese & others as Sandwich Islanders armed with Clubs & Spears." It was rather disconcerting for the Europeans to discover that, while they had been filling their journals with descriptions of strange customs, they too were being studied—so closely that they could easily recognize themselves in the pantomime.

After spending the winter in Hawaii, Vancouver returned to the Northwest Coast. By June, he was surveying Dean Channel; and there, one of history's fascinating near misses occurred. If he had delayed his survey by only seven weeks, he would have met Alexander Mackenzie, who emerged on the Pacific on 22 July 1793 to become the first European to cross North America by land.

Captain Vancouver's ship *Discovery*, shown here aground at Queen Charlotte Sound, was only 100 feet long but carried a crew of eighty-four accompanied by sixteen marines— crowded accommodations for a voyage expected to stretch for five long years.

"Fifty-four persons sat down to Dinner and the plates, which were solid silver, *was shifted five times, which made 270 Plates. The Dishes, Knifes and forks, and indeed every thing else, was of Silver and always replaced with spare ones."*
—seaman aboard *Columbia*

"I have read Vancouver's Voyage *and even tho' I accompanied him, I think it is one of the most tedious Books I have ever read."*
—Lieutenant Robert Barrie

CHAPTER 3

DOWN *the* WILD RIVERS

The coat of arms of the North West Company, which began in 1776 when a group of independent Montreal fur traders decided to work together to better compete with their American rivals and the Hudson's Bay Company.

THE MONTREAL FUR TRADERS who joined forces to form the North West Company had good reason for turning their attention to the west. The London-based Hudson's Bay Company (HBC) continued to enjoy a crown-granted monopoly over the trade around Hudson Bay and, with the end of the Revolutionary War, Americans had gained control over the fur-rich lands south of the Great Lakes.

By the end of the 1780s, the Nor'westers had worked their way to the Athabasca country (northern Alberta), and their efforts had been rewarded with rapidly rising profits. But, as the distances from Montreal became greater and greater, the transfer of furs and supplies became increasingly difficult, and the Nor'westers began to dream of an outpost on the western ocean.

On 9 May 1793, Alexander Mackenzie and nine travelling companions—his second-in-command Alexander Mackay, two Indian guides and six French-Canadian canoemen—embarked on their voyage of discovery from Fort Fork (near Peace River, Alberta). Aboard their 25-foot birchbark canoe, they carried 3,000 pounds of supplies: "goods for presents, arms, ammunition and baggage," and enough flour, rice and pemmican to last ten weeks.

Before them lay a daunting journey. They would follow the Peace River into the west—battling upstream against the current—paddling and poling; and when the current became too strong, dragging the heavy

canoe, sometimes pulling on a towline from the riverbank and sometimes wading through fast-flowing water made frigid by melting snow.

On their second day on the river, they were served notice of the difficulties that lay ahead. "The canoe, being strained from its having been very heavily laden, became so leaky that we were obliged to land, unload, and gum it," Mackenzie noted. And then, after the canoe was repaired and they were back on the river, he dropped his pocket compass into the water.

When they reached the eastern approach to the Peace River Canyon, Mackenzie was told that the Beaver (Dunne-za) people always skirted the canyon along a "carrying trail." But he hoped to avoid portaging, an arduous process that involved unloading the canoe and then carrying it, and all the supplies, overland on the backs of the men.

The next few miles on the Peace became a nightmare of poling, dragging and towing. After two exhausting days, Mackenzie admitted that their only choice was to climb out of the canyon, over Portage Mountain. Returning to the river above the falls, Mackenzie looked downstream at the terrible current they had avoided, "high, foaming, half-formed billows, as far as the eye could follow it." (This is now the site of Bennett Dam.)

On 31 May, when they reached the meeting of the Finlay and Parsnip Rivers (now under Williston Lake), Mackenzie decided to take the advice of a Dunne-za elder who had told him that, if he followed the Parsnip, he would

Travelling upstream against the current often required poling and towing. Under better circumstances, voyageurs paddled at a rate of up to sixty strokes a minute. To keep their rhythm and raise their spirits, they sang.

"My winter interpreter . . . shed tears on the reflection of those dangers which we might encounter in our expedition, while my own people offered up their prayers that we might return safely from it."
—Alexander Mackenzie

In 1793, Alexander Mackenzie was twenty-nine years old, "strong and well-built," blessed with a constitution "equal to the most arduous undertakings" and convinced that a water passage to the Pacific existed.

"They [voyageurs] make Gods of their bellies, yet when necessity obliges them, even when destitute of every kind of nourishment, they will endure all the fatigue and misery of hard labour & cold weather &c. for several Days following without much complaining."
—Daniel Harmon

find a carrying-place to a large river. The Parsnip proved to be a difficult river. The current was too swift for paddling, the water too deep for poling, the banks so thick with willow that the towline could not be used. "We proceeded by hauling the canoe from branch to branch," Mackenzie wrote.

On 10 June, they paddled across a small lake and found "a beaten path leading over a low ridge of land" that led to another small lake. Mackenzie counted off the distance: "Eight hundred and seventeen paces." They had crossed the continental divide. From here, rivers flowed toward the Pacific Ocean. Soon, they were travelling downstream for the first time since leaving Fort Fork more than three weeks earlier.

As they voyaged down the Bad River (James Creek), the current grabbed the canoe, forced it sideways and slammed it into a rocky bar. Mackenzie and the men jumped into the river. Before they could align the canoe, they were swept into deeper water. They lost their footing and clambered back aboard. Moments later, the canoe was driven into a rock that smashed its stern, and then was slammed into another rock that crushed its bow. One man, hoping to stop the canoe, grabbed an overhanging branch but was jerked out of the boat and left dangling over the water as the canoe careered on.

Lurching through the rapids, the canoe began to fill with water. The steersman yelled to the men to let go and save themselves. Stay where you are, Mackenzie ordered. And the men obeyed, holding fast to the boat in the tumbling water. Clinging to the canoe, they were carried over a cascade, and then suddenly, they found themselves in a back eddy, in a patch of shallow water. As the canoe settled on the bottom, they found their feet. By the time they unloaded the boat and gained the riverbank, their legs were so numb from the frigid water that they could barely stand.

The canoe seemed beyond repair and most of their provisions had been ruined. The men were light-headed with relief, for now, surely, the expedition would have to be abandoned. But Mackenzie had no intention of turning back. He waited until they had had "a hearty meal and rum enough to raise their spirits." And then he told them that they were going on.

The next morning, they set off—four men easing the canoe down the river, the rest packing as much gear as they could carry along a trail they hacked through the bush. That night, after fourteen hours of desperately hard work during which they covered only 4 miles, they gathered round a blazing fire, and Mackenzie doled out the rum.

Just below their camping place, the river thundered over a falls, and Mackenzie was forced to order a portage. Staggering through deep mud, struggling over fallen trees, persecuted by mosquitoes, sweating under an unrelenting sun, Mackenzie and his men spent the whole long day travelling 2 miles. Late the next evening, they arrived at the bank of a river (Herrick Creek). "At length we enjoyed, after all our toil and anxiety, the inexpressible satisfaction of finding ourselves on the bank of a navigable river," Mackenzie rejoiced. And then it began to rain.

The following day, they entered the "great river" (Fraser River). By 19 June, they were paddling past the point where the river is joined by the Nechako, a river Mackenzie failed to notice in the heavy mist. They portaged around the rapids of Fort George Canyon and flew through Cottonwood Canyon. They had passed the mouth of the Quesnel River when Mackenzie received bad news. At a Carrier (Dakelh) village, an old man assured him that no canoe could travel the length of the "great river." However, he said,

TUTCHONE

TAGISH

INLAND
TLINGIT

TLINGIT

KASKA, DENA

**FIRST NATIONS TERRITORIES
AND EXPLORERS' ROUTES**

Liard River

TAHLTAN

Stikine River

DENE-THAH

Finlay River

SEKANI

NISGA'A

DUNNE-ZA

Nass River

NAT'OOTEN

Peace River

(1804)

GITXSAN

(1802)

Skeena River

HAIDA

Parsnip River

Haida
Gwaii
(Queen
Charlotte
Islands)

HAISLA

WET'SUWET'EN

TSIMSHIAN

(1806)

SAULTEAUX, CREE

Nechako River

DAKELH

THOMPSON

PEREZ (1774)

Dean Channel

NUXALK

HEILTSUK

MACKENZIE (1793)

(1812)

STONEY

OWEEKENO

Fraser River

SECWEPEMC

(1799)

TSILHQOT'IN

North Thompson R

Columbia R

Pacific Ocean

KWAKWAKA'WAKW

STL'ATL'IMX

Thompson River

S Thompson R

FRASER (1808)

(1807)

NLAKA'PAMUX

KTUNAXA,
KINBASKET

DRAKE (1579)

NUU-CHAH-NULTH

Nootka Sound

COAST
SALISH

(1811)

OKANAGAN

Vancouver
Island

Strait of Georgia

VANCOUVER (1794)

COOK (1778)

VANCOUVER (1792)

DITIDAHT

Okanagan River

Cape
Flattery

Juan de Fuca Strait

KALISPELL

0   100 kilometres

Sir Alexander Mackenzie's
rock at Bella Coola.

A stocky, bull-necked man,
Simon Fraser joined the fur
trade when he was sixteen.
As ambitious as he was brave
and energetic, he was not
impressed by Alexander
Mackenzie—not by his explorations and still less by the
knighthood Mackenzie
received following the publication of his journals. The
desire to outdo his predeces-
sor only added to Fraser's
resolve, and in composing
his own journals, he missed
few chances to disparage
"the knight."

there was a much easier route to the western ocean. The Dakelh traded with the Bella Coola (Nuxalk) who lived near the coast. The trail was well-marked and it would take them only seven days to reach the Nuxalk.

Mackenzie ordered the men to turn about. On 3 July, they entered a waterway (West Road River) that flowed out of the west. Four or five miles upriver, they cached most of their supplies and set off on foot, each voyageur packing 90 pounds of pemmican, and Mackenzie and Mackay carrying 70-pound packs, together with their arms and ammunition. Soaked by continuous rain and hail, they followed the trail through the woods. Two weeks later, they crossed the mountains (Mackenzie Pass) through snow, hail and rain. And then, they glimpsed a river in the distance, they killed a small deer for their supper, and their mood improved. Mackenzie celebrated by shaving his beard and changing his underwear.

Later that day, they reached the Bella Coola River and after dark stumbled into a Nuxalk encampment, where they were fed on roast salmon and treated to salmon-roe delicacies. A fire was prepared for them, and boards were laid on the earth for their beds.

In two borrowed canoes manned by Nuxalk paddlers, Mackenzie and his men sped toward the sea. On 20 July, seventy-two days after leaving Fort Fork, they reached the western ocean (North Bentinck Arm at the head of Burke Channel). They paddled along the shore of King's Island and into Dean Channel, where they encountered a party of Bella Bella (Heiltsuk). "They examined everything we had in our canoe with an air of indifference and disdain," Mackenzie wrote. "One of them in particular made me understand, with an air of insolence, that a large canoe had lately been in this bay, with people in her like me, and that one of them, whom he called *Macubah* [Vancouver] had fired on him and his friends."

Expecting trouble, Mackenzie collected his men on a rocky islet at the entrance to Elcho Harbour, where they kept watch through the night. "My people were very anxious to get out of the reach of the inhabitants of this coast," Mackenzie noted. The next day, he marked a rock as evidence of their presence and announced that the time had come to turn back. Thirty-two days later, on 24 August, they arrived back at Fort Fork. "Here my voyages of discovery terminate," Mackenzie wrote.

Mackenzie and his men were the first Europeans to cross the continent north of Mexico, but to the North West Company, the expedition was a failure. Mackenzie had not discovered a water passage to the Pacific. His route to the coast could never be practical for trade.

THE NORTH WEST COMPANY clung to the hope of finding a navigable river route to the coast. In 1792, an American trader had discovered the mouth of a large river which he had named the Columbia after his ship. Since no European had found the mouth of the Fraser River, it was presumed that Mackenzie's "great river" was the Columbia. The Nor'westers decided to build trading posts west of the Rockies and to trace the "Columbia" to its mouth. Both tasks were assigned to Simon Fraser.

OF ALL the men who accompanied Simon Fraser down the Fraser River, only Jean Baptiste Boucher made British Columbia his permanent home. The son of a French-Canadian father and a Cree mother, he had signed on with the North West Company in 1803 when he was about thirteen years old. Listed in the company records as an interpreter, Boucher turned his hand to many tasks, excelling at all of them. To John Stuart, under whom he served for many years, he was "the best of the Class I ever met with." Known by his nickname "Waccan," he became the company's "gendarme and chief executioner in New Caledonia," the man sent to discipline problem employees, to round up deserters and to smooth over disputes with local Indians.

At Fraser Lake on 18 March 1811, Daniel Harmon noted in his journal, "My Interpreter (Baptiste Bouché) has taken to Wife the Daughter of one of the Carrier Chiefs & she is the first woman of that Tribe kept by any of the White People." That attachment was short-lived, and soon afterwards Boucher was allied to Nancy McDougall, the daughter of a trader and his country wife. By the time Waccan died at Fort

Billy Bouchie (right) and his wife, Lizette Allard, in front of their home, with a "government engineer."

Alexandria in 1849 "from a relapse of the measle," he and Nancy had produced seventeen children.

One of his sons, William, born at Fort Alexandria in 1831, followed his father into the fur trade. Known as "Billy Bouchie," he spoke seven languages, which he described as Cree, French, Chinook, Nicola Valley, Kamloops, Lillooet and English. "In general conversation," a friend observed, "he invariably used a few words of them all."

His principal duty was as a courier, packing Hudson's Bay Company correspondence between Fort Alexandria and Fort St. James. On those long journeys, he carried with him only the mail pouch, a pound of tea, a small sack of barley and a gun. That was enough, he explained. "I keel rab-

bit, and beaver, sometimes bear, and make him good barley soup."

A fine-looking man—tall, straight and broad-shouldered—and respected as the son of the famous Waccan, he caught the attention of HBC Chief Factor James Douglas, who used Billy Bouchie as his footman when he made official visits to far-flung outposts.

In 1864, Bouchie married Lizette Allard, a daughter of the fur trade. In the 1870s, he left the HBC and took up land on the west bank of the Fraser, opposite the little town of Quesnel. He and Lizette grew grain on their small holding, and Billy operated a canoe-ferry across the river.

When Billy Bouchie died at Quesnel in 1924 at the age of ninety-three, only one of his fourteen children survived him: his youngest son, Joe, born in Quesnel in 1888. Intensely proud of his heritage, Joe continued to reside on his father's old homestead until his own death in 1966.

Today, there are many descendants of Jean Baptiste Boucher throughout British Columbia. Near Quesnel, Bouchie Lake and Bouchie Creek commemorate Billy Bouchie.

Billy Bouchie and a boy, who may be his son Joe, on the Fraser River at Quesnel.

Joe Bouchie standing outside the old homestead in West Quesnel, by the well-known handwritten sign on which he proclaimed his heritage.

This page: Traders husbanded the supply of rum, doling it out only after the most difficult days, but they were always happy to get their hands on Indian dogs, regarded by the voyageurs as particularly tasty.

Facing page: A modern sketch suggests the difficulties Simon Fraser and his men encountered in the Fraser Canyon.

In 1805, Fraser followed Mackenzie's route to the forks of the Finlay and Parsnip Rivers. He then traced the Pack River to McLeod Lake, where he built Fort McLeod, the first permanent European settlement in what would become British Columbia.

The following summer, Fraser was on the "Columbia." He was delighted to discover the Nechako River. "This River is not mentioned by Sir A.M.K. which surprises me not a little, it being in full sight and a fine large River," he noted pointedly. He ascended the Nechako to Stuart Lake, where he left some of his men to build Fort St. James, while he sent others to Fraser Lake to build Fort Fraser. In 1807, he built Fort George (Prince George), at the junction of the Nechako and the "Columbia."

On his exploration of the "great river," Fraser led a party of twenty-one: his two clerks, John Stuart and Jules Quesnel, and nineteen voyageurs, including La Chapelle, Baptiste, D'Alaire, La Certe, Bourbonnais, Gagnier, La Garde and Jean Baptiste Boucher. They embarked from Fort George at five in the morning of 28 May 1808, aboard four canoes. Fraser set a brisk pace. By the time they stopped for breakfast six hours later, they had run down the rapids of Fort George Canyon; by the time they encamped at six that evening, they had passed the West Road River and were above Cottonwood Canyon.

By 3 June, they had reached Iron Canyon. "It is terrible to behold the rapidity and turbulence of the immense body of water that passes in this narrow gut," Fraser shuddered. After a four-hour portage around the canyon, he treated the men to "a dram."

At French Bar Canyon, they held their breaths and flew through. "I scarcely ever saw any thing so dreary, and seldom so dangerous in any country," Fraser wrote. "Whatever way I turn, mountains upon mountains, whose summits are covered with eternal snows, close the gloomy scene."

He ordered the men to continue on foot. Two days later, they arrived at a Lillooet (Stl'atl'imx) village where they learned that the sea was "ten nights" away. They plodded on.

On 13 June, encamped near Bridge River at the end of a hard day, Fraser wrote: "The country through which we passed this day was the most savage that can be imagined." Two days later, they came to a fortified village, a "metropolis," Fraser noted, "a fortification of 100 by 24 feet, surrounded with palisades 18 feet high." There, they negotiated the loan of a canoe.

On 18 June, near the junction of the Thompson River, they made contact with the Thompson (Nlaka'pamux) people, who gave them an enthusiastic welcome. After shaking hands with twelve hundred villagers, Fraser and his men were fed. "We had salmon, berries, oil and roots in abundance, and our men had six dogs."

With three Nlaka'pamux guides, they set off on the worst part of their journey—the stretch of the river from Lytton to Yale. Above Hells Gate, their guides ordered them out of the canoes and directed them up the face of a steep hill.

"One of the old men, a very talkative fellow, and we understand a great warrior, had been at the sea; saw great canoes and white men. He observed that the chiefs of the white men were well dressed and very proud, for, continued he, getting up and clapping his hands on his hips, then strutting about with an air of consequence, 'This is the ways they go.'"
—Simon Fraser

"I have been for a long period among the Rocky Mountains, but have never seen any thing equal to this country," Fraser wrote. "We had to pass where no human being should venture. Yet in those places there is a regular footpath impressed, or rather indented, by frequent travelling upon the very rocks." In places where the ledge disappeared, they were forced to climb upward, clinging to Indian ladders (two long poles with rungs of "sticks" tied with twigs) that were "so slack that the slightest breeze set them in motion—swinging them against the rocks." Where the cliff face overhung the river, they took to "bridges," structures that reminded Fraser of the shrouds of a sailing ship but more closely resembled a trapeze—a horizontal log hanging from hide ropes tied to either end and anchored on the clifftops.

By 28 June, they had passed Spuzzum and entered the territory of the Tait and the Stó:lō. At a village (near present-day Yale), they received the welcome news that the river below was navigable all the way to the sea.

On 2 July, paddling down the river in a borrowed canoe, they caught sight of "a gulph or bay of the sea" (Strait of Georgia). On the north shore, they saw a Musqueam settlement, a huge "fort," which Fraser estimated to be 1,500 feet long and 90 feet wide. After a brief skirmish with the Musqueam, "howling like so many wolves and brandishing their war clubs," he pressed on, following the shore as far as Point Grey. Then he turned back. He had failed to reach the open ocean. And his compass had already told him that he was too far north. The river he had descended was not the Columbia.

"We . . . directed our thoughts toward home," Fraser wrote.

The unknown river was not navigable. To the North West Company, it was useless. Fraser's efforts on the river that would come to bear his name were rewarded with a year's furlough; it was left to another man, David Thompson, to trace the Columbia to its mouth.

CHAPTER 4

SURVIVING *in* NEW CALEDONIA

NEW CALEDONIA, the name Simon Fraser gave to the area around Stuart Lake because it reminded him of his mother's descriptions of her native Scotland, soon came to apply to all of central British Columbia. To the men of the North West Company, it was the "worst side of the Rocky Mountains," a hardship posting, a "land of sin and misery."

Contributing to the misery was New Caledonia's remoteness. To take the furs out and return with supplies involved a 5,000-mile round trip. In early spring, with the snow still thick on the ground, furs collected over the winter were sent by dog teams to Stuart Lake, where they were bundled into "pieces," tightly packed bales weighing about 90 pounds. The pieces were then sent on to the McLeod Lake post to wait for spring breakup on the Peace River. In May, the brigade left in canoes for the portage around the canyon of the Peace, where the boats were cached and the men packed the furs on their backs over 14 miles of "amazing bad" country—up and down steep hills, through swamps, over fallen trees.

Fort St. James was established on Stuart Lake in 1806 by Simon Fraser.

Born in Vermont in 1778,
Daniel Harmon joined the fur
trade when he was twenty-
one. His union with Lizette
Duval, the daughter of a Cree
woman and a French
Canadian, was described as
"unusually happy." "We have
wept together over the early
departure of several children,
and especially, over the death
of a beloved son," Harmon
wrote in 1819.

On the east side of the Peace River Canyon, the furs were loaded into
canoes for the remainder of the trip east. It took five months to deliver the
furs and return to McLeod Lake with the annual "outfit," the trade goods
and the basic supplies, such as flour, sugar, tallow and tea, necessary to sus-
tain the traders for a year.

WITH REMOTENESS AND ISOLATION came a terrible loneliness.
The *engagés*, the French Canadian or métis labourers and boatmen, could
rely on each other for company. But an officer often found himself the only
English-speaking resident of a post. Officers knew French well enough to
direct the engagés, but they yearned for conversations in their native tongue.
To combat the "dreadful solitude," they often made long and dangerous
journeys in the depth of winter to visit another post for the luxury of
talking to another trader. At Fraser Lake in the spring of 1822, John
McDonnell confided to the post journal: "I am today enjoying the greatest
if not the only happiness I can expect in this country: the company of
an intelligent friend—Mr. George McDougall having arrived here at 1 PM
from Fort St. James."

News from home—from Scotland or Montreal or Vermont—took months
to arrive. The answer to a letter sent out with the annual returns might not
reach New Caledonia until the arrival of the following year's outfit.

Most of the officers and men eased their loneliness by taking "country
wives," Native or métis women whom they married "by the custom of the
country." Many of the traders looked upon their liaisons as temporary.

Some men considered their associations more permanent—if only for
so long as they remained in New Caledonia. In 1805, when Daniel Harmon
took Lizette Duval, a young métis woman, as his country wife, he confided
to his journal: "My intentions now are to keep her as long as I remain in
this uncivilized part of the world, but when I return to my native land shall
endeavour to place her in the hands of some good honest Man, with whom
she can spend the remainder of her Days in this Country."

As it happened, Harmon's initial resolve weakened. By 1819, when he
left New Caledonia for a year-long furlough, he discovered that he could not
bear the thought of leaving his "beloved" children in the "wilderness," but
neither could he bring himself to separate them from Lizette. "How could I
tear them from a mother's love and leave her to mourn over their absence?"
he asked himself. And he took Lizette and the children with him when he
returned home to Vermont.

Other men chose a different course. William Connolly was only seventeen when he took fifteen-year-old Suzanne as his country wife. They had
been together for twenty-eight years when Connolly, while on furlough in
Montreal, decided to repudiate Suzanne and marry his cousin, the "ami-
able" and "cultivated" Julia Woolrich.

In addition to isolation and loneliness, clouds of biting insects added to
New Caledonia's reputation as "a vile country." No sooner were the lakes and
rivers free of ice than mosquitoes appeared. In May 1811, the trader at
Stuart Lake recorded: "This afternoon the Ice in this Lake broke up—and
Musquetoes begin to come about and troublesome fellows they are." And
after the mosquitoes came the blackflies. "The men as busy as yesterday,"
John Stuart reported in 1820, "but the flies are so numerous that they
cannot stand it."

The son of a Scots plantation manager and his Barbados-born mistress, James Douglas was born in Demerara, British Guiana, in 1803. After being schooled in Scotland, he joined the fur trade, and in 1825 he was sent to New Caledonia.

In 1828, while serving at Fort St. James, he married, "by the custom of the country," Amelia, the sixteen-year-old daughter of the trader William Connolly and his Cree wife, Suzanne. Amelia and his children became the "tender ties" that bound James Douglas to the west.

In 1832, Hudson's Bay Company Governor George Simpson penned a shrewd assessment of James Douglas: "A stout powerful active man of good conduct and respectable abilities . . . Well qualified for any Service requiring Bodily exertion, firmness of mind and the exercise of Sound judgment."

Those qualities stood Douglas in good stead. In 1849, he was given the important role of chief factor in charge of Fort Victoria. Two years later, he was appointed the second governor of the Colony of Vancouver Island. And

in 1858, when the Colony of British Columbia was formed, he became its first governor. Criticized by some as being too authoritarian, he would hold both positions until 1864, when he was replaced by two men and was rewarded with a knighthood.

In an age when social class meant everything, Governor Douglas kept to hand a copy of Burke's *Peerage, Baronetage and Knighthood* to check the antecedents of colonial appointees, and he was acutely aware of his own humble origins. To maintain his authority, he adopted a stern demeanour. According to his son-in-law, Dr. John Helmcken, Douglas was "not humorous—never joked." Others found the governor "imperious," "stiff and formal" and "Pomposity itself."

While most colonists agreed that Douglas was the right man for the times, others felt he had been promoted beyond his position in life. Annie Deans, semi-literate and the wife of an indentured farmworker, thought herself superior to the governor: "He has been all his life among North American Indians and has got one of them for a wife so how can it be expected that he can know

Sir James Douglas, Knight Commander of the Order of the Bath.

Between 1829 and 1854, Amelia Douglas gave birth to thirteen children, only four of whom survived her.

anything at all about Governing one of England's last Colony's in North America."

As the governor's wife, and later as Lady Douglas, Amelia was at the peak of colonial society, but she played no official role. Some found her "modest as a wood violet" and attributed her absence from public life to shyness. But Amelia was also known as practical and strong-willed. Her choice to remain in the background may have been based, in part, on her

reluctance to expose herself to snobbery.

Amelia loved to tell her children the stories she had learned from her Cree mother. "As a little girl I used to listen to these legends with the greatest delight," Martha Douglas remembered. "When written they lose their charm, which was in the telling. They need the quaint songs and the sweet voice that told them, the winter gloaming and the bright fire as the only light." But when Martha regaled her classmates at an English boarding school with her mother's tales, her father warned: "I have no objection to your telling the old stories but pray do not tell the world that they are Mamma's."

By the time he died in 1877, Sir James Douglas had become a British Columbia icon. "Today the whole Province is in tears," the *British Colonist* mourned. "Truly he has set an example of greatness and patriotism worthy of being copied by future generations of British Columbians."

When Amelia Douglas died in 1890, the *Colonist* recalled her "unwavering kindness" and "unostentatious Christian charity."

The Douglas family's Victoria home stood on the south shore of James Bay. The site is now occupied by the Royal British Columbia Museum.

But, when it came to hardship, nothing—not isolation, not loneliness, not the exhausting work of the brigades, not the idleness and boredom of the frozen winters—compared to the appalling monotony of the food. In order to cut the costs of supplying New Caledonia, posts were expected to be as self-sufficient as possible. In 1811, Daniel Harmon started a garden at Stuart Lake. Late in May, he planted potatoes and sowed barley and turnip seeds: "The first we ever sowed, on this west side of the mountain." It was hardly worth the effort. New Caledonia was still gripped by the lingering effects of the centuries-long period of cold weather known as the Little Ice Age. "In every month of the year, there are frosts," Harmon noted. With so few frost-free days, gardens failed to thrive. And so the people of New Caledonia were forced to rely on dried salmon, the "New Caledonian staff of life."

No one complained about fresh salmon, which was consumed with enthusiasm, but dried salmon was quite another matter. Salmon was preserved by splitting and hanging in the air to dry, a process that rendered a 10-pound salmon into a hard, 1-pound "shingle," with "little more substance than a piece of rotten wood." No matter how unpalatable it might be, New Caledonians depended on the "misery of Damned Dried Salmon" for much of the year. And they consumed it in vast quantities. The daily ration of four dried salmon (when other food was available) rose to seven or eight during the winter.

As well as being unbearably boring—"How long, oh Lord," one trader moaned—a steady diet of dried salmon was so lacking in calories and vitamin C that some men began to show symptoms of scurvy, and almost all became weak and sickly. To make matters worse, dried salmon could be a powerful laxative. "It is quite *Medicinal*," Thomas Dears wrote to a friend. "This very morning one of my men in attending on the calls of nature evacuated to the distance of six feet . . . often we are troubled in this way."

"Our men are the greatest gormandizers that I have ever come across, yesterday Evening they got two of the largest Salmon Caught weighing without exaggeration 40 lbs Net and 12 dog Salmon which they devoured without having a fish [left] this morning— this is between 3 Men 1 Woman & 2 Children."
—post journal, Fort St. James

"You Know I am generally a slender person. What would you say if you saw my emaciated Body now? I am every morning, when dressing, in danger of slipping through my Breeks and falling into my Boots. Many a night I go to bed hungry and craving something better than this horrid dried Salmon we are obliged to live upon."
—Thomas Dears

Jean Baptiste St. Paul Lolo served as the interpreter at Fort Kamloops. In this 1865 photograph, he appears with his wife and younger daughters. An older daughter, Sophia, married John Tod, the trader at Fort Kamloops.

On special occasions, the usual fare was enlivened by the addition of fattened dogs, known as "New Caledonia bears," a great favourite of the engagés and best eaten boiled. One diarist wrote on 25 December 1824: "This being Christmas Day, the Men did nothing & got a dram each, with 2 dogs as their Christmas Goose."

Yet, New Caledonians realized they could not survive without dried salmon. If salmon had not returned to the rivers by August, people began to worry. On 2 August 1811, the officer at Stuart Lake admitted his concern: "Five Salmon is all the Provisions we have in the Fort & we are no less than ten persons . . . what will become of us unless the Salmon begin soon to make their appearance in the River." A week later, he sent all the men, women and children at the post out to gather berries. His relief was palpable on 2 September: "One of the Natives has taken a Salmon therefore it is to be hoped that in a few Days they will be plentiful." By the end of October, he felt he could relax. "We now have 25,000 Salmon in our Store which will be a sufficiency for all hands till next autumn."

In New Caledonia, it was said that "if the salmon fails, all fails" and "both the Natives and the Traders may be said to exist rather than to live." If there were no salmon, there would be no furs.

Left: After enjoying the company of several country wives, John Tod married a Welshwoman, Eliza Waugh, who within two years went mad. "The fact is that Mrs. Tod's state of health, or rather I should Say Mind, is Such that I must return her again to England," Tod confided to a friend. As his next and last wife, he chose a woman capable of enduring a fur trader's life.

Right: In 1843, sixteen-year-old Sophia Lolo became John Tod's country wife. They settled in Oak Bay in 1851, becoming the first people to choose southern Vancouver Island as their retirement home.

THE HUDSON'S BAY COMPANY had noted the success of the Nor'westers in the west, and an intense rivalry, which at times verged on open warfare, had developed between the two companies. In 1821, under pressure from Britain's Colonial Office, the companies merged under the HBC's banner. George Simpson was given responsibility for the Northern District, which included New Caledonia, as well as the more southerly and less profitable Columbia District, which had been the HBC's area of activity.

Simpson decided to shift the brigade route from the Peace to the Columbia River. Beginning in 1826, furs were carried to Fort St. James, where they were loaded into canoes and sent down the Stuart and Nechako Rivers to the Fraser, and down the Fraser to Fort Alexandria, built in 1821 at the point at which Alexander Mackenzie had turned back. At Alexandria,

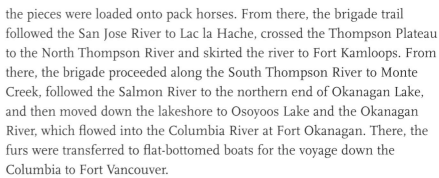

Fort Kamloops was established in 1812 at the junction of the North and South Thompson Rivers. John Tod, who took over the fort in 1841 and to whom this painting is attributed, noted: "The Shuswap [Secwepemc] Indians called the place 'Kahm-o-loops,' meaning 'the meeting of the waters.'"

the pieces were loaded onto pack horses. From there, the brigade trail followed the San Jose River to Lac la Hache, crossed the Thompson Plateau to the North Thompson River and skirted the river to Fort Kamloops. From there, the brigade proceeded along the South Thompson River to Monte Creek, followed the Salmon River to the northern end of Okanagan Lake, and then moved down the lakeshore to Osoyoos Lake and the Okanagan River, which flowed into the Columbia River at Fort Okanagan. There, the furs were transferred to flat-bottomed boats for the voyage down the Columbia to Fort Vancouver.

Compared to the route over the mountains, the Columbia route was shorter by half, involving a round trip of 2,400 miles. And because there were no difficult portages, the route was easier on the men. It was, however, extremely hard on the horses. Their backs sagged under the heavy packs. Some died on the trail. Many went lame, their unshod hooves worn away by the rocky terrain.

When horses first began to be used, they were at the mercy of fur traders. "None of our men understand much about horsemanship," William Connolly admitted. During the winter of 1826, seventy animals—three quarters of the herd overwintering at Fort Alexandria—starved to death. In years when the salmon runs failed, horses were picked off and eaten by starving Indians, and, if provisions at a post ran low, officers were prepared to sacrifice some of the "useful Animals" for food.

THE HBC HAD BUILT Fort Vancouver on the north bank of the Columbia River in the hope that, when the time came to divide American and British possessions, the boundary would follow the river. If the 49th

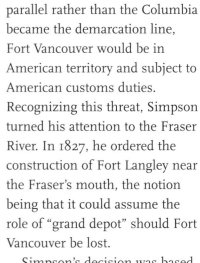

Sir George Simpson, Governor of the Hudson's Bay Company.

parallel rather than the Columbia became the demarcation line, Fort Vancouver would be in American territory and subject to American customs duties. Recognizing this threat, Simpson turned his attention to the Fraser River. In 1827, he ordered the construction of Fort Langley near the Fraser's mouth, the notion being that it could assume the role of "grand depot" should Fort Vancouver be lost.

Simpson's decision was based, in part, on his hope that the Fraser River might prove to be navigable after all. In the autumn of 1828, when the river was low, and with "three of the most skillful Bowsmen in the country," he spent two terrifying days descending the river from its junction with the Thompson to Fort Langley. He emerged from the experience with a new

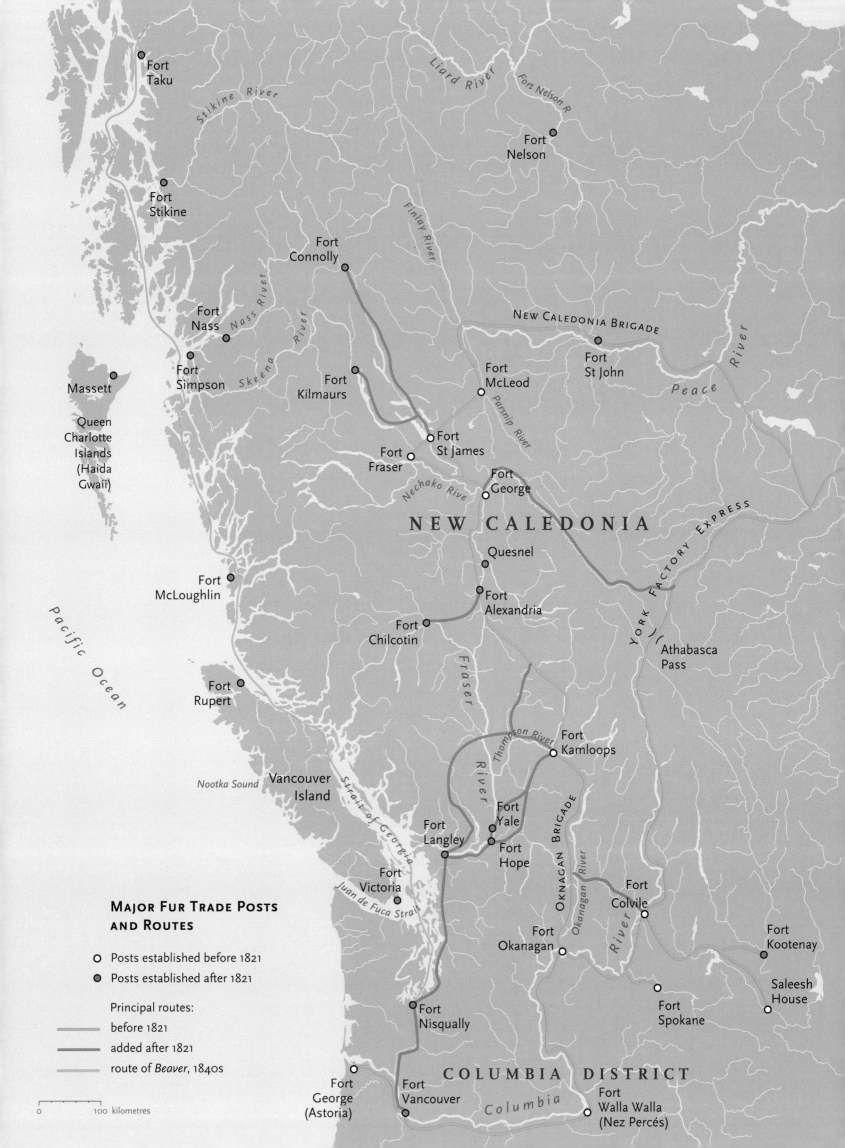

Fort Taku

Stikine River

Liard River

Fort Nelson R

Fort Nelson

Fort Stikine

Fort Connolly

Finlay River

New Caledonia Brigade

Fort Nass

Nass River

Fort St John

Peace River

Massett

Fort Simpson

Skeena River

Fort Kilmaurs

Fort McLeod

Parsnip River

Queen Charlotte Islands (Haida Gwaii)

Fort St James

Fort Fraser

Fort George

Nechako Rive

NEW CALEDONIA

York Factory Express

Fort McLoughlin

Pacific Ocean

Quesnel

Fort Alexandria

Athabasca Pass

Fort Chilcotin

Fraser River

Fort Rupert

Nootka Sound

Vancouver Island

Thompson River

Fort Kamloops

Strait of Georgia

Fort Yale

River

Oknagan Brigade

Fort Langley

Fort Hope

Fort Colvile

Fort Victoria

Okanagan River

Fort Kootenay

Juan de Fuca Strait

MAJOR FUR TRADE POSTS AND ROUTES

○ Posts established before 1821

● Posts established after 1821

Principal routes:

before 1821

added after 1821

route of *Beaver*, 1840s

Fort Okanagan

River

Saleesh House

Fort Spokane

0   100 kilometres

Fort Nisqually

COLUMBIA   DISTRICT

Fort George (Astoria)

Fort Vancouver

Columbia

Fort Walla Walla (Nez Percés)

Making a portrait was an arduous process that required men to unload the canoe, and then carry it and more than a ton of furs or trade goods and supplies overland on their backs. The route from Lillooet to the Fraser River via Harrison Lake was rejected because it called for seven portages.

respect for Simon Fraser and a firm opinion. "Frazers River," he wrote, "can no longer be thought of as a practicable communication with the interior."

If the Fraser could not be used, then an overland route from Fort Kamloops to Fort Langley must be found. In 1845, Alexander Caulfield Anderson, the trader at Fort Alexandria, trekked along the Fraser to Lillooet. From there, on foot and by canoe, he followed Seton and Anderson Lakes to Harrison Lake, and went down the Harrison River to the Fraser and Fort Langley. Concluding that the Harrison route could never be practical for the brigades as it involved at least seven portages, Anderson tried again. Setting out from Fort Langley, he followed the Fraser to the Coquihalla River and marched over the Cascades to the headwaters of the Similkameen. But that route, too, proved unusable, since the path rose so high that mountain snows would render it impractical.

The final brigade trail moved overland from Fort Kamloops, descended to the Fraser at Spuzzum and, after crossing the river by boat or barge, looped over the hills before returning to the river. At that point, where it was possible to descend the Fraser by boat or canoe, the HBC built Fort Yale. For returning brigades, Fort Hope was built at the head of upstream navigation.

There was another problem to overcome. Fort Langley could never fill the role of central depot, the post at which ships sailing from England delivered trade goods and collected furs, because the sandbars and shifting shallows at the Fraser's mouth were too serious an obstacle to navigation for all but the most shallow-draughted vessels. Searching for a better site, the Hudson's Bay Company turned its attention to Vancouver Island.

CHAPTER 5

A PERFECT EDEN

In 1842, when James Douglas selected the site of Fort Victoria in Songhees (Lekwammen) territory, he enthused: "The place itself appears a perfect 'Eden' in the midst of the dreary wilderness of the Northwest coast."

IN 1842, the Hudson's Bay Company dispatched James Douglas from Fort Vancouver to survey Vancouver Island's southern shore for a suitable site for a new fort. One particular location he found to be ideal. It had a good, safe harbour and a supply of fresh water, and it was surrounded by open, grassy fields, dotted with Garry oaks. "Valuable tillage and pasture land," Douglas noted.

Fort Victoria was built in 1843. Three years later, the Oregon Treaty settled on the 49th parallel, rather than the Columbia River, as the international boundary. In 1849, the HBC transferred the role of central

Charles Ross, who supervised the building of Fort Victoria, described his wife, Isabella: "She is not indeed fitted to shine at the head of a nobleman's table, but she suits the sphere [in which] she has to move much better than any such toy—in short, she is a native of the country, and as to beauty quite as comely as her husband!" Isabella outlived her husband by forty-one years. Using money from his estate, she purchased 100 acres near Fort Victoria and became the first woman of European descent to own property in British Columbia.

"Sunday at the Staines school is to this day, a day
of terror to me. After morning prayers we had breakfast,
such as it was, bread and treacle and tea
without milk. Church at 11 in the mess hall to which we
were summoned by the ringing of the Fort bell,
then dinner, potatoes, meat, sometimes fish, then a dreary
afternoon learning the Collects; how I hated them."
—James "Jimmy" Anderson

"The Hudson's Bay Company have kept their territories as
inaccessible as the Jesuits kept Paraguay . . . The agents of
the Hudson's Bay Company have discouraged settled habits
among their Indians, and communicated to them the worst
vices of civilised society without its redeeming qualities."
—London Daily News

depot to Fort Victoria and sent James Douglas north as chief factor in charge of the fort; the focus of the fur trade shifted from the Columbia River to Vancouver Island.

The HBC had decided to recruit a schoolmaster for the children growing up uneducated in New Caledonia and the Columbia District. Now, the Company's school would be established at Fort Victoria. Run by Reverend Robert Staines and his wife, Emma, the first school in what would become British Columbia was private, fee-charging and sectarian. It was available only to the children of the Company's officers, who paid for the privilege of enrolling them, and the doctrines of the Church of England were an important part of the curriculum. The French-speaking, Roman Catholic offspring of engagés were left to their own devices. And for that they may have been grateful. As Jimmy Anderson, one of Staines's pupils, recalled, the schoolmaster was "of rather uncertain temper and disposed at times to be unduly severe in administering corporal punishment."

Children from mainland posts attended the school as boarders, their dormitory the upper floor of the Bachelors' Hall. One night, Jimmy Anderson discovered he was sharing his bed with a rat bent on carrying off the crust of bread he had hidden under the covers. "With a quick movement I pinned him to the side of the bed with my blanket covered arm," Jimmy remembered. He was determined to catch it—Reverend Staines paid a bounty of a shilling a dozen.

BRITAIN WAS CONCERNED about American dreams of gaining control of all the coast from California to Alaska, expressed in the slogan "Fifty-four Forty or Fight!" Washington and Oregon territories were filling with settlers. If Vancouver Island was to remain British, it would have to attract a population loyal to the crown. In 1849, the Colony of Vancouver Island was formed. Fort Victoria became its capital, a governor was dispatched from England, and the Hudson's Bay Company was given the task of administering the new colony. The HBC became "true and absolute lords and proprietors" of the island for a period of ten years. The Company agreed to encourage colonization and to use 90 per cent of the revenues produced by land sales to provide civic amenities such as roads and bridges.

Few colonists were expected. In the nearby American territories, land could be had for nothing. In the Colony of Vancouver Island, land cost £1 an acre, the minimum purchase was 20 acres, and for every 100 acres a colonist acquired, he was required to bring with him five single men or three married couples as farm workers. In addition, gold had been discovered in California, and it was becoming difficult to keep the Company's servants on the island, let alone attract newcomers. "It is in my view worthless as a seat for a colony," the HBC's secretary, Archibald Barclay, huffed. "It is about the last place in the globe to which (were I going to emigrate) I should select as an abode."

But a colonist arrived, just the same. Captain Walter Colquhoun Grant, late of the Scots Greys, was the first person to see a chance to make a fresh start. His debts were "numerous" and his creditors "pressing" when he sold his commission in the army and shipped out for Vancouver Island, with £4,000 in unpaid bills waiting for his return.

British Columbia's first independent settler set an almost unmatchable standard for incompetence. When he reached Fort Victoria in August 1849, he was flat broke and encumbered with all manner of useless items, such as cricket bats and wickets, that he considered essential for a gentleman farmer. For the incidentals—the food to keep him and his workmen alive during their first winter, and the oxen, cattle and horses to stock his estate—he depended on the Hudson's Bay Company. He had signed on as the colonial surveyor (becoming British Columbia's first civil servant) for £100 a year. Just deduct from his wages whatever he owed, he suggested airily.

Captain Walter Colquhoun Grant, British Columbia's first independent settler, christened his farm "Mullachard" after his ancestral home in Scotland. "The house was a shanty," a visitor scoffed.

As a surveyor, Grant was a disappointment. At the Royal Military College, Sandhurst, he had made only a nodding acquaintance with the subject. On Vancouver Island, he had expected to lead a party of experienced men. Instead, he discovered that he was required to accomplish the surveys alone, a task he found particularly difficult since he possessed almost no sense of direction, on one occasion becoming lost in the woods and "in very bad shape" when he was found five days later.

During the winter of 1850, Grant, finding himself gripped by seasonal depression, discovered an antidote that continues to serve British

Richard Blanshard was appointed the first governor of the Colony of Vancouver Island in 1849.

"Window glass unknown, some used oiled paper instead. Furniture none, round logs for seats, bunks for bedsteads, deer, bear and sheep skins for carpet, bugs innumerable, fleas without limit."
—Charles Bayley

"I have long since given up the thoughts of going to lay my bones in the land of my Fathers. I must seek out some retired spot, where my savage habits & mode of life will be less under the eye of ceremonial observance, and where my liberty is not likely to be hemmed by Game laws."
—John Tod

"I am aware that my family, being natives of this country, would not be fit for society, but . . . they are mine and I am bound to provide for them."
—John Work

Columbians. He hopped aboard a ship bound for the HBC's post in the Hawaiian Islands and spent two months warming himself in the sun. "I returned from the Islands with fresh vigour," he announced.

Captain Grant hung on for another year, and then quit the colony for good. Possessing an irresistible charm, he left behind many bad debts but no bad feelings. He had, a creditor sighed, "a peculiar talent for getting into the pockets of his friends."

RICHARD BLANSHARD, the first governor of the Colony of Vancouver Island, was an ambitious young barrister. He must have hoped that the position would lead to more prestigious appointments, and on paper, at least, the responsibilities he was assuming had the potential to launch a successful career. As governor, he had the power to raise and command a militia. He was also empowered to appoint an advisory council and to arrange for the election of a general assembly. With the advice and consent of those two bodies, he was to enact all laws and ordinances required for the "Peace, Order and good Government" of the colony. But all this supposed that there would be colonists to govern and land sales to provide revenues.

Blanshard may have begun to suspect that things would not go well as soon as he arrived. On 11 March 1850, when he disembarked from HMS *Driver* to read the proclamation announcing his appointment, a foot of snow lay on the ground. He was "rather startled by the wild aspect of the country," James Douglas observed.

Only eight months after arriving in the colony, Blanshard wrote to London requesting permission to resign. Ten months would pass before the dispatch, relieving him of office, arrived from England. Suffering agonies from tic douloureux and plagued by recurring bouts of malaria, Blanshard spent much of the time in bed, smoking his pipe, nursing his ailments with morphine and writing dispatches critical of the HBC's role as colonial administrator.

The policies pursued by the Company, Blanshard insisted, tended to "exclude free Settlers and reserve the Island either as an enlarged Post of their own, or a desert." He had a point. The HBC had reserved for its own use a large tract of the best land on southern Vancouver Island. That land was available only to the Company, or the Puget Sound Agricultural Company (a subsidiary of the HBC) or retired HBC employees.

The HBC operated three farms: Beckley Farm, North Dairy Farm and, near Cadboro Bay, 1,030-acre Uplands Farm. Four large farms, ranging from 600 to 1,000 acres, were established by the Puget Sound Agricultural Company (PSAC). Each PSAC farm was managed by a bailiff, a gentleman-farmer who was expected to assume the role of a country squire. The farms were worked by indentured servants who, in exchange for free passage from Britain, signed a five-year work contract, and who would, when their contracts expired, be granted 20 acres of land.

To HBC retirees, the Colony of Vancouver Island was like an answer to prayer. For men who had spent thirty years in the wilderness, returning to civilization had little appeal, but remaining in New Caledonia, with its harsh winters and its summertime insect hordes, also lacked charm. Southern Vancouver Island provided an attractive alternative. Winters were mild, summers were warm and dry, mosquitoes were rare, blackflies non-existent.

In 1848, when he retired from the fur trade, John Tod spent £100 to purchase a holding at Oak Bay, an easy walk from Fort Victoria. Soon, other HBC men began to follow his example. But three years after the creation of the colony, there were still no more than twenty landowners on Vancouver Island.

Blanshard's instructions had required him to appoint an advisory council and to arrange for the election of a general assembly. With so few settlers, he had seen no reason to hurry. He did not accomplish the first part of his mandate until 27 August 1851, when he appointed James Douglas, John Tod and Captain James Cooper to his advisory council. Three days later, when the council assembled for its first meeting, Blanshard announced his resignation, and James Douglas took his place as governor.

The Works' Hillside Farm was renowned for its hospitality. To Charles Wilson, a Royal Engineer posted in Victoria in the 1860s, it was a home away from home: "The Works are about the kindest people I ever came across. 'My western home' I call it." Wilson celebrated New Year's Day 1861 at Hillside Farm: "There were about 30 at dinner—such a display of fish, flesh and fowl and pastry as is seldom seen. We danced until 12 & then all hands sat down to a sumptuous supper and then set to work dancing again until a very late hour."

Like Blanshard, Douglas felt no pressing need for advice. Seven months passed before he called together his council, and then only because the colony was so chronically short of funds. After the council balked at the idea of imposing import duties, Douglas suggested licensing the sale of alcohol. That seemed a surefire revenue producer. As one settler put it, "It would take almost a line of packet ships, running regular between here and San Francisco, to supply this Island with grog, so great a thirst prevails among its inhabitants." On 29 March 1853, the council reluctantly agreed to charge £100 for a wholesale licence and £110 for retail, and then got down to the business of approving the construction of two schools.

In London, the colonial secretary began to worry about the state of affairs on Vancouver Island. He wrote to Governor Douglas in February 1856, pointing out that the time to institute an elected assembly had long since passed. The instructions provided by the Colonial Office restricted the franchise to men who owned freehold property of at least 20 acres, a qualification that limited the electorate to forty-three. Even fewer could put themselves forward as candidates, since to run for office a man was required to own property valued at £300. "At first it seemed difficult to find

Craigflower was one of the two schools financed by liquor taxes. Built in 1855, it is the oldest schoolhouse in British Columbia.

people qualified or willing to become representatives," an observer noted. But, after it was discovered that the election would be lubricated by alcohol, the electors got into the spirit of things. And on 12 August 1856, the first elected assembly west of the Great Lakes was sworn into office in the common room of the Bachelors' Hall.

A seven-member assembly, a three-member council and a royal governor seemed rather more government than the colony required. A census published in 1855 revealed that the European population of Vancouver Island numbered only 774, almost half of whom were children.

RICHARD BLANSHARD HAD SEEN IT as his duty to "repress and over-awe the natives." When James Douglas became governor, he adopted a different approach. In his role as HBC chief factor, he had placed great importance on maintaining good relations by negotiating with local Native people to purchase the land required by the Company. The first conveyance, signed by See-sachasis and ten others, was dated 29 April 1850. By February 1851, Douglas had obtained title to all the land within the fur trade reserve near Fort Victoria, as well as blocks of land near the coal outcrops at Fort Rupert and Nanaimo, for a total outlay of about £750.

In the event of trouble, Douglas was prepared to act on the principle that it was "unjust to hold *tribes* responsible for the acts of *individuals*." In 1852, when an HBC shepherd was murdered, Douglas identified two culprits: one man was a Cowichan, "the most numerous and Warlike tribe on Vancouver Island"; the other was the son of a Nanaimo (Snuneymuxw) chief. On 4 January 1853, 130 officers and men from HMS *Thetis,* under the command of Governor Douglas, sailed out of Victoria for the mouth of the Cowichan River. There, Douglas dispatched messengers to inform the Cowichan people of the reason for their visit.

Early next morning, Douglas's force took up a "commanding position" and waited. "In the course of two hours the Indians began to drop down the River in their war canoes and landed a little above the position we

"How many times the candidates visited every freeholder in the district, how many bottles of whiskey were drunk, how many songs sung, deponent sayeth not. It was a good time for some of the voters and a break in monotony, a small game of fisticuffs did no harm."
—Dr. John Sebastian Helmcken

"Soon rolling down the river came the melancholy boom of the war-drums, and far-off cries resolved themselves into war-songs, as a fleet of large canoes, lashed together in triplets, paddled furiously round a bend of the river and headed for our position at full speed . . . Over 200 tall warriors, their height exaggerated with head-plumes, faces terrifically painted with red ochre, decked with loin-ropes of shells which met their deer-skin leggings and clattered with every movement as they leaped from the canoes."
—Lieutenant John Moresby

occupied," Douglas reported. After a brief standoff, followed by lengthy negotiations, the fugitive was produced and taken prisoner.

Douglas proceeded to Nanaimo, where he succeeded in arresting the second suspect. On 11 January 1853, aboard the HBC's ship *Beaver*, the two men were tried before a jury of naval officers. Found guilty and sentenced to death, they were hanged on a gallows erected on Protection Island in Nanaimo harbour. The two men, who "met their death with steady fortitude," had been tried by the first jury empanelled in British Columbia and were the first to be sentenced to death.

Cannonballs stored at Esquimalt naval base, 1860s. Governor Richard Blanshard believed in the efficacy of gunboat diplomacy. In 1850, when news reached Fort Victoria that three white men had been murdered by the Newitty (Nahwitti), Blanshard sailed to the northeast coast of Vancouver Island aboard the nineteen-gun HMS *Daedalus*, fired on the Nahwitti village suspected of harbouring the murderers and burned it to the ground.

The first steamer on the Pacific Coast, the Hudson's Bay Company's *Beaver* arrived on the Columbia River in 1836. In 1888, steaming out of Vancouver harbour, *Beaver* ran aground near Prospect Point. Not considered worth salvaging, the ship's hulk was left on the rocks and became a favourite destination for Stanley Park picnickers.

FORT VICTORIA was built in 1843. Cedar logs, supplied by the Songhees (Lekwammen) people in exchange for Hudson's Bay Company blankets, were driven into the ground to form a palisade almost 20 feet high, enclosing a quadrangle 300 by 330 feet. An octagonal two-storey bastion, built of heavy squared logs and provided with eight cannon bays, stood at the southwest corner. (The bastion's cannon claimed only one victim, Charles Fish, who died in 1851 after his arm was blown off when the cannon was fired to celebrate the arrival of a ship.)

A bell that hung in the bell-tower near the centre of the fort was rung to mark times for rising and meals, the beginning and end of the working day and Sunday services. Each peal was met by a chorus from the fort's dogs and an answering chorus from the dogs in the Lekwammen village across the harbour.

The military-like organization of the Hudson's Bay Company separated the officers, who were usually Scots, from the engagés, the labouring class composed mostly of French Canadians and métis but also including a few Kanakas, recruited in the Hawaiian Islands. Only officers were invited to dine at the chief factor's house. During James Douglas's term of office, dinners

The bastion at Fort Victoria.

were sombre affairs, the chief factor greeting any undue levity with a stern frown. It was with some relief that young officers escaped to the conviviality of their own quarters, the Bachelors' Hall, to enjoy a pipe and to savour more than a few post-prandial brandies.

Years later, the town that grew around Fort Victoria would become famous for its Englishness. But during the 1840s, the main influence was French Canadian or métis. And, like other fur trade

posts in New Caledonia and the Columbia District, Fort Victoria was built using the French-Canadian method of post-on-sill construction. Logs, squared by axemen so expert that a hand passed over the finished surface would not contract a splinter, were fitted into vertical grooved posts—unlike the American style, which utilized round logs. Most of the engagés, like the blacksmith, Beauchamps, who was renowned for his "blood curdling bad lan-

guage in French and English," spoke some English, but the principal language spoken in the fort was French.

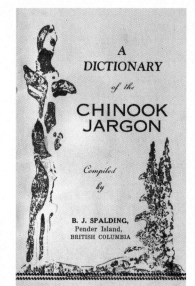

A DICTIONARY of the CHINOOK JARGON

Compiled by

B. J. SPALDING, Pender Island, BRITISH COLUMBIA

Chinook jargon, a mixture of French, English and various Native dialects and languages spoken from the Columbia River to Nootka Sound, became British Columbia's *lingua franca*, used by fur traders and missionaries, and later by Cariboo miners and Victoria businessmen. Superintendent of Indian Affairs Israel Powell commented, in 1873: "The Chinook Jargon . . . is very little used or understood by the natives outside of white settlements, and is generally (I think justly too) despised by them, as being far inferior in every way to their own tongue."

Interior view of Fort Victoria showing the bell tower, chief factor's residence (left) and Bachelors' Hall (right).

The marines and seamen of HMS *Thetis* had proven their usefulness, but the British Admiralty remained averse to assigning a ship for the colony's year-round protection. It took a faraway war to start the Admiralty down the road to a change of policy.

In 1854, Britain declared war on Russia. Although most of the action centred on the Black Sea and the Crimea, the Royal Navy's Pacific fleet, based at Valparaiso, Chile, launched an attack on the Russian fortifications at Petropavlovsk on the Kamchatka peninsula. In October of that year, three Royal Navy ships entered Esquimalt harbour, carrying eighty men wounded in the assault. But Fort Victoria and its farms had few medical supplies and no hospital, and the small fleet was forced to sail on to San Francisco.

The following year, Governor Douglas was informed that a second attack was being planned and that he should be prepared for the arrival of three or four ships in July. They would require coal, fresh meat and vegetables, and a building that could serve as a temporary hospital. On a parcel of

In 1865, the British Admiralty named Esquimalt the base for its Pacific squadron. The presence of the Royal Navy became an essential ingredient in the rare mix that created Victoria's character as "a little bit of old England."

land on Duntze Head at the entrance to Esquimalt harbour—a site later described as "most unsuitable" and calculated to "encourage and invite" a shelling—Douglas ordered the construction of the "Crimea huts," three small buildings housing a kitchen, surgeon's quarters and an operating room.

When the British fleet arrived at Petropavlovsk, it found the fort deserted. Instead of dozens of wounded men, the Crimea huts were called upon to house only one seaman suffering from scurvy. Still, the strategic importance of Esquimalt as a supply base had been established, and with the Crimea huts, the navy found itself in possession of shore facilities.

With Britain's attention now focussed on the north Pacific, more ships began to call at Esquimalt, and the officers and men of the Royal Navy

Top: HMS *Zealous* served on the Esquimalt station from 1867 to 1869.

Bottom: Officers from HMS *Zealous* performed plays and pantomimes for the entertainment of the colonists. In the centre, wearing the flowery dress, is Lieutenant Sydney Smith Haldimand Dickens, fifth son of the novelist Charles Dickens.

began to influence the character of the colony. The arrival of a naval ship invariably occasioned a round of parties. Soon after HMS *Monarch* and HMS *Trincomalee* dropped anchor at Esquimalt in August 1856, Governor Douglas hosted a ball at the fort, with music provided by *Monarch's* band. "A very pleasant party, kept up until 4 o'clock in the morning," a lady colonist confided to her diary. Festivities were not limited to the governor's ball. Riding parties collected at Colwood Farm to explore the countryside. Naval officers hosted shipboard dinners and dances, and volunteered ships' bands to play at any celebratory occasion.

The governor and the leading families usually restricted their guest lists to officers. Ordinary seamen and the members of the colony's labouring class were seldom part of the festivities. "Great Ball held at Victoria, riff-raff excluded," Robert Melrose, an indentured farm worker, complained.

Farm workers amused themselves by heavy drinking. The seamen did likewise. Melrose, who carefully calculated the degrees of inebriation enjoyed by himself and his friends, experienced feelings of solidarity when he informed his diary, "One of Neptune's sons, belonging to the 'Trincomalee' got himself hurt by falling from a tree, after drinking a bottle of Grog on top of it."

BY 1857, the Colony of Vancouver Island was being described as "a kind of England attached to the continent of North America." Within a year, it would become "a little bit of old San Francisco." The groundwork for the American invasion was laid when an Indian discovered gold on the Thompson River. Supplied with shovels and pans by the trader at Fort Kamloops, the "whole tribe forthwith began to collect the glittering metal."

Douglas hoped to keep the discovery quiet. There was no government on the mainland, no one to exercise British authority over the goldfields. But the word spread, and a few Americans began to move north to the Thompson River.

Saturday 3	Andrew Hume ¾ Drunk, James Whyte & James Liddle ½ Drunk
Tuesday 6	J. Wilson & the Author ¾ Drunk
Saturday 17	The Author ¾ Drunk. James Wilson ½ Drunk
Saturday 24	James Wilson Whole Drunk. James Liddle ¾ d. The Author ¼ Drunk.

—Robert Melrose, diary

"About 1857 Governor Douglas at the mess shewed us a few grains of scale gold which had been sent him from the North Thompson. This was the first gold I ever saw and probably the first that arrived here. The Governor attached great importance to it and thought it meant a great change and a busy time."

—Dr. John Sebastian Helmcken

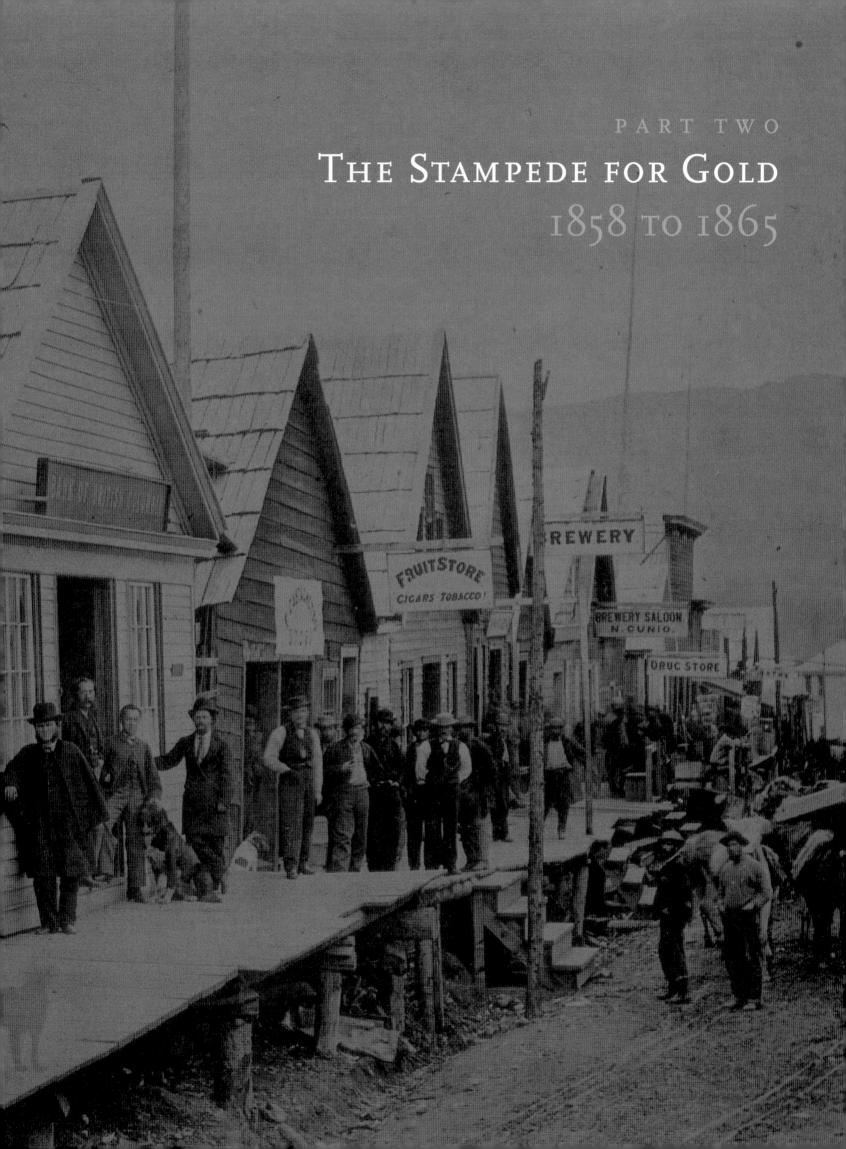

PART TWO

THE STAMPEDE FOR GOLD

1858 TO 1865

CHAPTER 6

GOLD FEVER

Previous page: The gold-rush town of Barkerville.

This page: The first goldseekers travelled north from San Francisco aboard the *Commodore.* "The good people of Victoria were at church when we arrived, and were perfectly astounded when they came out, and beheld between 400 and 500 Yankees, armed with revolvers and bowie knives," a passenger reported. By summer, every available craft had been pressed into service. On one July day alone, five vessels disembarked 1,732 passengers at Victoria.

FOR SEVERAL YEARS, rumours of northern gold had been drifting around Washington and Oregon territories and down the coast to California. And so the pump was primed when, in February 1858, word leaked out that the Hudson's Bay Company steamboat *Otter* had arrived in San Francisco with 800 ounces of gold found in New Caledonia, near the junction of the Fraser and Thompson Rivers.

Within days, "Fraser River fever seized hold of the people." By April, hundreds had already left California and thousands were preparing to go north. Then, in May, news reached San Francisco that two men, working on the Fraser at Hill's Bar, near Fort Yale, were taking out more than 10 ounces of gold a day. In the California city, a day's wage for a carpenter was $7 and for a bricklayer $8.75; the going rate for gold was $16 an ounce. The thought of two men earning $160 a day was simply phenomenal.

Donald Fraser, the San Francisco correspondent for *The Times* of London, reported in June: "The effect in California has been astounding. People seem to have suddenly come to the conclusion that it is their fate to go . . . None are too poor and none too rich to go. None too young and none too old to go—even the decrepit go. Many go with money, many go without. People of all nations are going. Men who can't speak a word of English are going. Some are going out of curiosity, some to gamble, and some to steal and, unquestionably, some to die."

The wonder is that many did not die on the voyage to Fort Victoria. San Francisco ship owners pressed every available craft into service and charged outrageous fares—$60 for "nobs" and $30 for "roughs"—to travel on "crazy old vessels" into which men and women were packed "like herrings in a barrel."

By summer's end, upwards of thirty thousand goldseekers would make their way to the Fraser, two thirds of them streaming through Victoria. Soon the fort and the town that had begun to grow around it were surrounded by a city of grey canvas tents—a rowdy, boisterous, transient settlement redolent of cigars and whisky, and alive with the sounds of "badly-played instruments, roisterous songs, the rattle of the dice-box, angry words, and oaths too terrible to name."

From Victoria, miners had to cross the Strait of Georgia to the Fraser's mouth. Some purchased dugout canoes; others built makeshift craft—"punty, awkward-looking things, about as good imitations of coffins as anything else." Hundreds of people were never heard from after leaving Victoria, and suspicions arose that many inexperienced sailors had lost their lives when their boats were swamped by sudden squalls.

However harrowing the trip across the strait might be, the really difficult part of the journey began at the Fraser's mouth. At first, the river was wide and slow, but gradually it narrowed and the current became strong. Above Fort Langley, the safest course was to hire a canoe and paddlers. As one traveller recalled: "We were advised to use an Indian canoe because the Indians were the most reliable guides on account of their knowledge of the river and their

Lieutenant Charles Wilson of the Royal Engineers arrived in Victoria in July 1858: "Vancouver Island itself is quite beautiful, but turned quite upside down by the gold discovery, a regular San Francisco of 49 . . . the whiz of revolver bullets around you goes on all day & if anyone gets shot, of course it's his own fault."

A sternwheeler heading up the
Fraser River from Fort Hope.

experience with canoe work." For those who did not follow that advice, the results could prove disastrous. As early as May, when the rush was only a month old, James Douglas noted that a great number of canoes had been dashed to pieces and their passengers "swept to eternity." By summer, it became almost commonplace to find dead bodies floating in the lower reaches of the river.

On 6 June, the American sidewheeler *Surprise* managed to battle the current all the way to Fort Hope—a feat she accomplished thanks to the help of an Indian pilot, Speel-est, with her boilers threatening to explode and her smokestack throwing off showers of sparks that burned holes in hats and coats. Thanks to the *Surprise*'s success, Fort Hope became the head of steamboat navigation and, when melting snows raised the height of the water, forcing men off the river, it boomed into a rowdy town. "In the summer of 1858," David Higgins recalled, "several thousand people made Hope their trading-post. The business of saloons, restaurants, gambling houses and stores were nearly all carried on in tents . . . Trading and gambling went on all day and night. The rattle of dice and the rolling of rondo balls across the tables, mingled with the curses of the unfortunate gambler or the inebriate mad with drink."

Fort Hope's role as a major town lasted only until an American entrepreneur introduced a sternwheeler to the Fraser. Sidewheelers, like the *Surprise*, were not the most suitable craft for the river. They were designed for ocean travel; their deeper draughts made navigating shoals a risky business and their side-mounted paddlewheels made them vulnerable in narrow river canyons. On the other hand, sternwheelers could snug up to canyon walls and drew so little water that they could land almost anywhere, simply nudging the bow onto a bank and then, with a reverse thrust, pulling back into the river. And as for the shallows, it was said that experienced skippers could "*walk* a steamer over a sandbar on its paddle wheel."

In July, the American sternwheeler *Umatilla* made it all the way to Fort Yale. There was no question of any boat travelling farther upriver. Above Yale, the Fraser boiled through a series of canyons. "Here all navigation ceases, not even the boldest and most reckless boatman daring to attempt its passage."

Beyond Fort Yale, men travelled on foot. When the water was low, they could make some headway by scrambling over boulders on the riverbank. When the water was high, some took to the upper trail, the narrow footpath that Simon Fraser had found so daunting fifty years earlier. Crawling along on hands and knees, and dangling from Indian ladders as they moved from ledge to ledge, 800 feet above the churning waters, dozens of men made their way through the canyons. Others chose a safer route, following the Douglas Portage, the old brigade trail that swung away from the Fraser on a detour around the lower canyon, rejoining the river at Spuzzum. There, an American, Franklin Way, had built a rope ferry to take travellers to the other side of the river, where they could join the trail that avoided the upper canyon, climbing to a plateau 2,500 feet above the river before swinging back to the Fraser at Boston Bar.

Nothing could hold them back. "The cry is 'Up.' Higher and higher in the hope of finding the real 'Dorado." The push was to reach "The Forks" (Lytton) where the Thompson River joined the Fraser. By late summer, several hundred men were working the river between Yale and Lytton, at places like New York Bar, Boston Bar and China Bar.

The fish-drying racks of Nlaka'pamux people lined the Fraser's canyons to catch warm August winds. Miners found places like Hells Gate (pictured here) particularly daunting. "On both sides of the river rise rocky mountains almost perpendicularly for hundreds of feet, so that, in some places, if a stone were dropped from their top, it would drop direct into the water."

THE SKIPPERS of Fraser River steamboats became legends in their own time. A favourite story concerned Captain Tom Wright, whose small, underpowered steamboat was one of the first on the lower Fraser. Unable to make way in the rapid current, Wright hollered, "All passengers overboard to haul at the tow line." No one moved. "How much steam on, engineer?" he shouted. "Already 175 pounds, sir," the engineer called. "Then put on 25 pounds more and blow her to hell!" the captain ordered. And, as the engineer responded, "Aye, aye, sir," every man jumped overboard and grabbed the towline.

The threat of explosions was very real. On 14 April 1861, the sternwheeler *Fort Yale* was steaming past Union Bar when she exploded with such force that a 90-pound chunk of her boiler was thrown a quarter mile inland. Five people were killed, including the captain, Smith Baird Jamieson, whose body was never found.

A month earlier, Smith Jamieson's brother, Robert, captain of the *Portland*, had been killed when his ship lost way in the current and was swept over the falls on the Willamette River at Oregon City. And then, on 2 August 1861, less than four months after the *Fort Yale* explosion, the steamer *Cariboo* was blown apart as she was leaving Victoria harbour. Among the dead

The sternwheeler *Enterprise* at Soda Creek.

were her captain, Archibald Jamieson, and George Jamieson, her assistant engineer. Of the four Jamieson brothers who left Scotland to take up steamboating on the west coast, none survived.

On the run from Soda Creek to Quesnel, the man to remember was Woodbury J. Doane of the *Enterprise*. Born in Maine into a seafaring family, Doane was a big, bluff hearty man, full of good will and bonhomie. "Very jolly fellow," an acquaintance smiled. "Happiest man I ever saw." Captain Doane had good reason to be happy. As the steward of the *Enterprise* confided to a passenger, "The Captain takes a cocktail every ten minutes while on board."

Dr. Cheadle, who was touring the goldfields as companion to

Viscount Milton, a peripatetic but sickly young aristocrat, encountered Captain Doane when he and his charge boarded the *Enterprise* at Soda Creek in October 1863. "After we had been on board a short time the Captain, finding out who we were, gave us the use of his cabin, a comfortable little room & supplied us with cigars & a decanter of cocktails. We were fetched out every few minutes to have a drink with some one, the Captain taking the lead by standing champagne all round. We had some dozen before supper; no one the least affected."

Still, Doane had a successful career on the Fraser River and later on Puget Sound, and he lived into ripe old age. "My old hulk is all in," he told his friends. "I have tried hard to keep her going, but it's no use. I can't keep this old ship going much longer." He died in 1903, at the age of seventy-eight.

THE BRITISH COLONIST

Thursday Morning, April 18, 1861.

TERRIBLE CATASTROPHE !

EXPLOSION OF STEAMER "FORT YALE."

Several Killed and Wounded !

The steamer Caledonia, Capt. Frain, arrived from the river at 4½ o'clock, yesterday, bringing the sad intelligence that the steamer Fort Yale had been blown up, and that several lives were lost. An EXTRA COLONIST, containing the melancholy news,

Woodbury J. Doane, captain of the *Enterprise*.

Most goldseekers contented themselves with claims on the lower Fraser, and by September, thousands of men (and a very few women) were encamped on the river's gravel bars. They were a cosmopolitan lot. "Americans were in the majority. Then followed Germans, French and Chinese. Next came Italians, Spaniards and Poles," one observer noted. *The Times*'s man, Donald Fraser, encountered "Russians, Swedes, Danes, French, Norwegians, Austrians and other Germans, English, Scotch, and Irish, and other nationalities besides."

Every rocky bar had been given a name, and each had developed a distinctive character. Murderer's Bar, above Fort Langley, was home to over a hundred Cornishmen who were building log cabins to see them through the winter. On Mosquito Bar, above Fort Hope, twenty-five men "growled horribly" because they were making as little as a dollar a day. Union Bar was worked by 150 Americans with "a military turn," who had built a fort— a stockade flanked with bastions and christened "Fort Union." Canada Bar, deserted by its original miners for "better diggings higher up," was occupied by half a dozen men "squatted on the ground in a happy state of idleness" trying to decide what to do next. At Santa Clara Bar, 250 men were building huts for winter but complaining of making only $6 a day. Their gold was very fine and much of it was washing away. "Told us that higher up a man's daily earnings were $35 a day," Donald Fraser reported. "The *rich* places are always either 'down' or 'up,' never where you are at the moment."

During the summer of 1858, a tent town appeared on the Fraser River below Fort Langley. The settlement's most prominent landmarks were two tents bearing the names "Growler House" and "Our House," whose owners "sold meals at all hours" but whose real profits came from selling brandy "on the sly."

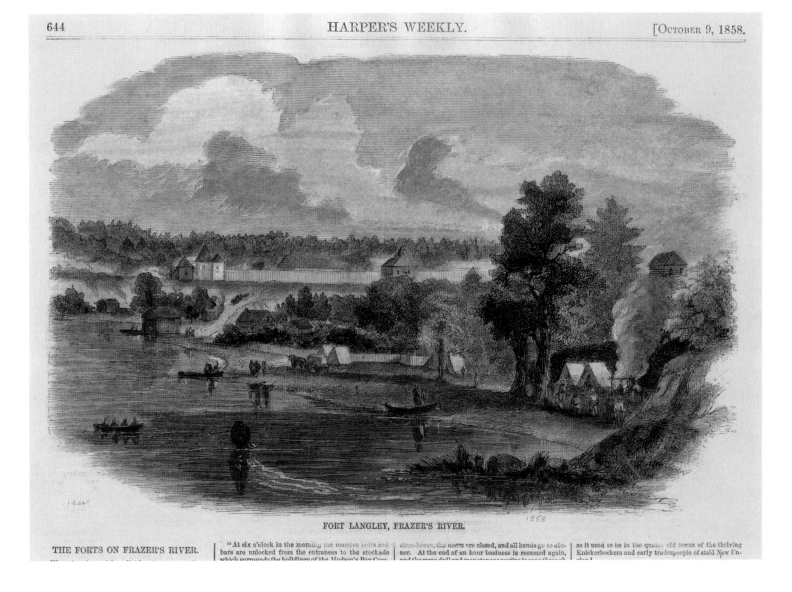

FORT LANGLEY, FRAZER'S RIVER.

THE FORTS ON FRAZER'S RIVER.   "At six o'clock in the morning the massive bolts and bars are unlocked from the entrances to the stockade which surrounds the buildings of the Hudson's Bay Com-   store-house, the doors are closed, and all hands go to din- ner. At the end of an hour business is resumed again, and the same dull and monotonous routine is gone through   as it used to be in the quaint old towns of the thriving Knickerbockers and early tradespeople of staid New En- gland.

"[At Fort Yale's American Restaurant]
the only table was occupied by three wild-looking men.
In spite of our repugnance, we were compelled
to sit at the table, and while awaiting our food, they talked
with us and invited us to drink with them,
but we refused on the pretext that we drank nothing but
water. They were quite insulted by our refusal . . .
but we remained calm and casually showed our weapons."
—Dr. Carl Friesach

At American Bar, a group of old Californians was mining with the help of a Chinese crew working for hire. Texas Bar was worked by men so keen that they were now down to the third layer of gravel. John Daly, an Irishman who had been unsuccessful in California but who was now taking $10 to $12 a day, was building a log cabin for his wife, "the only leddy on the bar." Emory's Bar was home to a "jolly lot" of miners who were putting up log huts and shingle cabins. Above Emory's Bar, a party of Frenchmen, Americans and Irishmen was earning only $4 a day but full of hope about doing better. On Hill's Bar, creature comforts were being provided by "a fair haired comely little woman" who was offering room and board, or "boarding by the Meales" as her handwritten sign put it. "The men are all very brotherly," she assured a questioner, but "there are not many sisters to be sisterly."

Fort Yale had become a tough little town, notorious for gambling, drinking and violence. Its population of about eight hundred (of whom only six were women) lived in tents and wooden shacks. There was only one public eating house, the American Restaurant, a large one-roomed log house with a dirt floor, "cramped and hot as an oven." But saloons and gambling houses abounded.

To Donald Fraser, the town was "filthy and unsavoury," a "modern Sodom." To David Higgins, it was hell on Earth: "In every saloon a faro-bank or a three-card-monte table was in full swing and crowded to suffocation. A worse set of cut-throats and all time scoundrels than those who flocked to Yale from all parts of the world never assembled anywhere . . . Decent people feared to go out after dark. Night assaults and robberies, varied by an occasional cold-blooded murder or a daylight theft, were common occurrences."

The casual violence of which Americans were capable worried James Douglas. He suspected that some of the new arrivals were criminals, the "outscourings" of the jails of California, "the very dregs, in fact, of society." And he was concerned that, as the country filled with revolver-packing Americans, they would challenge British authority over the mainland goldfields.

As governor of Vancouver Island, Douglas had no authority over New Caledonia. But because months would pass before a letter of his could receive a reply from London, he felt he had no choice but to take matters into his own hands. On 8 May 1858, he announced that no one would be allowed on the Fraser without a $5 miner's licence issued by the Colony of Vancouver Island. To enforce his proclamation, he sent the two naval vessels based at Esquimalt to patrol the entrance to the river. Then, he wrote to London to plead for an increased naval presence and for additional troops.

A party of sixty-five Royal Engineers and their officers, whose assignment was to survey the 49th parallel, had already sailed from England in April, before the gold rush began. But they would not arrive until July, and the goldfields were continuing to fill with men, many of whom made no secret of their anti-British sentiments, and many of whom were ready to take the law into their own hands.

Douglas's worst fears seemed about to be realized in August. Until the arrival of the miners, the Thompson (Nlaka'pamux) people had controlled the gold trade. Now, according to Douglas, they "felt annoyed at the large quantities of gold taken from their country by the white miners." When the

Kinahan Cornwallis described his accommodations at Fort Hope in 1858: "After dark, the skins were brought in and spread along either side of the tent . . . They were soon covered with the lounging and recumbent bodies of the miners, who kept on talking and medicinal-brandy drinking till about ten o'clock, when silence supervened or rather snoring was substituted for talking. All slept with their revolvers and gold under variously improvised pillows."

headless corpses of two Frenchmen were fished out of the river at Yale, it seemed that reprisals had begun. Militia companies were organized in Yale and headed up the canyon. Soon, an appalling story reached Victoria. Forty-five vigilantes had been massacred and their bodies had been thrown in the river.

The reports of the "massacre" were quickly denied. Still, James Douglas felt duty bound to visit Yale, and he considered it prudent to divert a party of Royal Engineers from their boundary survey to accompany him. Arriving at Yale, he satisfied himself that the stories had been wildly exaggerated. But he was aware that the American vigilantes had formed themselves into an armed force larger than any he could hope to muster. To discourage men from taking the law into their own hands, he appointed a chief constable and five assistants—an act greeted with some merriment by one observer, who opined that it would take 250 policemen at Yale, a similar number at Fort Hope and as many again at the Forks to preserve order. Douglas hoped for the best and waited for instructions.

Although Douglas did not know it as he made his way back down the Fraser that September, London had already taken steps not only to affirm his authority but also to send him reinforcements. In July, an act to grant colonial status to New Caledonia had been introduced in the House of Commons, and the colonial secretary had written to inform Douglas that he was to be appointed the new colony's governor and that another party of Royal Engineers would be sent immediately.

On 2 August 1858, "An Act to Provide for the Government of British Columbia" was given royal assent. By September, the Royal Engineers were on their way across the sea. The main body was sent on the longer, cheaper route via Cape Horn and would not reach the colony for six months. Aware that Douglas needed assistance as soon as possible, the colonial secretary dispatched an advance party of twenty men via Panama. They would be at Douglas's side in two months.

In September, Matthew Baillie Begbie, who had been appointed judge of British Columbia, embarked from Liverpool. He carried with him the commission, signed by Queen Victoria, appointing James Douglas governor of the new colony. Within hours of arriving at Victoria, Begbie found himself accompanying Douglas to Fort Langley.

James Douglas was determined that his swearing-in be as imposing an occasion as possible. On 19 November 1858, when he disembarked from the *Beaver* at Fort Langley, he was received by an honour guard of Royal Engineers and greeted by an eighteen-gun salute. Judge Begbie read the queen's commission to the assembled crowd. And the Colony of British Columbia was officially born.

THE RUSH TO THE FRASER transformed Fort Victoria. When Alfred Waddington arrived in the spring of 1858, he found "a quiet village of about 800 inhabitants. No noise, no bustle, no gamblers, no speculators . . . a few gentlemanly-behaved inhabitants, chiefly Scotsmen, secluded as it were from the whole world." Within six short weeks, over two hundred new buildings appeared on the narrow streets, and town lots that had sold for $50 in April were bringing $5,000 and more.

Annie Deans, who had been in the colony since 1853, recorded her amazement: "In the morning there be bonny green grass, at night there be

---

"In consequence of the very bad reports from the mines up Fraser River, Major Hawkins has gone up with a body of men, to help the Governor keep the peace. I volunteered several times to go up as a little fighting would be much more to my taste than this work; but I was left behind . . . there has been a good deal of fighting up there & wise heads in these matters say we are going to have a regular Indian war."
—Lieutenant Charles Wilson

"The only name which is given to the whole territory in every map the Queen has consulted is 'Columbia,' but there exists a Columbia in South America, and the citizens of the United States call their country also Columbia, at least in poetry, 'British Columbia' might be, in the Queen's opinion, the best name."
—Queen Victoria

"The enterprise you [the Royal Engineers] go to is indeed glorious. Ages hence industry and commerce will crowd the roads that you will have made; travellers from all nations will halt on the bridges which you will have first flung over solitary rivers . . . children unborn will, I believe, bless the hour when Queen Victoria sent forth her sappers and miners to found a second England on the shores of the Pacific."
—Sir Edward Bulwer Lytton

"Yesterday, the birthday of British Columbia, was ushered in by a steady rain, which continued perseveringly throughout the whole day, and in a great measure marred the solemnity of the proclamation of the Colony."
—Victoria Gazette

A miner panning for gold.

Sister Mary Angèle was one of four French-speaking nuns of the SIsters of St. Ann recruited in Québec before the gold rush began to teach the children of the Hudson's Bay Company's French-Canadian employees. "We had been told that some twenty bark-roofed cabins housed a few people who had made their homes near the fort and that was all," she said in amazement when she arrived in the gold-mad town.

Free-born in Philadelphia, Mifflin Gibbs was among fifty or sixty black people who left California to escape legislation limiting their property and voting rights. A successful businessman, Gibbs reached Victoria in June 1858.

"If either of us had arrived here two months ago, worth $1000, we could have been worth $10,000 today," he informed his San Francisco partner.

a house on it." Saloons and hotels and shanties crowded around the palisades of the fort. Businesses like the California Saloon and the Sacramento Restaurant wooed American miners with familiar names. "It is the San Francisco of 1849 reproduced," an observer reported. "The same hurry-scurry, hurly-burly, dirt, dust, inconvenience, bad living, bad housing, cheating and lying."

During dry summer months, the town was choked by swirling dust. Water was in short supply and far too expensive to be used for sprinkling the streets. According to one observer, it would have been cheaper to dampen the roadways with HBC rum. "Liquor was cheaper than water," he recalled. "We remember on a hot day in July seeing a perspiring man enter a saloon on Yates Street to ask for a glass of water. 'Water!' gasped the astonished barkeeper. 'Why, stranger, I'll *give* you a glass of rum but two bits is the price of water in this yere bar.'"

In winter, the streets became a quagmire. "The mud is so deep that it comes up to the horses' girths & foot passengers can only cross on planks laid across," one visitor recorded. And whatever the season, the air was rank with the aroma wafting from outhouses and privies, which were sited for their users' convenience, with little thought given to neighbourly aesthetics.

Victoria soon found itself in need of a hospital. Before the gold rush, patients requiring care were simply visited by the doctor in their homes, but that simple arrangement could not continue once the town filled with transients. In August 1858, when a Fraser-bound miner fell ill, his companions could think of nothing to do but carry him from his tent and deposit him in Reverend Cridge's garden.

Petitioned to provide funds for a hospital, the House of Assembly responded that "such benevolent objects should be left to the good feeling and charity of the Public." Fundraising balls and concerts were organized, and in November 1858, a cottage was rented, a caretaker was hired, and a

doctor agreed to call. A few months later, the first hospital in British Columbia was under construction on the Lekwammen reserve.

Like any wood-built town, with straw-filled stables and with saloons, hotels and dance halls lit by oil lamps and heated by woodstoves, Victoria was particularly vulnerable to fire. In 1859, when the jail and police barracks were built in the centre of town, they were constructed of brick and deemed to be "fire-proof." But when Governor Douglas approved the construction of buildings to house Vancouver Island's colonial government, he chose a site on the south shore of James Bay, a safe remove from the threat of any civic conflagration.

While the Colony of Vancouver Island was gracing its capital city with exuberantly fanciful government buildings, the Colony of British Columbia was having second thoughts about its chosen capital. At Derby, the site

"The gutters in the main streets are at times choked with putrescent filth," Amor De Cosmos scolded in the *British Colonist*. He was not far wrong. Victoria had no sewer system. Cesspools overflowed into the drainage ditches lining the streets. The soapy streams released by public bathhouses mingled with the mud churned up by horses' hooves.

Designed by Herman Otto Tiedemann, Vancouver Island's government buildings were known as the "Birdcages," partly because they reminded people of the ornamental birdcages popular at the time and partly because the road that separated the legislative precinct from the governor's land had been named Birdcage Walk, after the London street that runs from Buckingham Palace to the Houses of Parliament.

As depicted by Reverend W. Burton Crickmer (shown here preaching from a barrel), Derby in 1859 was a lively place. Among those gathered to listen to the sermon are American miners, Royal Engineers, Chinese merchants and a group of Stó:lō people, one of whom is wearing a Royal Engineers' tunic.

"Viewed from the Gulf of Georgia across the meadows on entering the Fraser, the far distant giant mountains forming a dark background—the City would appear throned Queen-like & shining in the glory of the midday sun. The comparison is so obvious that . . . everyone joins in thinking the appropriate name would be Queensborough."

—Colonel Richard Moody

near Fort Langley selected by James Douglas, town lots had been surveyed and sold, and construction had begun on a barracks for the Royal Engineers. But when Colonel Richard Moody, commanding officer of the Royal Engineers, visited Derby, he was quick to register his disapproval of Douglas's choice. Located on the Fraser's south bank, with nothing but a few miles of easily crossed land separating it from American territory, Derby would be impossible to defend against attack.

In its place, Moody selected a site on the river's north bank, near the Pitt River. On 14 February 1859, Douglas ordered the relocation of the capital and suggested it be named Queensborough. "Queensboro is not only prosaic," the colonial secretary sniffed, "it is also the quintessence of vulgarity." In July, Governor Douglas announced that Her Majesty had been "graciously pleased to decide" that British Columbia's capital should be known as New Westminster.

But the New Westminster site presented problems of its own. It was important for the colony to control the Fraser by establishing an official presence, but the sandy shallows at the river's mouth made navigation difficult. A much better potential port existed to the north, at Burrard Inlet. In 1859, Moody put his men to work on a trail connecting the Royal

Holy Trinity Anglican Church in New Westminster, 1860. Of his rectory, the log cabin in the foreground, Reverend John Sheepshanks wrote: "It was rather draughty, as the wind came in at the interstices between the logs; so I gathered moss and stuffed it well into the crevices. The floor was only mud, but I had some boards put down, and put in a sheet-iron stove and a stove pipe."

Engineers' headquarters at Sapperton to the head of Burrard Inlet; and around the inlet, he set aside a number of strategically located military reserves. (One of those reserves is now the University of British Columbia Endowment Lands; another forms the nucleus of Stanley Park.)

New Westminster's value as a port was further hampered by the Fraser's habit of becoming clogged with ice during the winter. "A wonderful sight it is to see the huge fields of ice being hurried along by the rapid current, grating against the fringe of strong ice that clings to the shore," a New Westminster resident wrote. "It is grand and solemn to hear morning, noon and night that continual crashing going on."

Sometimes, the Fraser froze solid. "Sleighs were rapidly made, and presently the ladies were being driven about in rough equipages, made smart with skins and jingling with bells," Reverend John Sheepshanks reported. "Hockey sticks were cut from the forest, and the male portion of the population, officials, parsons, storekeepers, woodsmen and Indians, were engaged in this exciting game on the broad river. Occasionally, carts come down the river on the ice, and cattle are driven across to the other side."

In winter, New Westminster could be cut off from the outside world for weeks at a time, bringing business to a "standstill" and leaving Victoria the functional capital of both colonies. Mainlanders did not take kindly to Victoria's superiority, and resentment of the island city began to grow.

"When I awake in the morning the bucket of water for my bath is frozen solid. My blind fell down the other day, and I fastened it up again by driving a nail in with my sponge. I cannot easily comb my hair, for it is frozen together. My upper-most blanket is hoary with my frozen breath. But, notwithstanding, I like the weather."
—Reverend John Sheepshanks

*"The accounts of the gold discoveries
at Cariboo are perfectly fabulous."*
—Lieutenant Charles Wilson

CHAPTER 7

STRIKING IT RICH

FOR A TIME, it seemed as though the gold rush might falter. The winter of 1858–59 was brutally cold, and the men who stuck it out at their claims had a miserable time. "When you are out on the river you haven't got anything to eat but bread, beans and pork," miner Frank Matthias complained. "We were all sick with swollen legs and rheumatics." Thousands of men who had not been able to stake good claims began to grumble that the Fraser was "A Great Humbug!" By the end of a second hard winter, as many as twenty-five thousand goldseekers had given up and gone home, but five thousand hardier and more determined prospectors hung on.

By 1860, the gravel bars on the lower Fraser were believed to be played out and had been abandoned to the Chinese by less patient men who were pushing farther into the country. Some went along the Thompson River, others struck out to the Similkameen; but the most successful were

Chinese miners worked the Fraser's gravel bars after other men deserted the river for better digging higher up. The man on the right is using a rocker, constructed like a child's cradle, with sides sloping gently inward. The rocker was fed with sand and gravel and water, then rocked back and forth, allowing the heavier particles to sink to the bottom while the lighter sand and dirt were washed away. If the gold was very fine, quicksilver (mercury) was added to bind to the gold. A rocker could use up to 10 pounds of quicksilver a day.

those who followed the Fraser up to Fort Alexandria and on to Quesnel. That summer, six hundred men were working along the Quesnel River and making as much as $60 each per day.

In September 1860, four prospectors set out from Keithley Creek, crossed the Snowshoe Plateau and descended into the valley of Antler Creek. There, they found the richest deposit yet discovered, a single pan yielding as much as $100 in gold. Word spread quickly. "To the old experienced gold miner these reports were much as a war bugle is to the old war horse." Within a few months, four hundred men were burrowed into the snow along Antler Creek, waiting for spring and a chance to work their claims.

William "Dutch Bill" Dietz decided to leave Antler Creek and poke about the country. After crossing Bald Mountain and descending into an unexplored watershed, he lost his footing and landed flat on his back in the depression of a creek. Thinking he might as well give it a try, he clawed away the snow, retrieved some gravel and found gold. He returned to Antler and then went on to Quesnel Forks for equipment and supplies. As Dietz returned to the creek (named Williams Creek in his honour), "the whole population of Antler" followed the path of his snowshoes and "within two or three hours of his arrival, the whole creek was staked off into claims over ground covered with 8 feet of snow."

The town of Richfield grew around Dutch Bill's claim, and while some men made strikes on Lightning Creek, Lowhee Creek and Grouse Creek, most worked their way down Williams Creek. The gold deposits on Williams Creek were found above a 15-foot thick layer of blue clay, which everyone assumed was underlaid by bedrock. But in the summer of 1861, a miner named Abbott, passing the time while his partner was off getting supplies, dug through the clay and was amazed to discover a layer of gold-bearing gravel. Two days later, when his partner returned, Abbott presented him with 50 ounces of gold. And it was not the light, dusty gold of the lower Fraser. Here, it could be found in fist-sized nuggets.

"Large fortunes have been made, from £6,000 to £10,000 earned in a month or six weeks," Lieutenant Charles Wilson of the Royal Engineers noted in his journal. "Old miners say they never saw anything like it in the best days of California in 49 and 50."

People from around the world scrambled to get to the Cariboo. But by 1863, travellers on their way to the goldfields were being met by a returning army of discouraged men. "Day after day we met groups of men, chiefly young men and Englishmen, turning back, never having reached the mines, disappointed, broken down, haggard, furious with those whose lying representatives (as they said) had brought them to this accursed country." To all who would listen, they detailed their complaints: "Provisions are at famine prices. The men are starving. All have gone back except the thieves and gamblers. Oh, this God-forsaken country!"

Still, people came. Catherine Schubert followed one of the most difficult routes. In May 1862, she and her husband were living in Fort Garry (Winnipeg) when they heard about the Cariboo from a party of men who

Artist Frederick Whymper did his best to make Richfield look picturesque, but even artistic licence could not conceal the fact that the towns along Williams Creek were depressingly bleak, with mud everywhere and hillsides denuded of trees.

"The Cariboo is a dreadful place to get at . . . right up in the mountains . . . and inaccessible for 7 or 8 months out of the year from snow and even in summer it is nearly as bad."
—Lieutenant Charles Wilson

An 1882 map showing the gold regions of the Fraser River and Cariboo.

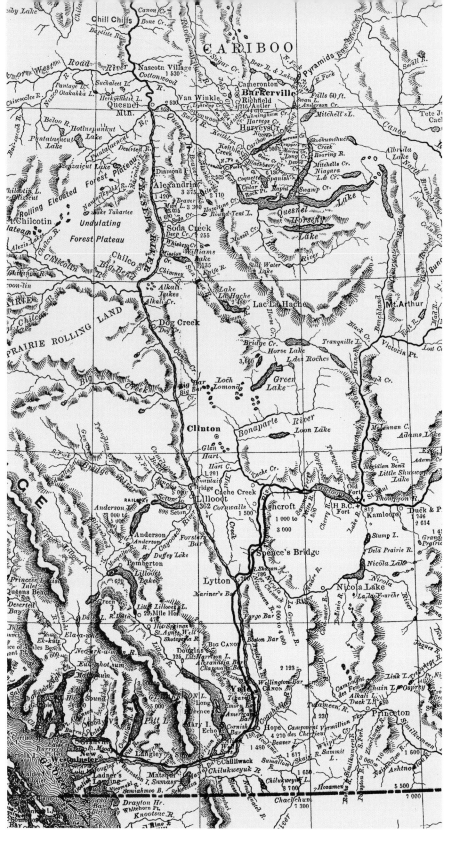

A page from a pamphlet, "The New Gold Fields of British Columbia and Vancouver Island, Handbook for Emigrants," published in London in 1862. It was similar to other guides circulating in the United States and Britain. "There is a great scarcity of unmarried females throughout the colony," the author advised, "and no sooner do they arrive than they receive substantial offers of matrimony and future happiness."

had left Ontario and were travelling overland to the goldfields. Catherine, who had three children under the age of six and was pregnant with her fourth, readily agreed to her husband's suggestion that they throw in their lot with the "Overlanders."

Travelling on horseback and with oxen pulling Red River carts, they left Fort Garry on 2 June, crossed the prairies and reached the Yellowhead Pass by the end of August. After struggling over the pass, the Schuberts walked to the headwaters of the North Thompson. They swept down the river in a canoe and, when the canoe fell apart, on a raft, reaching Fort Kamloops on 14 October. A few hours later, in a tent pitched on the riverbank, Catherine gave birth to her daughter, Rose.

Catherine had endured four-and-a-half months on the trail. She had eaten moss, boiled in water, when their supplies ran low. She had come close to drowning on several occasions. And after all that, she said, they "found only hard work & no gold."

The Overlanders had known little of the difficulties they would encounter. But even people who knew all about the problems were not immune to the pull of gold. Since 1859, an American miner, Watson Hodge, had been running a wayside house above Yale, dispensing bacon, potatoes, coffee and illegal whisky. But in 1863, he threw in the towel, hammered a notice on his door and headed for the Cariboo:

> My whisky's gone, and credit too,
> And I've put out for Cariboo
> So if you want rum or rye or ale,
> You'll have to get it down at Yale.
> (And pay for it.)
> HODGE

Four hundred difficult miles lay between Yale and the goldfields. Beyond the big canyon, the trails that had been beaten down by men and mules as they tramped into the wilderness were a nightmare. "It is difficult to find language to express in adequate terms the utter vileness of the trails of Cariboo," Lieutenant Palmer of the Royal Engineers reported: "Slippery, precipitous ascents and descents, fallen logs, overhanging branches, roots, rocks, swamps, turbid pools and miles of deep mud."

As the demand for supplies increased, mule trains grew to include up to fifty animals. The passage of so many hooves turned trails into gumbo. Sucked down into the sticky mud, heavily laden mules became immobilized. "In many places are dead mules standing straight up, having hopelessly sunk down above the girths and been left to perish miserably in that position."

It occurred to one visionary that camels might do better than mules. A camel could pack up to 600 pounds, twice as much as a mule; its long legs would enable it to plow through snowdrifts, and the American army had used a camel corps in the southwest with some success. In 1862, an American entrepreneur imported twenty-five camels to the coast and offered them for sale at $300 each. They were purchased by a syndicate

As shown in this sketch, "To the Diggings and from the Diggings," disappointed gold-seekers were "a pitiful looking lot." On his way up the Fraser River in 1859, Charles Major met a party of returning miners: "They are what the Yankees call dead broke. They have been six hundred miles up the river. When they got there they had no shoes on their feet. Some had pieces of shirt and trowsers, but even these were pinned together with small, sharp sticks. They had nothing to eat for one week, and not one cent in money. This is gold mining for you!"

"The trail [over Jackass Mountain] is frequently dangerous. We ascended to great heights on the almost perpendicular side of a mountain gorge, on which one false step would mean certain death.
Today we met a man with a pack train, in a gloomy mood. He had just witnessed one of his mules rolling over and down the mountain, being dashed from crag to boulder until the mighty torrent below received it and carried it away."
—Reverend George Hills

Mule trains, some of which included as many as fifty animals, hauled supplies from the coast to the Cariboo.

"They [the camels] beat any transport we have, either ox, wagon, mule or cayoosh ponies," a Lillooet correspondent enthused in 1863. "They are now acclimated and will eat anything from a pair of pants to a bar of soap."

"Was bothered all day by the camels of which there are about a dozen here who have a neat idea of walking over your tent and eating your shirts."
—Henry Guillod

fronted by Frank Laumeister, a native of Bavaria who ran a Victoria saloon and brewery. When the camels arrived in Victoria that spring, they were a sorry-looking lot: losing their winter coats, they presented "a very scalpy appearance." Still, they were on the trail by June.

All did not go well. "The mules and horses, which were on the roads and trails, did not take at all kindly to the strangers, and would stampede on every occasion they hove into sight, now and then plunging over a precipice with their packs in sheer fright." Designed for walking on sand, rather than over boulders and through mud, the camels "became footsore." After two summers, they were withdrawn from service. Some were turned loose and left to their own devices. "A magnificent camel" was spotted grazing along the road near Clinton in October 1863. Another was butchered for its meat by the proprietor of a wayside house near Lac La Hache, who discovered that none of his guests had a taste for camel. A few others were taken by a rancher at Westwold, one old female surviving for thirty or more years, until, feeble and falling down, she was put out of her misery and turned into a floor rug.

In 1861, Governor Douglas ordered the construction of an 18-foot-wide wagon road through the Fraser Canyon and all the way to the goldfields. By May of the following year, the Royal Engineers were blasting away at the rock face between Yale and Spuzzum, and private contractors, who were granted the right to charge tolls to defray their costs, were at work on other sections. By September 1863, the Alexandra Suspension Bridge, built by contractor Joseph Trutch (later British Columbia's first lieutenant-governor), had replaced the old ferry at Spuzzum and the road had been completed all the way to Soda Creek, where it connected with sternwheelers running up to Quesnel. The road from Quesnel to Cottonwood was put through in 1864, and the following year it reached Williams Creek.

The Alexandra Suspension
Bridge opened for traffic
in September 1863. Freight
crossing the bridge was
required to pay a toll of $7.40
per ton.

Freight wagons at China Bluff on the way to Boston Bar. The construction of the Cariboo Road meant the introduction of freight wagons and stage-coaches. Travelling by stage-coach in 1864, Henry Jones reported: "The stage was hung on stout leather belts, instead of springs. The belts swung fore and aft, so that I soon got seasick and was very wretched for some hours."

As work on the Cariboo Road progressed, stagecoaches and freight wagons were introduced. And as shipping supplies became easier and prices went down, more people were able to spend the winter in the Cariboo. During the winter of 1864–65, twelve hundred people overwintered along Williams Creek, but their lives were far from easy.

Beef and mutton were readily available, large numbers of livestock having been slaughtered in the fall. "They were soon frozen solid and thawed out as required," Harry Jones reported. However, eggs and milk were unobtainable, and beer was almost impossible to come by. One saloonkeeper imported forty-eight bottles, but only eighteen survived the trip. He recovered his investment by selling them for $5 a bottle, twice the price of a restaurant meal—that is, twice the price for everyone but the Reverend John Sheepshanks. Tall and thin, Sheepshanks had an enormous appetite: "A leg of mutton was only an ordinary meal to him." After watching him devour one or two all-you-can-eat $2.50 meals, restaurant keepers upped the price to $5.

Most married men in the Cariboo had left their wives behind and were terribly lonely. "Mary, I have thought of you more, prayed for you more, and if possible loved you more this summer than ever before," John Thompson wrote to his wife in July 1862. "I sometimes wonder how I ever came to leave a kind and affectionate wife to sojourn in this land."

Women of easy virtue were also in short supply, and some of those who made themselves available were alarmingly unappealing. In September 1862, the *British Colonist* reported the arrival of nine prostitutes at Williams Creek. "They dress in male attire and swagger through the saloons and mining camps with cigars or huge quids of tobacco in their mouths, cursing and swearing.

After trying his luck in the California goldfields, Billy Barker followed the rush to the Fraser River. On Williams Creek in 1862, he struck it rich. He sold his claim, enjoyed a few comfortable winters in Victoria and then went back to the Cariboo. Pursuing gold excitements here and there, he never again met with success. Barker died in poverty in 1894 and was buried in an unmarked grave in Victoria.

Judge Matthew Baillie Begbie travelled on horseback to bring justice to the Cariboo mining towns. Where no courtroom was available, he heard cases while perched on a stump or sitting astride his horse. He revelled in the outdoor life but missed society's pleasures. From Richfield, he wrote to a friend: "When you write, you should write *gossip*. I can't send you any gossip from this place—the unisexual character of the population almost precludes it."

"Some enterprising farmer about two hundred miles down the road sent up a barrel of milk, frozen of course, for Christmas Day. I bought a pound, chipped off the block with an axe, and carried it home in my pocket. Two frozen turkeys also arrived, and were raffled for $125. I took a chance, but did not get a prize."
—Harry Jones

"On one occasion, when I was walking down the Creek to see a sick miner, I met a man and woman coming up. 'Wal, doc, me and this young woman were coming up to look for you. We want to know if you can marry us?'

'Oh yes, certainly, if all is right, and after proper notice.'

'Wal, y' understand, it is only to be for the season.'"

—Reverend John Sheepshanks

The town that grew around Billy Barker's claim became the largest on Williams Creek. Barkerville's planked sidewalk was raised to avoid the streams of water that washed off the bare hillsides and made a river of the main street.

JOHN ANGUS "Cariboo" Cameron spent a few years poking around the California goldfields before returning to his Ontario hometown in 1860 to marry Sophia Groves. The following year, Cameron decided to try his luck in British Columbia. In March 1862, he and Sophia were in Victoria when their infant daughter fell ill and died. They buried her in the Quadra Street cemetery and headed for the mines.

Cameron and a few partners took up a claim on Williams Creek. By autumn, they had found a promising amount of gold. Cameron's excitement was rising when Sophia contracted "mountain fever" (typhoid). As she lay dying, she begged her husband to bury her in her family's vault in Ontario. After her funeral, attended by all of the ninety men who were overwintering in Richfield, Cameron put her coffin in an empty cabin. While Sophia froze solid in the Cariboo winter, he returned to his claim. Soon, he was taking out gold by the pound.

In January 1863, Cameron loaded the coffin and a 50-pound bag of gold onto a toboggan and, accompanied by his partner Robert Stevenson and a party of miners hired to drag the load, he set off on the 600-mile trek to Victoria. "There were six or seven feet of snow," Stevenson remembered, "and two feet on top of that, newly fallen." Struggling with the heavy toboggan through blizzards and temperatures that dipped to 35 degrees below zero, eighteen men gave up before they reached Quesnel. At Beaver

John Angus Cameron.

Sophia Cameron.

Creek, the remainder deserted, but there Cameron was able to buy a horse, and he and Stevenson pushed on alone. By the time they reached Victoria, they had been on the road for over two months.

John Cameron explained his problem to a Victoria undertaker. He had promised to take Sophia home, but first he must to return to his claim. The undertaker placed Sophia's body in a tin casket, poured in 25 gallons of alcohol and sealed the coffin in lead. After burying Sophia beside her baby, John headed back to the mines. In six short months, he took out $250,000.

In October 1863, Cameron returned to Victoria, disinterred Sophia's coffin and took her home to Ontario, where she was laid to rest in her family's vault. His duty done, John built a fine new house, married a local woman and began to entertain lavishly. But his neighbours began to ask unpleasant questions. He had left the town penniless and accompanied by Sophia; he had returned with a fortune and a coffin. Was Sophia in the coffin, or was there some sinister story waiting to be discovered?

Ten years after "Cariboo" Cameron's return, the story was taken up by the American press.

The *Syracuse Sunday News* reported breathlessly: "For the past ten years she has been the unwilling prisoner and wife of an Indian chief to whom Cameron had traded her for the claim that had yielded him all his wealth."

There was nothing to do but open the coffin. Several hundred people joined Sophia's relatives as the vault was opened and the coffin laid on the grass. As the lid was pried open, the crowd leaned forward to peer inside. "The body was disclosed in a most wonderful state of preservation, with the exception that the eyes had somewhat fallen in and the lips slightly contracted. But the general fullness and contour of the visage was so well preserved as to be instantly recognizable."

"A triumphant vindication!" Cameron's friends rejoiced. But his troubles were not over. His investments turned sour and his fortune slipped away. He was "broken in health and spirit" and a "wreck of his former self" when he returned to British Columbia in 1886. He died in Barkerville two years later, "an emaciated old man" of sixty-eight.

John Cameron's claim on Williams Creek.

Each has a revolver or bowie knife attached to her waist." Other, less intimidating, members of the demimonde tended to forge a series of seasonal relationships, rather than entertain customers. "We have learned to live without the support of a woman," a miner grumbled.

To fill the void, the British Female Emigrant Society recruited sixty more-or-less marriageable women in England and shipped them to Victoria aboard the *Tynmouth*. "An odd assortment of women," a fellow passenger mused. "Wives for our Bachelors!" the *Colonist* cheered. The bride ship dropped anchor at Esquimalt in September 1862. As five hopeful Victoria men, "arrayed in their best, with clean white shirts and garotte collars," circled the *Tynmouth* in a rowboat, the *Colonist*'s man scrambled aboard to inspect the women. "They are mostly cleanly, well-built, ages varying from 14 to an uncertain figure," he reported.

Bachelors on Vancouver Island were as eager as Cariboo miners, and few women reached the goldfields. There remained only one solution to the lack of female company—the "hurdy-gurdies." They were young women who had been brought out from Germany by a "Boss Hurdy" and who were required to work for him until their expenses had been paid, "about a thousand percent for his outlay." They were not prostitutes, although many people thought they were. "Morally speaking, they are really not what they are generally put down for," a man, who was in the position to know, protested. They were hired out at a dollar a dance, and they were expected to encourage men to drink.

*"The hurdy style of dancing differs from all other schools.
If you ever saw a ring of bells in motion,
you have seen the exact positions these young ladies
are put through during the dance, the more
muscular the partner, the nearer the approximation
of the ladies' pedal extremities to the ceiling,
and the gent who can hoist his 'gal' the highest
is the best dancer."*
—*Cariboo Sentinel*

The popularity of Barkerville's hurdy-gurdy girls (shown here) prompted Sawney (James Anderson, the Cariboo bard) to celebrate them in 1866 in a song, "The German Lasses," which included the chorus:

Bonnie are the hurdies, O!
The German hurdy-gurdies, O!
The daftest hour that e'er I spent,
Was dancing' wi' the hurdies, O!

Miners at Ne'er Do Well Dump on Grouse Creek, c. 1868. Men in the Cariboo developed a language of their own. Worthless claims were described as "fizzled" or "caved" or "gone up the flume." The phrase "in a hog's eye" was equivalent to "no, you don't." Strong liquor was known as "chain lightning" or "scorpion juice" or "mountain howitzer." And to "vamoose the ranch" meant to leave for points unknown.

For some men, the poor living conditions, combined with their lack of success, became unbearable. "In the intensity of their disappointment, many committed suicide," miner Robert Stevenson remembered. A man named Pin walked into the woods and took poison. James Craig, who had been forced to resign his position at a bank after allowing too many uncollectable debts, tried mining with no luck and, "in a moment of despair," took his life. But the suicide that touched people most was that of John Fraser, son of the explorer Simon Fraser.

In 1862, when his father died, John Alexander Fraser was twenty-nine years old. After mortgaging the family home, he arrived in the Cariboo with several thousand dollars to invest. Spreading his money wide and far, he "launched out into mining ventures in all directions" and became "one of the leading men of Cariboo": president of the Literary Society, the Glee Club and the Library Association. He was popular and seemed to be doing well, but one May night in 1865, he cut his jugular vein with his penknife. "I never knew there was so much blood in the body of a person before," a friend, Harry Jones, shuddered.

To escape the cold and loneliness, hundreds of miners chose to overwinter on the coast. Each autumn, as snow began to fall in the Cariboo, Victoria boomed. Across the harbour, the Lekwammen settlement on the Esquimalt road experienced a similar boom as northern Indians were drawn down the coast by the opportunity to trade. In Victoria, they sold salmon and baskets door to door. They worked for wages in restaurants and hotels and in private homes.

The mouth of the Homathko River, Bute Inlet, scene of the first outbreak of the Chilcotin War, painted by Frederick Whymper, who brought the news Victoria.

During the spring of 1862, as many as two thousand northern Indians were encamped on the Lekwammen reserve and along the ravine that marked Victoria's northern boundary. At the same time, the town was full of miners preparing to return to the Cariboo. With the two communities mingling freely, the stage was set for tragedy on a huge scale.

In March, a man recently arrived from San Francisco fell ill with smallpox. "Imagine for a moment what a fearful calamity it would be, were the ... Indians on the outskirts of the town to take the disease," the *British Colonist* worried.

Caused by a virus, smallpox is highly contagious. After the onset of the first symptoms—a sudden spike of fever, accompanied by a blinding headache and a knifing pain in the back—a flush of tiny red spots appears. Soon, the spots become blisters, and the blisters develop into pustules, painful hot pockets of pus. In severe cases, the pustules grow together until the skin resembles a cobblestoned street.

Dr. John Helmcken did what he could. Using the crude but effective arm-to-arm method, he vaccinated the Lekwammen and then turned his attention to their Native visitors from the north. He managed to vaccinate several hundred in the first few weeks of the outbreak, but that was far too few.

THE CHILCOTIN (Tsilhqot'in) people were devastated by the smallpox epidemic of 1862. Later, their fear of the disease led to the uprising that became known as the Chilcotin War.

Alfred Waddington, who had fetched up in Victoria during the gold-mad spring of 1858, became convinced that the best route to the Cariboo mines lay up Bute Inlet and the Homathko River. His idea won favour with Victoria businessmen who were happy to invest in the construction of a route that avoided New Westminster. Work on Waddington's road began in 1862.

Two years later, a work party returning to the inlet after overwintering in Victoria, discovered that a supply of flour, left behind in a log storehouse, had been plundered. Waddington's agent, sure that the Tsilhqot'in were responsible for the theft, warned: "All the Chilcoatens are going to die. We shall send sickness into the country, which will kill them all." The Tsilhqot'in remembered a similar threat and the smallpox epidemic that followed it.

Near dawn a few weeks later, Edwin Mosely, a member of a work crew encamped beside the Homathko River, was asleep in a tent when he was jolted awake by a "whoop" and the sound of gunfire. "I saw knives on each side of me come through the canvas and pierce the bodies of my two companions," he recalled. As the Tsilhqot'in moved off to another tent, Mosely scrambled away and hurled himself into the river.

Fifteen men were dead. Two posses were sent in search of the raiders. One, led by gold commissioner William Cox, proceeded from Fort Alexandria. The second, led by Governor Frederick Seymour, sailed up the coast to Bella Coola, where they learned that a pack train had been attacked and three men killed.

The principal suspects, Klatsassin (Lhatses'in, Klatsassine) and Telloot (Tellot) were pursued until 15 August 1864, when they agreed to surrender. By then, the death toll had risen to twenty-one whites and three Tsilhqot'in. Klatsassin and his men considered themselves to be prisoners of war, and they expected to negotiate their surrender with the gover-

nor. But to their pursuers, they were murderers.

Six men were tried at Quesnel before Judge Matthew Baillie Begbie. Klatsassin, Telloot, Tahpit (Tapeet), Pierre and Chessus were found guilty and sentenced to death. "It seems horrible to hang 5 men at once—especially under the circumstances of the capitulation," Begbie admitted. "Yet the blood of 21 whites calls for retribution."

The sentence was carried out on 26 October 1864. As the prisoners were led to the gallows, Tahpit called to his fellows to have courage. "One instant more and the signal was given; the drops fell. All was done so quietly and so quickly it was difficult to realize that the frightful work was over." The men were buried in a wood near the Cariboo Road.

Waddington's road was abandoned. Eight years later, while in Ottawa on business, Waddington was approached by an acquaintance, a doctor, who clasped Waddington's hands warmly in greeting. In response to a polite inquiry, the doctor exclaimed, "I have just left the worst case of confluent smallpox I have ever

seen." Waddington snatched back his hands and, trembling violently, stumbled to a chair. He died shortly afterward of smallpox.

More than a hundred years after the end of the Chilcotin War, the unmarked graves of the five men lay under the asphalt of a hospital parking lot, but they were far from forgotten. According to Judge Anthony Sarich, who conducted the Cariboo-Chilcotin Justice Inquiry in 1993, "That episode of history has left a deep wound in the body of Chilcotin society." The Tsilhqot'in felt the men should be pardoned, and Sarich agreed. "It is time to heal that wound . . . it is appropriate that Victoria grant a posthumous pardon to those chiefs, and I so recommend."

On 26 October 1999, a plaque, acknowledging that the executed men had been involved in war rather than murder, was unveiled at Quesnel.

The Tsilhqot'in feared smallpox and also resented the construction of a road through their territory.

Europeans had lived with smallpox for centuries and had developed some immunity to the disease. Even for those who had not been vaccinated, the survival rate was encouraging. In mild cases, most victims recovered; in the worst cases, chances of survival were better than 50 per cent. However, as this Tsimshian mask suggests, the prospects for Native people were grim.

◼

"At the present rate of mortality, a Northern Indian will be an object of curiosity in two years from now."
—British Colonist

◼

"Poor creatures, they [the Nuxalk people] are dying and rotting away by the score, & it is no uncommon occurrence to come across dead bodies lying in the bush. They have now dispersed from their villages, but it seems to be spreading through the valley."
—Lieutenant H. Spencer Palmer

◼

By April, thirty Tsimshian were dead or dying, and the disease had spread to the Haida. Alarmed townspeople demanded that Indians be banished from the town and confined to the Lekwammen reserve. When that proved unworkable, the shacks on the reserve were burned and the visitors ordered away. In June, a party of thirty Haida, who had been on their way home from Victoria, were found dead at Ogden Point near the harbour mouth. Out at Isabella Ross's farm, a score of Stikine people had collapsed on the beach in the last stages of the disease.

News from the north was appalling. On a beach near Nanaimo, a passing sailor counted twelve bodies "festering in the noonday sun." The captain of a schooner sailing along the coast reported: "So soon as pustules break out on an occupant of one of the canoes, he is put ashore; a small piece of muslin, to serve as a tent, is raised over him, a small allowance of bread, fish and water doled out and he is left to die alone." Then the rest of the party continued their journey, unaware that they were carrying the disease to their homes.

When the trader at Fort Kamloops heard that there was smallpox on the coast, he began vaccinating all the Shuswap (Secwepemc) people who called at the post. Reverend John Sheepshanks, who was travelling from New Westminster to Williams Creek, vaccinated any Indians he met. "Sitting down upon a fallen tree and taking out my lancet, I told the chiefs that I wished to cut them all slightly on the arm and put in a little good medicine which I hoped—I tried to express myself carefully—would preserve them from the bad disease."

But still the disease spread. From Bella Coola, smallpox moved along the "grease trail" to the Chilcotin plateau. In October, four men travelling from Fort Alexandria to Bella Coola, along a trail that took them past the village of Nancootlem on Anahim Lake, found no people, only bodies— some buried, others covered by brush or wrapped in blankets, and still others lying inside deserted houses. At the end of the lake, they came upon a "horribly pockmarked" man, sitting alone by a small fire. "When he saw us he rose to his feet. He had a knife in his hand, and from the look of anger and hatred in his face, I wondered if he would attack us all."

"'Cultus [worthless] white man,' he shouted," adding that the white man had brought smallpox and killed his people.

That winter, two miners travelling from Williams Lake to Lac La Hache began to notice "snow graves," bodies left unburied and now covered by mounds of snow. At one encampment, they counted 120 graves and "only three full grown Indians left."

The 1862 outbreak took two years to burn itself out. By the time smallpox finally retreated, it had carried off at least a third of the Native population—a death toll estimated to be as high as twenty thousand.

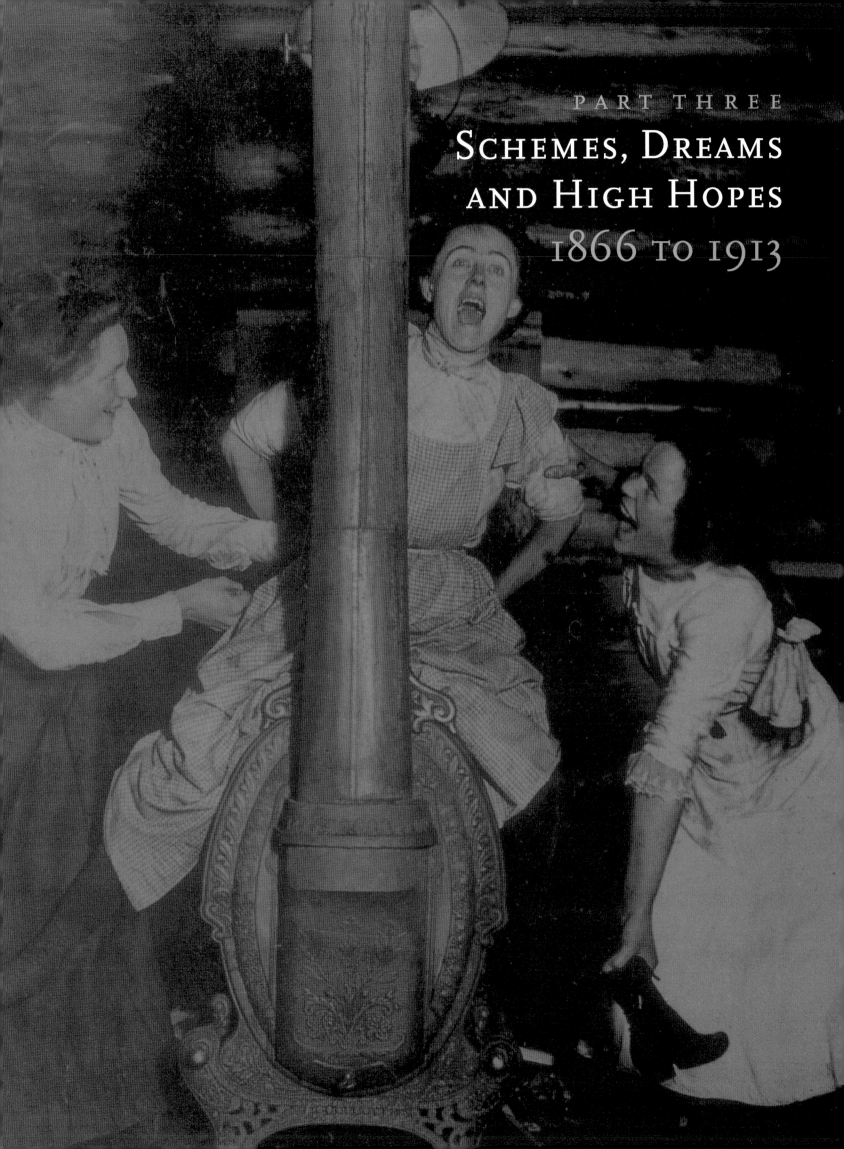

SCHEMES, DREAMS AND HIGH HOPES

1866 TO 1913

"We are a conquered country
& the Canucks take possession tomorrow."
—E. G. Alston

CHAPTER 8

DIVIDED LOYALTIES

Previous page: Mattie
Gunterman (centre) and Rose
and Ann Williams worked as
cooks at the Nettie L. Mine in
the Lardeau. In 1898, Mattie,
her husband and five-year-old
son walked most of the 600
miles from Seattle to Upper
Arrow Lake. A horse packed her
heavy camera, tripod and glass
plate negatives. She helped the
family income by cooking in
mining camps and spent her
spare time developing her
photographs in a woodshed.

BY 1864, it had become clear that, while the Colony of Vancouver
Island was profiting from the gold rush, the Colony of British Columbia
was not. Steamers from San Francisco, laden with supplies for the goldfields, called at Victoria rather than New Westminster. Victoria counted
its population in the thousands, New Westminster in the hundreds.
New Westminster's newspaper, the *British Columbian*, might dismiss the
senior colony as that "insignificant little Island which forms the natural
breakwater to British Columbia," but mainlanders were convinced that
Governor James Douglas, who continued to reside in Victoria and who
owned a large estate in the city, was deliberately setting policies that
favoured the island colony over British Columbia.

When Douglas announced his resignation from the governorship of both colonies, mainlanders were delighted. The news that he would be replaced by two men—Arthur Kennedy on Vancouver Island and Frederick Seymour in British Columbia—was cause for rejoicing. At last, British Columbia would have a governor of its own.

Frederick Seymour arrived at New Westminster in April 1864 to a delirious reception from the town's residents, who proclaimed him to be "our first governor." Still frail from "Panama fever" picked up during an earlier colonial appointment in the tropics, Seymour warmed to his welcome, but he could not help but notice that New Westminster seemed "played out." He set about lifting the spirits of the colony by improving his official residence (Colonel Moody's former home in Sapperton). After adding "a spacious and handsome ballroom, capable of handling two hundred dancers," he hosted his first ball, a glittering affair held to celebrate the Prince of Wales's birthday. The *Columbian*, taking aim at Victoria, declared it to be "the most brilliant social event yet to take place west of the Rocky Mountains," and New Westminster boasted of feeling like "a real capital" at last.

Facing page: The Victoria Fire Brigade gathered in front of the Birdcages to be inspected by Arthur Kennedy, who became the third governor of the Colony of Vancouver Island in 1864.

This page: Governor Seymour's first impression of New Westminster was not good: "I had not seen even in the West Indies so melancholy a picture of disappointed hopes as New Westminster presented on my arrival. Many of the best houses were untenanted. The largest hotel was to let, decay appeared on all sides, and the stumps and logs of the fallen trees blocked up most of the streets." In this 1867 painting depicting Queen Victoria's birthday celebration, Government House appears in the background.

Seymour found it easy to adopt the mainland's view that British Columbia had been treated as if it were nothing more than "a gold mine at one end of a line of road." He did what he could to set matters right. He approved the completion of the Cariboo Road to Williams Creek. And when he heard of new gold discoveries on the Big Bend of the Columbia, he agreed to an extension of the Dewdney Trail. To divert trade away from the port of Victoria to the "deep, placid & undevious entrance to the Fraser," he approved the plan to mark the sandbanks at the river's mouth with a lightship and buoys. But, in the end, he had to face the fact that the gold rush was waning.

"The merchants and owners of Town lots in Victoria in the comparatively unimportant Colony of V.I. have drawn nearly all the share of the profits of the gold discoveries in this Colony which have not been absorbed by California."
—Governor Frederick Seymour

In the summer of 1864, Governor Frederick Seymour and his official party (shown here near Lillooet) travelled along the Cariboo Road. Seymour was impressed by his welcome: "If the white people were loyal in their demonstrations, H.M.'s Indian subjects were by no means behind them."

The mainland colony was deeply in debt. To raise revenues, Seymour increased fees for licences and for registering claims, and he instituted heavy duties on goods shipped to the mainland from the duty-free port of Victoria. The results were predictable. Prices rose, imports fell, and revenues declined. Most of the surface (placer) mines were played out, and much of the mining activity had shifted to the deep digging that only organized companies could afford. Faced with increased fees and new charges, the "floating population" of the colony began to drift away.

In Victoria, rents fell by half and merchants were forced into bankruptcy. The population that had peaked at over six thousand sank to thirty-five hundred. "No city on the Pacific Coast occupies a more deplorable condition commercially than Victoria," the American consul reported.

The annual cost of running the two colonies was $954,000, the revenues less than $207,000. Both colonies were drowning in debt: British Columbia owed $1,002,983; Vancouver Island, $293,698. As a cost-cutting measure, the island's house of assembly proposed the union of the two colonies. That idea, opposed by Governor Seymour and the mainlanders, found acceptance in London. In August 1866, Queen Victoria gave royal assent to the British Columbia Act, and on 19 November, the union was proclaimed in Victoria and New Westminster. "There was no enthusiasm or excitement shown in either town," Seymour observed.

Governor Frederick Seymour invited chiefs from the Interior to New Westminster to celebrate Queen Victoria's birthday in 1864. They presented the governor with a plea for protection. The governor presented them with a decorated staff and a pipe.

By the mid-1860s, successful gold mining was limited to companies with sufficient capital to support the expense of hydraulic mining.

"The Ships of war fired a salute. A funeral procession . . . would have been more appropriate to the sad melancholy event," James Douglas grumbled. Like other Vancouver Islanders, he had assumed that the mainland would be annexed by the senior colony. But by the terms of the act, the reverse was true. The united colony would be known as British Columbia. The governor of the new colony would be Frederick Seymour, the mainland's governor. Vancouver Island's elected house of assembly would be replaced by a less democratic legislative council; of its twenty-three members, only nine would be elected, and of those nine, only four would be from Vancouver Island. Victoria lost its status as a free port; customs duties and other charges that had prevailed on the mainland would now apply to the island.

Worst of all, the act was silent on the subject of the capital city. That decision was left to the governor, and Seymour was known to favour New Westminster, "the most respectable, manly and enterprising little community with which I have ever been acquainted." However, he was reluctant to risk the ire of Vancouver Islanders by choosing New Westminster. Instead, he hoped that the legislative council would name its preference; he could then be seen as following its advice.

In 1867, when the new legislative council met at New Westminster, Dr. John Helmcken, an elected member from Victoria, seized the opportunity to introduce a resolution "recommending the removal of the Seat of Government to Victoria." The arguments in favour of the island city were telling. Not only did Victoria enjoy the status of being the first colonial capital

but also it was British Columbia's largest, most substantial city, the centre of business and commerce. With the Royal Navy based in nearby Esquimalt, it was easier to defend than New Westminster. And, as some of Seymour's appointees could not help but agree, it was "civilized" and settled, a more pleasant town in which to reside than rough and raw New Westminster.

Helmcken's resolution carried by a five-vote majority. But Seymour, who had fervently hoped the vote would turn out differently, procrastinated, hoping that the council might have a change of heart. That his health was failing only added to his indecisiveness. As the question of the capital hovered in the air, the governor's secretary warned his medical advisor, "In a short time, you will have to give a medical certificate that he may be invalided if these cocktails all day go on as now."

When the second session of the British Columbia legislative council met at New Westminster, Seymour admitted that the government in London was becoming impatient: "I am commanded to come to a decision without further ado." The council voted a second time, and once again the members favoured Victoria, a result so infuriating to New Westminster that a mob assembled outside the Colonial Hotel, where a triumphant Dr. Helmcken and a clutch of Victoria supporters were celebrating. "You had better not go outside!" the landlord warned. "There is a crowd waiting for you and threaten to be revenged on you."

On 25 May 1868, Seymour reluctantly proclaimed Victoria the capital of British Columbia.

"Fairfield," the home of Cariboo Road bridge-builder Joseph Trutch, was set in an orchard a short walk from Victoria's business district. With the departure of so many American residents, the city's Englishness became more apparent: croquet on the lawn, tea in the afternoon, cricket in the park.

"Westminster was a very small place—a village, with virtually one street along the waterfront, with three or four good buildings. The people seemed peculiar—hated Victoria. What was Victoria—nothing! In a few years she would be wiped out—they would see that Victoria should not sponge on Westminster— Westminster was the place and the natural seaport of the Mainland."
—Dr. John Sebastian Helmcken

Top: Governor Frederick Seymour's reluctance to name Victoria the capital was based, in part, on his dislike of "Bleak House," the nickname for Cary Castle, the official governor's residence of the Colony of Vancouver Island. Sited on a gale-swept rocky hill, Cary Castle was damp, draughty and bone chillingly cold.

Bottom: Governor Frederick Seymour died on 10 June 1869 aboard HMS *Sparrowhawk* while travelling on official business. The ship's medical officer explained: "I found him suffering from great gastric irritation, nervous tremors, sleeplessness and other symptoms of alcoholism." In spite of the doctor's warning, Seymour "succeeded in getting hold of a bottle of brandy and drinking it off" the night before his death.

OF ALL THE MEN who hauled freight into Lillooet, Quesnel and Barkerville, the most famous was Jean Caux, known as Cataline, "the first and the last of the old Cariboo packers." Born in about 1829 in the kingdom of Béarn, on the border between France and Spain, Cataline joined the Mexican packers who came north from California in 1858.

A striking man, with broad shoulders, narrow hips and luxuriant, wavy hair falling to his shoulders, he spoke a few words of Spanish and English, combined with a sprinkling of Chinese and Chinook. For his pack trains of forty to sixty mules, he used the language of the Mexican packers: the man in charge was the *corregidor*; the second in command, the *segundo*; the saddle, the *aparejo*. His packers were a picture of pioneer British Columbia. His corregidor was Ah Gun, a Chinese; his segundo was Dave Wiggins, the son of a Lillooet woman and "Judge" Wiggins, a black man who liked to say, "I was the first white man that ever went over Pavilion Mountain." His muleteers were Mexican, Indian and Chinese.

Cataline, an acquaintance recalled, "lived hard, worked hard and consumed liquor in the same manner." He seemed to be impervious to the cold. Whatever the weather, he never wore socks. At dawn one frosty morning, a friend encountered him asleep by the trail, fully clothed down to his spurs but with no blanket covering him. "I stood for a few minutes watching his deep, steady breathing; his chest rose and fell in regular beat and his hair, beard and clothing were heavily covered with a white frost. He was enjoying a good night's rest."

Cataline earned a reputation for being both honest and reliable. He could not read or write, so he kept all his accounts in his head, and he developed tricks of the trade to be sure that fragile cargo arrived undamaged. When packing cases of eggs, he removed the shoes from the mule selected to carry them. "No shoe, he go out there and maybe ten mile or fifteen mile, his feet get sore," Cataline explained. "He walk easy, just like a cat. Not break one egg."

With the coming of the railroad, Cataline moved his headquarters from Yale to Ashcroft and later to Hazelton. By the time he retired, he had been on the road for fifty-four years. He spent his last years alone in a little cabin outside Hazelton.

He had two children with Amelia, a Nlaka'pamux from Spuzzum, but she had remained with her community, and their children did not accept him as their father. His granddaughter, Annie, remembered: "Those pack trains had little bells, and they would go ding, ding, ding. And Cataline would come along and my father [Cataline's son] would be watching by the fence, and Cataline . . . would come down and give money to my father, but my father wouldn't take it because he didn't know his father . . . They say that Cataline was the most generous man. But my father couldn't use that name, Caux, because my grandmother wasn't married to him."

When Jean Caux died in Hazelton in 1922, his grave was marked by a small stone cairn and a brass plate carrying the words "Jean Caux—Cataline, the packer."

Top: Jean Caux c. 1897, after he had been on the road for almost forty years.

Bottom: Cataline with his packers, c. 1910. The man on the left is likely Dave Wiggins, his segundo.

Lilloett, on the Fraser River.

Lillooet in 1863 was "a town of one street" and sixteen hundred inhabitants.

While mainlanders and islanders were arguing over the capital, two American army officers were travelling around the colony "on official duties," carefully recording their impressions. Lieutenant Colonel Robert Scott and Major James Hoyt became convinced that the colony's economic salvation lay in annexation by the United States and that most British Columbians favoured following that route.

The union of the two colonies had not resulted in the desired savings. In 1867, the governor presented to the legislature a proposed budget of over $700,000—a taxation level of $87.50 for each of the eight thousand non-Native residents of the colony. Duties on American imports, including the food on which the colonists depended, rose to crippling levels: $3 per head on cattle, $2 on hogs, 10 cents on a pound of butter, 12 ½ cents on a dozen eggs.

The cost of living rose and revenues declined. Road work was suspended and schools were closed. The governor offered to take a $3,000 cut in his $20,000 salary and reduced the salaries of senior officials, but those salaries were considered much too high to begin with. It cost $64,000 to support the governor and his colonial officials, the same amount that was being spent to run the state of California with its half million residents and almost six times the amount being paid by the twenty thousand residents of neighbouring Washington to support their territorial government.

In November 1867, Scott and Hoyt submitted a confidential report: "Victoria presents a melancholy spectacle of premature decay and financial ruin. Day after day we saw large wholesale trading establishments without a customer, the proprietors looking gloomily over their open ledgers in which no transactions were being entered. The merchants who remain are in despair . . . Grass is literally growing in the thoroughfares formerly crowded with teams and busy drays."

New Westminster, too, was the picture of gloom. "We found the place nothing more than a small village built among the stumps of the forest," Scott and Hoyt reported. "There was not more than half a dozen stores open, and their business is minimal. The business on the wharves is very light, and steamers going up the river often have neither passengers or freight."

Everywhere the two Americans went, they were told that the only solution to the "utter prostration" of business was annexation by the United States. In fact, they found annexation to be the "constant theme of conversation."

It was not an unreasonable solution. Great Britain had little interest in maintaining its Pacific colony. British Columbia seemed far too remote to attract large-scale emigration from Britain, and the Royal Navy did not regard the colony as having any strategic importance.

"We are satisfied that beyond any question a large majority of the inhabitants (whites) of the colony are in favor of the immediate annexation of the colony to the United States."
—Lieutenant Colonel Robert Scott and Major James Hoyt

John Tod may have been thinking of these fellows, whiling away the hours at the Branch Hotel at Yale, when he wrote in 1867: "The country is being deserted of its white inhabitants . . . the few who remain, and who, having lost their all, cannot well leave, sit brooding over their blighted prospects and ruined fortunes in sullen silence and hopeless despair."

Nova Scotian William Smith
changed his name to Amor
De Cosmos ("lover of the uni-
verse") by an act of the
California legislature. In 1858,
he arrived in Victoria and
began publishing the *British
Colonist* newspaper. Later the
second premier of British
Columbia, he was renowned
for his eccentricities, the passion of his opinions and the
unpredictability of his temper.

Most items necessary for day-to-day life in the colony were imported
from America. The Americans were already in possession of Alaska, having
purchased the former Russian territory in March 1867. If British Columbia
were annexed by the United States, coastal trade would flourish, unimpeded
by customs duties, from California to Alaska. Although thousands of
Americans had left the colony, many remained, and they continued to give
their first allegiance to the republic. Gauging public sentiment from his
office in Victoria, the American consul was sure that "the people of
Vancouver Island and British Columbia are almost unanimous in the
desire for annexation to the United States."

There was, however, an alternative: union with the Canadian federation
to the east. In March 1867, London was finalizing the British North America
Act, which would gather the colonies of Upper and Lower Canada (Ontario
and Quebec), New Brunswick and Nova Scotia into a federal union. On
8 March, Amor De Cosmos rose to his feet in the British Columbia legislative council to propose that the members go on record as supporting the
union of British Columbia with the new federation.

"No one knew much about this subject save De Cosmos," Dr. John
Helmcken admitted. But the council gave unanimous approval to a motion
requesting the governor "to take such steps, without delay as may be
deemed by him best adapted to insure the admission of British Columbia
into the Confederation on fair and equitable terms."

South of the 49th parallel, pro-annexationists were not in the least discouraged by the council's vote. In the first place, they thought it unlikely that
Canada would welcome a bankrupt colony, pointing out that while per capita
debt in the Dominion of Canada was a manageable $23.50, in British Colum-
bia it was a whopping $187.50. And even if Canada was so misguided as to
accept the colony, then that would just simplify matters. After all, within ten
years, the Dominion of Canada would be pleading to join the United States.

Among British Columbians, support for Confederation was far from
unanimous. The most vocal supporters were, like De Cosmos, former
residents of the new federation. But neither Canadians nor their opinions
were well regarded in British Columbia, where they were considered
"poor mean slow people" and accused of counting pennies in a colony
where the smallest change was "two bits." Many of the British residents,
from whose ranks most government officials had been selected, preferred
colonial status partly out of genuine loyalty and partly to protect their
appointments. American residents could think of nothing more desirable
than annexation by the United States.

The colony's future remained unsettled in December 1869, when
American president Ulysses S. Grant received a "memorial" signed by forty-
three Victorians. "We earnestly desire the ACQUISITION of *this Colony*
by the *United States*," the signatures pleaded. The *British Colonist* was quick
to dismiss the petition as "a sublime bit of cheek" and the work of "foreign-
ers." But while it was true that the majority of the petitioners were men
of European ancestry who had come to the colony by way of San Francisco
or New York, it was also true that they represented a powerful element
in Victoria's once-thriving business community and that their views were
shared by more than a few British colonists.

However, the pressure to join Canada was becoming inexorable. The
colonial secretary had made it clear that Britain was determined to see

British Columbia enter Confederation. And after Governor Seymour's death, his place was taken by Anthony Musgrave, hand-picked for his strong pro-Confederation opinions. Still, there was little real enthusiasm for union with Canada.

The spark was lit only when the colonists learned the truly bold demands that British Columbia intended to make. Governor Musgrave had given the task of drafting the terms of union to his executive council, expanded by the addition of Dr. Helmcken, who was known to oppose Confederation but whose connections and credentials were impeccable. Helmcken suggested they require the construction of a railway from the lower Fraser River to Kamloops, and a wagon road from Kamloops through the Rocky Mountains. Joseph Trutch, who had built the Alexandra Suspension Bridge and who was now serving on the executive council as commissioner of lands and works, came forward with a more audacious proposal.

"Helmcken, your idea of a waggon road and railroad are good," he said, "but on thinking the matter over I think Confederation will be valueless without a railway to the Eastern Canada!"

"Heavens, Trutch," Helmcken exclaimed, "how are they to build it!—and as to operate it—I do not see the way."

"I am a loyal Briton, and would prefer living under the institutions of my own country, were it practicable. But I, like the rest of the world of which we are each an atom, would prefer the flag and institutions of the United States with prosperity, to remaining as we are, with no prospect of succeeding as a British colony."
—British Columbian

Drying salmon at Shuswap Lake. Native people welcomed Confederation because they believed they would fare better under the federal government than they had under the colonial administration.

"Well I do," Trutch assured him.

Trutch's railway became part of the package introduced to the legislative council. Governor Musgrave sweetened the pot by promising that, if British Columbians accepted the terms, he would proclaim a new colonial constitution, replacing the partially appointed legislative council with one that was wholly elected.

The legislative council accepted the terms with nary a dissenting vote, and in May 1870, three delegates left Victoria for Ottawa to negotiate the union. When Canada agreed to all the significant items, Governor Musgrave was astounded. "And the Railway, Credat Judaeus! *is guaranteed* without a reservation!" he exclaimed.

Members of the legislative council of British Columbia in front of the Birdcages in 1871, the year that the colony joined Confederation.

On 18 January 1871, the council voted in favour of the terms, and on 1 April, the House of Commons in Ottawa approved British Columbia's entry into Confederation. On 16 May, Queen Victoria gave assent to the union, and 20 July 1871 was set as the date of British Columbia's admittance to Canada.

On 19 July, Governor Musgrave proclaimed the promised new constitution, which provided for an elected legislative assembly of twenty-five members, twelve from the island and thirteen from the mainland. And as the clocks ticked toward midnight, British Columbians prepared to celebrate "the super-excellent terms" that had brought them into Canada.

On the mainland, flags flew and buildings were draped with bunting. In Barkerville, the day was greeted with gunfire and the ringing of the fire bell. At midnight in Victoria, church bells pealed, gunfire crackled, fireworks lit the sky, and people thronged the streets and "cheered, and cheered, and cheered!"

"British Columbia is a sea of Mountains . . .
It has been pronounced by British
Ordnance officers Impractical for a Railroad."
—Northern Pacific Railway Company

CHAPTER 9

WAITING *for the* RAILWAY

In 1871, Victoria's population was 3,270. Ten years later, it had risen to only 5,925. Still, it was the largest city in the province. "The English character of the place is particularly noticeable," a visitor observed in 1875. "Victoria seems almost lifeless in business."

THE BENEFITS OF CONFEDERATION were a long time coming. Until the transcontinental railway was completed, no large-scale settlement schemes could be contemplated. Emigrants arrived in a trickle rather than a flood. In 1871, British Columbia's non-Native adult population stood at about 10,500. Not until 1881 did the numbers rise again to gold-rush heights.

Commercial development languished. But even as economic depression hung over the land, there were pockets of progress. On the east

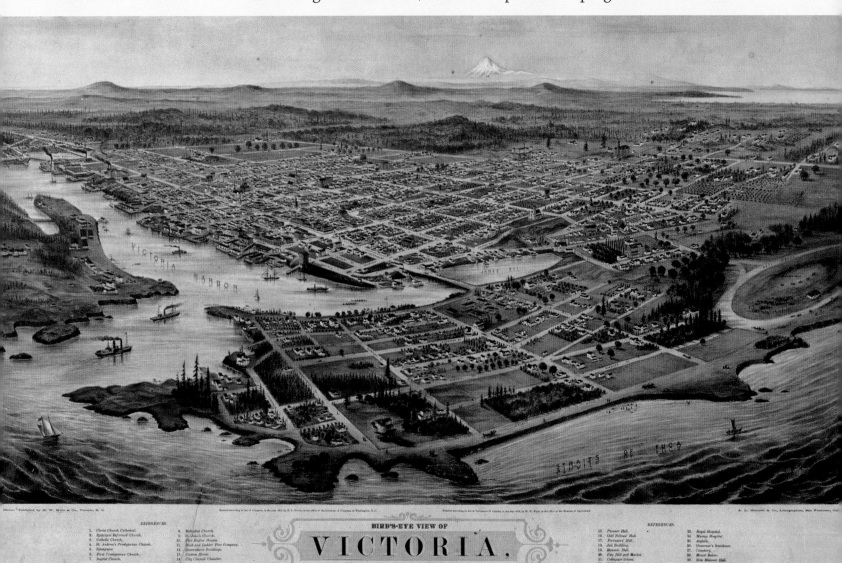

BIRD'S-EYE VIEW OF
VICTORIA,
Vancouver Island, B.C. 1878.

coast of Vancouver Island, on the lower Fraser River, along the shores of Burrard Inlet, in the Okanagan valley and on the Chilcotin plateau, a few men were beginning to exploit resources other than the fur and gold on which the colony had depended.

Of all the industries that blossomed in the 1870s, lumbering had the longest history. Almost one hundred years earlier, John Meares had instructed his captains, bound for Nootka Sound, to fill every space in their ships' holds that was not occupied by furs with "spars, and sawing planks, particularly boat knees and timbers—all of which bear a good price in China." In 1830, Fort Langley had sent cedar shingles and planks to the Hawaiian Islands and, a dozen years later, when James Douglas was inspecting Vancouver Island's south coast for a site for Fort Victoria, he had placed some importance on the proximity of a watercourse suitable for the establishment of a sawmill. In 1848, the water-powered mill, manned by Kanakas (Hawaiians), went into operation at Millstream and found a ready market for piles and timber in San Francisco, where builders were scrambling to meet the demands created by the California gold rush.

In 1855, the Muir family of Sooke opened a steam-powered sawmill using machinery salvaged from a shipwreck and began to export lumber to Hawaii, Australia, Hong Kong, Shanghai and England.

In 1859, Captain Edward Stamp, an English shipmaster in whom the entrepreneurial light burned bright, suggested to Governor Douglas that he would construct a steam-powered sawmill, provided he was given exclusive timber rights to at least 10,000 acres. With Douglas's approval, Stamp selected land at the head of the Alberni Canal, a long, slender inlet extending east from Barkley Sound. At first, the mill was wildly successful. In 1863, its exports totalled thirteen hundred spars and 11 million feet of sawn lumber. But after only three years of operation, mill manager Gilbert Sproat admitted that he had run out of trees.

Captain Stamp had timber rights to 15,000 acres, but the easily accessible trees had "only lasted about a year and a half." To reach the mill, logs were either floated down rivers to the canal or

Captain Edward Stamp, whose maritime career included the command of a troopship during the Crimean War, was active in two pioneer industries, lumbering and salmon canning. In 1866, he was elected to the united colony's first legislative council.

For residents of New Westminster, Burrard Inlet was a favourite picnic spot. The group pictured here includes James Douglas's daughter Agnes and her husband, Arthur Bushby.

Teams of oxen were used to haul logs to Burrard Inlet sawmills.

hauled overland by oxen. The trees remaining to be logged were "in Sheltered patches." The intervening country was too rough for oxen; the streams were too small and too shallow to carry logs. The mill shut down in 1864.

By then, Captain Stamp was involved in a more ambitious scheme on the shore of Burrard Inlet. A "lumber man's paradise," the inlet was home to the finest stands of accessible timber in either colony—tall, straight trees capable of producing "sticks" over 100 feet long and 36 inches square without a single knot.

A water-powered sawmill had been established on the inlet's north shore in 1863. After a year in operation, it was acquired by Sewell P. Moody, a native of Maine. "Sue" Moody improved and enlarged the mill and went after the export trade. Soon, timber was leaving the inlet for Australia, Mexico, China and Peru.

In 1865, Captain Stamp incorporated the British Columbia and Vancouver Island Spar, Lumber and Sawmill Company with capital of £100,000. Stamp's mill, steam-powered and located on the south shore of the inlet, opened for business in 1867.

Sue Moody's Burrard Inlet sawmill attracted a diverse workforce. Mill workers and longshoremen included deserting seamen, Chinese sojourners, Kanakas from the Hawaiian Islands and men from the nearby Indian reserve.

"There used to be a great fleet of vessels in Burrard Inlet . . . The most I ever remember was forty-two vessels at one time: ships, barques, barquentines, brigs, brigantines, and three-or four-masted masted schooners . . . that was at the time Captain Stamp had the mill."
—John H. Scales

"A pretty hard crowd used to find their way to Burrard Inlet from other parts to escape arrest."
—Dr. W. Wymond Walkem

Burrard Inlet boomed. From January 1867 to June 1868, Stamp's mill loaded fourteen ships with 4 million feet of lumber, one hundred thousand shingles and two thousand spars, while Sue Moody's mill filled thirty-three vessels with almost 6 million feet and eight hundred thousand shingles. Moody responded to the demand by constructing a steam-powered mill and by building a wharf capable of docking a dozen ships. With Stamp's mill and Moody's two mills running steadily and employing three hundred men, the inlet became a busy place, and small settlements began to cluster around the mills.

Just as Captain Stamp's mill was hitting its stride, his company was dissolved amid recriminations and lawsuits. In 1870, its assets were sold to a San Francisco company. Stamp's mill became Hastings Mill and continued to profit under the management of Captain James Raymur.

Meanwhile, Sue Moody was doing so well that he had exhausted the trees on his north shore timber leases. He found a supply at Pitt Lake. Logs were sent down the Pitt River, collected into booms on the Fraser and then towed past New Westminster and around Point Grey to his mill.

"In those days," Dr. W. Wymond Walkem remembered, "no logs were taken, or even looked at, which contained a knot to mar the beauty of the flooring into which most of it was cut. The trees cut down were generally those which had not a branch below sixty or seventy feet from the ground." By 1877, the Burrard Inlet mills had achieved worldwide renown for the quality of their lumber.

AFTER TURNING HIS BACK on lumbering, Captain Stamp threw himself into the salmon-canning business. Salmon ranks third to lumber and fur as the export commodity with the longest history on the coast. In 1828, the governor of the Hudson's Bay Company, George Simpson, fresh from his hair-raising voyage down the Fraser River, had been happy to discover that Fort Langley might have a purpose other than as a supply base for upriver forts. "Salmon are so abundant," Simpson had written, "that a considerable quantity might be cured for Exportation if a market could be found."

A market was soon found in the Hawaiian Islands. By the 1830s, the islands had become the crossroads of Pacific trade—a supply base for whalers out of Boston, an easy swing to the west for ships that had rounded Cape Horn on their way to the north coast, a stopping-off place for ships sailing between the west coast of America and the Orient. In 1832, Fort Langley shipped a hundred barrels of salted salmon to Oahu, where they were sold for $10 a barrel to a trader who intended to resell them in Peru.

Captain Stamp had toyed with the idea of processing salmon when he opened his Alberni mill in 1863. What appealed to him now was the possibility of preserving salmon in compact tins, rather than bulky barrels. At Sapperton, he leased derelict buildings, transformed them into a cannery and then went looking for a tinsmith.

The tin cans were made by hand. Measured sections were cut from sheets of tin and wrapped around a wooden dowel to form a cylinder; then hand-cut circles were soldered to either end. Stamp found an able man in John Sullivan Deas. A free-born black from South Carolina, Deas had arrived in Victoria during the gold rush. He was working at his own business, producing stovepipes and tinware, when Stamp hired him in 1871.

In its first year of operation, Stamp's Fish Preserving Company shipped seven hundred cases of tinned salmon to England. The following year, Stamp dropped dead of a heart attack, and Deas decided to go into the canning business for himself. In 1873, he pre-empted an island (Deas Island) in the Fraser Delta, hired twenty Chinese workers and produced 4,250 cases, each containing forty-eight 1-pound cans.

Deas's success attracted competitors. By 1878, there were eight canneries on the Fraser, and production had risen to 107,000 cases—more than 5 million 1-pound cans. Four years later, thirteen canneries were operating. The largest, the Delta Cannery at Ladner's Landing, employed more than four hundred men and shipped 1,152,000 cases—more than 55 million pounds of salmon—to London and Liverpool. The business had grown so fast that the federal government was beginning to think that some regulations should be applied to the burgeoning, unfettered industry.

While Deas was establishing an industry on the lower Fraser, Robert Dunsmuir was proving that Vancouver Island coal was "black gold." Dunsmuir was not the first to see the potential for profit in island coal. In 1849, the Hudson's Bay Company had established Fort Rupert near the most promising outcrops, but then the fur traders had lost no time in proving that they knew little about mining or marketing coal, and even less about managing the men who raised it.

MODE OF CURING SALMON

As soon as a cargo of Salmon is caught, the natives bring it to the trading post in their canoes. A number of Indian women are employed by the traders, seated on the beach, with knives, ready to cut up the fish. The women . . . commence cutting out the backbones, and cut off the heads of salmon. They are then taken to the salter, and placed in a large hogshead, with a quantity of coarse salt. They remain there for several days, until they are quite firm. The pickle produced from these is boiled in a large copper kettle; and the blood, which floats by the boiling process to the top, is skimmed off, leaving the pickle perfectly clear. The salmon are then taken from the hogshead and packed in tierces [casks] with a little more salt; the tierces are then headed up, and laid upon their bilge, or widest part, leaving the bung-hole open; the pickle is next poured in, until the tierce become full; a circle of clay, about four inches high, is then made round the bung-hole, in which the oil from the salmon rises. This oil is skimmed off; and, according as the salmon imbibes the pickle, more pickle is poured in, so as to keep the liquid sufficiently on the surface, and afford facility for skimming off the oil. After the oil ceases to rise to the circle round the bung-hole, the salmon is then supposed to be sufficiently prepared; the clay circle is cleared away, and the hole is bunged up. Salmon, so cured, will keep good for three years.

—John Dunn, 1884

"In the way of preserved fish, we have tasted nothing so delicate as the canned salmon put up in New Westminster by Captain E. Stamp. The fish is ready for the table, and can be eaten either cold or, as some prefer it, warmed up in the tins previous to being served."

—Colonist

Salmon on the wharf of a Steveston cannery, c. 1899. The catch often exceeded the canneries' capacity and thousands of dead fish were thrown back into the river.

Neat piles of canned salmon at the Phoenix Cannery on the Fraser River, 1891. By the turn of the century, the salmon industry on the lower Fraser was employing several thousand people. The first workers—Chinese and Coast Salish—were beginning to be replaced by the Japanese.

The HBC had recruited experienced Scottish colliers, luring them to the coast with three-year contracts that guaranteed an annual salary of £50 and promised a bonus based on the amount of coal they raised. When the first party of miners arrived, they expected to find a working colliery. Instead, they were told to hunt for a workable seam. "We came out here to work for coal not to look for it," they grumbled. A few weeks later, when they laid down their tools, Captain William McNeill, the officer in charge of Fort Rupert, ordered them confined to the fort's bastion. At the first opportunity, they deserted, slipping away from the fort and making their way to San Francisco.

Robert Dunsmuir, who arrived with the second group of miners in 1851, was the only member of his party who chose to remain on the island after his three-year contract expired. By 1854, the HBC had moved its mining operations to Nanaimo, where richer deposits had been found. Dunsmuir worked at Nanaimo as an independent collier and later as a mine manager. He lived frugally, hoarded his money and spent every spare moment exploring the countryside, looking for a promising seam. In 1869, he found it.

The Native man in the centre earned the name Coal Tyee (coal chief) for drawing the attention of the Hudson's Bay Company to the coal to be found at Nanaimo.

Risking his savings and winkling considerable sums out of officers in the Royal Navy, he developed the Wellington Colliery. By 1873, his colliery was producing 16,000 of the 40,000 tons raised from island mines.

Dunsmuir realized that the key to success lay in getting his coal to the richest potential market—the booming city of San Francisco. Other colliery operators relied on "chance craft" to ship their coal down the coast. Dunsmuir formed a partnership with a San Francisco coal dealer who guaranteed annual sales of 48,000 tons at $12 a ton. By 1875, Dunsmuir's colliery was producing 50,000 tons annually, his miners were earning $5 a day, and he was on his way to becoming British Columbia's first millionaire.

COAL, SALMON AND LUMBER relied on ships to reach their best markets. Of all the industries that developed during the 1870s, only cattle ranching was waiting for the railway.

None of the men who became involved in the cattle business had come to British Columbia with that idea in mind. Jerome and Thaddeus Harper were Virginians, drawn north by the gold rush but quick to recognize that the real golden opportunity lay in the high price of provisions prevailing in the Cariboo. In 1862, the brothers travelled to Oregon, where they cobbled together a mixed herd of Texas longhorns, Herefords and "plain scrubs," and then drove them north along the old fur brigade trail to Kamloops,

Top: In 1851, when he arrived on Vancouver Island, Robert Dunsmuir was an indentured coal miner. By the time he died in 1888, he was British Columbia's first millionaire.

Bottom: Established in 1852 by the Hudson's Bay Company to exploit nearby coal outcrops, Nanaimo became the hub of the Vancouver Island coal industry.

across the Interior plateau to Clinton and on to Barkerville. The route covered 800 miles, but the effort was worth it. Cattle purchased for $15 a head in Oregon could bring as much as $150 in Barkerville.

That same year, Cornelius O'Keefe left his home in Canada West (Ontario) to look for gold. When he ran out of money and found himself working as a labourer on the Cariboo Road, he was happy to fall in with Newfoundlander Tom Wood, who, like the Harpers, was driving cattle from Oregon. In 1867, O'Keefe pre-empted 160 acres at the head of Okanagan Lake, with the idea of raising his own cattle.

The Harpers followed the same reasoning. During the 1860s, they concentrated on acquiring rangeland. To their original holdings—"a bit of land on the south side of the Fraser River near Pike's Riffle"—they added large blocks of land around Clinton, Quesnel and Kamloops.

Cattle thrived on the bluewheat bunch grass of the hot Interior valleys. By 1874, the Harpers' supply of home-grown cattle had outstripped local demand, and prices had fallen to $15 a head. Thaddeus Harper was forced to face the problem alone. His brother Jerome had slipped into insanity and removed himself to San Francisco, where he was found dead in his bathtub. Although Jerome had been the better businessman of the two, Thaddeus, "a pleasant man to meet, but no head," came up with an ambitious solution to the problem of oversupply: he would drive his cattle to

"Turtle soup out of a gold spoon is meagre fare compared to Kamloops beef. After a few samples at breakfast, we were willing to subscribe to all that has ever been said in favour of bunch grass as feed for the cattle of kings."
—Reverend G. M. Grant

Above: The Harper brothers' brand continued to be used after their land became known as the Gang Ranch.

Below: The high price of cattle prevailing in Barkerville—$150 a head—encouraged men to take up cattle ranching.

Utah and load them onto American railcars bound for Chicago. There, he was sure, he would realize a profit of $40 a head, even after paying transportation costs.

In 1876, Harper left Clinton with 800 head and drove them to Okanagan Lake, where Cornelius O'Keefe added 428 cattle to the herd. Harper was in Idaho when he learned that a drought in California had decimated local herds. Abandoning the idea of Chicago, he drove his cattle to San Francisco. "Mr. Harper's band are coming into market at San Francisco," the *Colonist* announced in April 1878. "The cattle are large and well-grown beeves, rolling in fat, and have been sold at $70 a head."

Barring similar heroic efforts, cattle ranching could not become a regular source of profit until the promised railway boosted local populations and provided access to markets in the east. By the time that happened, it was too late for Thaddeus Harper. In the summer of 1884, he was kicked by a horse. His jaw was broken, his front teeth were knocked out, and his head was caved in. He survived, but in the words of one of the doctors who treated him, "The man's mind was thoroughly unhinged."

Other ranchers managed to hang on. They acquired more rangeland, increased their herds and joined other British Columbians who were, with growing impatience, waiting for the railroad.

Cowboys (with cattle in the background) in the vicinity of Vernon, c. 1885. The details of their rigging reveal that they have all come from different places.

The province's Native people were waiting, too, but for something less tangible than a railroad. They were looking to the federal government for fair treatment. Under the old colonial administration, no treaties had been signed since those negotiated on Vancouver Island by James Douglas in the 1850s. As governor of the mainland colony, Douglas had set aside reserve lands, but the boundaries had not been surveyed, and some of the land had been pre-empted by others.

In 1864, after Douglas retired, a group of Interior chiefs presented Governor Frederick Seymour with a simple plea: "Please to protect our land that it will not be made small for us; many are pleased with their reservations, and many wish that their reservations be marked out for them."

Responsibility for establishing and defining reserves was given to the chief commissioner of lands and works, Joseph Trutch, who adopted a "ten acre per family" formula that greatly reduced the allotments envisioned by Douglas. By 1871, only eighty reserves, totalling 28,237 acres (approximately 5 acres per family) had been established. "We have been at a loss to understand the views of the Local Government of British Columbia, in curtailing our land so much as to leave, in many instances, but few acres of land per family," Chief Peter Ayessik of Hope worried.

BRITISH COLUMBIA'S first premier, John Foster McCreight, was an Irish barrister whose knowledge of the law was unsurpassed. In February 1872, he led the first sitting of the legislature through the passage of thirty-six bills, laying the legal framework for the operation of the new province. Otherwise, he proved to be an ineffective leader. Judged by some to be a "nervous fidgetty queer tempered man," he was unable to win the personal following on which power depended before the introduction of the party system. Before the year was out, McCreight resigned as premier and immersed himself in his law practice. In 1880, he led the

Homathko River. During the pursuit, McLean had been ambushed and killed. He left behind a family of young children, including nine-year-old Allen, two-year-old Charlie and Archie, as yet unborn. Their mother, Sophie, was given an annual government pension of £100 for five years, but she lost the Hat Creek ranch and her boys grew up resentful and undisciplined.

In 1879, the "wild McLeans," and their sixteen-year-old friend, Alex Hare, went on a spree, stealing horses and saddles and generally making a nuisance of themselves up and down the Nicola Valley. "This is a fine state of things to be terrorized over by four brats," a Kamloops resident

Ussher cried out. As he lay on the ground, he was shot in the head by Archie McLean. After a long pursuit during which the fugitives encountered and killed James Kelly, a new sixty-man posse tracked them to a log cabin near Douglas Lake.

In March 1880, the McLeans and Hare were tried for murder at New Westminster. As prosecutor, McCreight called a series of witnesses to the killing of Johnny Ussher and also presented evidence of the boys' previous bad behaviour, including an 1878 charge against Charlie McLean "for biting off an Indian's nose at Kamloops." The defence, which presented no witnesses, entered a plea for mercy based on the youth

Ussher in cold blood. "Neither life nor property is safe while they are at large," he insisted. In less than an hour, the jury returned a verdict of guilty, and the judge sentenced Hare and the three McLean brothers to death.

On 31 January 1881, at the New Westminster jail, seventeen-year-old Alex Hare, and the McLean boys, twenty-five-year-old Allen, eighteen-year-old Charlie and seventeen-year old Archie, were hanged for the murder of Johnny Ussher.

prosecution at the trial of the McLean boys and their friend Alex Hare.

In some ways, the McLeans could be regarded as victims of the Chilcotin War. They were the sons of Donald McLean, who in 1864 had ridden from his Hat Creek ranch to join the posse pursuing the Tsilhqot'in who had killed members of the crew working on Waddington's road on the

complained. Johnny Ussher, the constable at Kamloops, organized a posse to bring them in. Ussher, who knew the boys well and had treated them with consideration in the past, thought he would have no trouble arresting them. But when he walked into their campsite, unarmed and calling on them to surrender, he was attacked with a knife by Alex Hare. "Don't kill me, boys,"

of the accused, and suggested that they had been seized by "a sudden burst of insane excitement" and were guilty of manslaughter, but nothing more.

In his address to the jury, McCreight branded the prisoners as "outlaws" who had terrorized the people of Kamloops. Their actions had been "deliberate" and "systematic"; they had shown no remorse; they had killed Johnny

Left to right: Alex Hare, Allen McLean, Charlie McLean and Archie McLean, all in chains, awaiting execution at the New Westminster jail.

Native peoples found reason for optimism when British Columbia joined Confederation and Ottawa assumed responsibility for Indian affairs. As Chief Ayessik noted: "We are fully aware that the Government of Canada has always taken good care of the Indians, and treated them liberally, allowing more than one hundred acres per family."

Hope was soon replaced by pessimism as it became clear that British Columbia would oppose more liberal federal policies every step of the way. After provincial politicians protested that the 100-acre formula was much too generous because most Native people supported themselves by fishing rather than farming, the federal government agreed to a compromise that limited reserves to 20 acres per family. And there was no guarantee that the land would be arable. The Tsawwassen reserve included land that was "swampy" and unsuitable for crops. Along the Fraser River, reserves did not include water rights, and without irrigation the land was useless for agriculture.

The provincial and federal governments were still wrangling over policy when an extraordinary meeting took place. On 17 July 1879, twelve hundred Nlaka'pamux people gathered at Lytton to establish a basis for self-government. They elected a head chief and thirteen councillors and, after debating for two weeks, settled on the policies the chief and his council

Metlakatla, founded in 1862 by Anglican missionary William Duncan as an "assault on heathenism" of the Tsimshian people at Port Simpson, was designed as a self-supporting "industrial mission" and boasted a sawmill, blacksmith shop, bakery, weaving shop, sash factory and trading post. The church (shown here) could seat eight hundred. It was described as "one of the most orderly, respectable and industrious communities to be found in any Christian country." To live there, Tsimshian people had to agree to abandon their traditional life and customs.

An example of individual initiative, Richard and Hannah Maynard operated two businesses in Victoria. On the ground floor, Richard sold boots and shoes; upstairs, Hannah established one of the first photographer's studios in Victoria. Later, Richard also became a photographer.

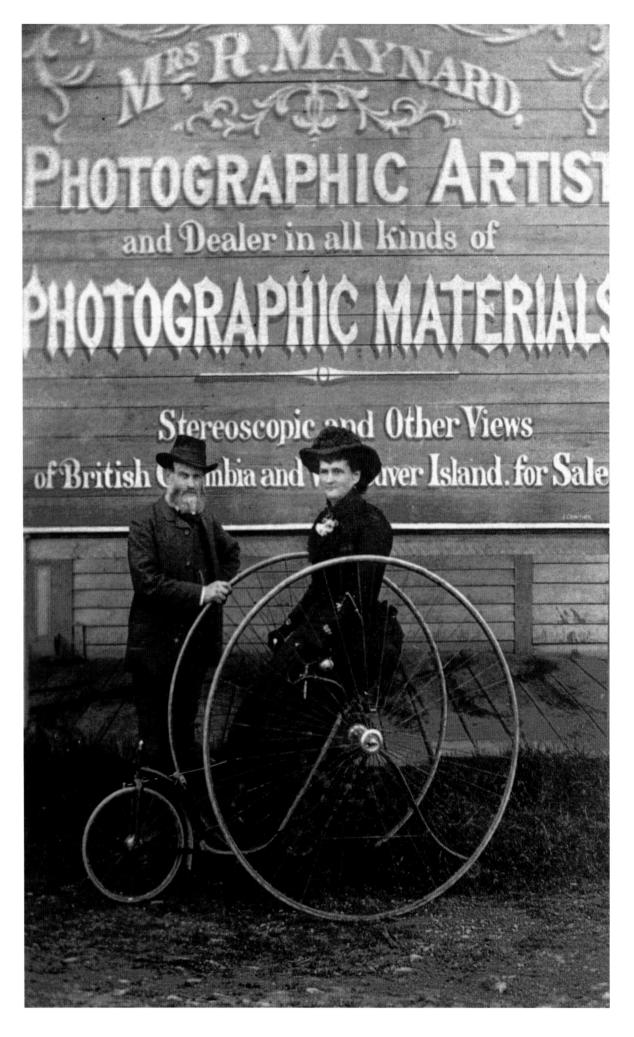

"Discouragement and depression have come upon our people [by 1874]. Many of them have given up cultivation of land, because our gardens have not been protected against encroachments of the whites. Some of our best men have been deprived of the land they had broken and cultivated with long and hard labour, a white man enclosing it in his claim, and no compensation given."
—Chief Peter Ayessik

would be called upon to pursue. A white doctor would be hired; a school would be built at Lytton and a teacher hired; fines would be levied for potlatching, drunkenness and gambling; hunting and fishing would be regulated; villages would be "made to look well."

Gilbert Sproat, the province's Indian commissioner, attended the meeting and was enthusiastic about the results. But settlers reacted with alarm. How were Indians to be controlled if they were permitted to unite and direct their own destiny? Faced with vociferous opposition, Ottawa refused to recognize the Nlaka'pamux council. Indians must remain completely dependent on the crown.

British Columbians waited fourteen years for the railway, but the province's Native people would have to endure for more than a century before their issues were addressed.

"I don't know how many millions you have,
but it is going to cost you money
to get through those canyons."
—Walter Moberly

CHAPTER 10

The GREAT RAILWAY

JUST THREE YEARS after joining Confederation, British Columbia began to talk secession. In 1871, the federal government had guaranteed that construction of the railway would begin in two years and be completed in ten, but by 1874, there had been no apparent progress. Worse still, Sir John A. Macdonald, the Conservative prime minister who had championed the railway, had been voted out of office, and his successor, the Liberal prime minister Alexander Mackenzie, had made it clear that he regarded Macdonald's promise as "insane" and "a bargain made to be broken." Irritated by the delay, British Columbia's premier, George Walkem, dug in his heels. "Secession is the next card to be played," a British Columbia correspondent warned the prime minister.

After two more years passed without a spade having been turned on the British Columbia section of the railway, the governor general, Lord Dufferin, was sent west as a conciliator. He spent ten days meeting with delegations of unhappy British Columbians. "Lord Dufferin," his private secretary informed the prime minister, "bids me add that he has great difficulty in keeping his temper with these foolish people." But the foolish people had good reason to try the governor general's

In Victoria, buildings decorated to mark the governor general's visit carried banners that pointed out British Columbia's unhappiness. "United without Union," one read. "Confederated without Confederation," proclaimed another. And "Our Iron Railway Rusts."

patience. Five years had passed since the terms of union had been negotiated, and the route through the province had *still* not been determined.

FROM THE BEGINNING, surveyor Walter Moberly had known the route the railway should follow. In 1866, he had discovered and named Eagle Pass through the Monashee Mountains. There, he claimed, he had emblazoned a tree with the motto "This is the Pass for the Overland Railway." In 1871, as soon as he learned about the promised railway, he hied himself to Ottawa and offered his services to Macdonald. "You can commence construction of the line six weeks after I get back to British Columbia," he assured the prime minister.

Moberly began his surveys in July 1871. His route followed the Fraser River to Lytton, moved along the Thompson River to Kamloops, continued up the South Thompson to Shuswap Lake, moved up and over Eagle Pass, travelled north and then south, skirting the Selkirk Mountains by following the trench created by the Columbia River, and then crossed the Rockies through Howse Pass (just north of Kicking Horse Pass). However, Sir Sandford Fleming, engineer-in-chief of the railway, favoured a more northerly route; he ordered Moberly to abandon his surveys and join him at the Yellowhead Pass.

"D. interviewed people from ten till five. They are very angry with Canada, and he has hard work."
—Lady Dufferin

By 1874, $500,000 had been spent on surveys. The result was an embarrassment of choices. Of the two major routes, one met the sea at Bute Inlet, the other at Burrard Inlet. To British Columbians, it mattered a great deal which was chosen. Settlers on the Lower Mainland preferred the route that emerged on Burrard Inlet. Residents of the Cariboo and Chilcotin allied themselves with Vancouver Islanders, who were passionately committed to Bute Inlet.

In 1873, Prime Minister Macdonald had named Esquimalt the official terminus of the transcontinental railway. If the tracks met the sea at Bute Inlet, then it would be a relatively simple matter to bridge Seymour Narrows and follow the east coast of Vancouver Island to Esquimalt and Victoria. If the railway met the sea at Burrard Inlet, terminal status for Esquimalt seemed highly unlikely. Victorians realized that their city's commercial pre-eminence was hanging by a thread. "In Victoria," Lord Dufferin reported, "the one idea of every human being is to get the railway to Esquimalt. It is upon this chance that the little town must depend for its future."

In December 1877, Macdonald's successor, Prime Minister Alexander Mackenzie, announced that the Burrard Inlet route had won out. When he rescinded the Order-in-Council that had named Esquimalt the terminus, Vancouver Islanders were outraged. On 9 August 1878, the legislature passed a resolution to be presented to the queen. If construction had not commenced by May 1879, the province would withdraw from Confederation.

Spirits rose when the federal election of 1878 returned the Conservatives to power. Optimism soared when John A. Macdonald, having been defeated in his home riding, chose Victoria as the safe seat that returned him to the house in a by-election. But Macdonald, too, had come to accept the Burrard Inlet route. To assuage the feelings of his constituents, he promised that work would soon begin on the "Island section" of the line—75 miles of orphan track running from Nanaimo to Esquimalt that made no sense at all now that the Bute Inlet route had been rejected.

In 1880, the Macdonald government signed an agreement with the syndicate of railwaymen and financiers from England, France and the United States who had formed the Canadian Pacific Railway Company (CPR). The CPR guaranteed completion of the line by May 1891—ten years behind schedule, as far as British Columbia was concerned. To calm Canada's westernmost province, the CPR promised to begin work immediately on the British Columbia section and to complete the line between Yale and Kamloops by 1885.

When Andrew Onderdonk won the contract to build the line from Port Moody to Savona's Ferry, he was asked to guarantee that he would not employ Chinese. Onderdonk calculated that he would need a workforce of ten thousand, but in 1880, there were hardly that many white males in the entire province. He promised to hire locally, and if he could not find enough men in British Columbia, to try to recruit French Canadians. But, if those measures failed, then he would hire Chinese. Onderdonk went through the motions of keeping his promises, but he had little hope of success. And besides, he was on a budget. White labourers would demand $1.50 a day. Onderdonk could hire Chinese for a dollar.

"How very disgracefully little W[alkem] has been behaving. Our poor Province is groaning and bleeding at the indignities and dishonor cast upon her representatives at home and abroad."
—Senator William Macdonald

""The railway is coming. The iron-horse will soon cause the hills to tremble before his giant tramp, and all other advantages that succeed development will arrive. The outlook is very pleasant. Business must revive and the hopes of hundreds realized. Empty houses will be filled; unoccupied fields tilled, new resources developed, old enterprises strengthened and new ones inaugurated."
—Colonist

This page: Andrew Onderdonk was only thirty years old when he signed the contract to construct the rail line from Port Moody to Savona's Ferry. "He is a very nice quiet man, with a good-natured fat little wife and some pretty children," Sarah Crease wrote in 1880. "They are all Americans but Mr. O. has none of their unpleasant peculiarities."

Facing page: In its 1881 Christmas issue, the *London Graphic* depicted British Columbia in a manner that was meant to be amusing but probably came close to the view most Europeans had of the province.

BARTERING FOR THE CHRISTMAS DINNER

CHRISTMAS MORNING—HOISTING THE BRITISH FLAG

MAKING THE PUDDING

IT TURNED OUT RATHER RAW

AND INDIGESTIBLE

A HALF-BREED BALL

Drawn north from California by the gold rush, the first Chinese arrived in British Columbia in 1858. Although they were often referred to as "Celestials" or "Heathen Chinee," they provoked little real enmity because they worked claims that white miners had already abandoned or took jobs no one else wanted. But after the colony raised fees and taxes to cope with its debt, resentment began to grow. The Chinese did not buy miners' licences. They escaped other taxes because they did not smoke cigars or drink whisky, and there were no import duties on rice. Instead of spending their money in towns, they saved it, looking forward to the day they could return to China.

During the 1870s, with jobs in short supply, some people thought the Chinese were destroying opportunities for other workers. In 1878, the Workingmen's Protective Association was organized for "the mutual protection of the working classes of British Columbia against the influx of Chinese, and the use of legitimate means for the suppression of their immigration." The following year, it reformed itself into the Anti-Chinese Association and insisted that no Chinese be employed on the railway. The association's president went so far as to state that he "would rather

A Chinese miner.

Many Chinese men, like this one who worked for a prosperous Victoria merchant, became domestic servants.

vote against the construction of the transcontinental railway than see Chinese employed on it."

Whatever the association's opinions, the railway went ahead, and the majority of the men working on the British Columbia section were Chinese. Three thousand, mostly from Hong Kong, arrived in 1881; by 1884, the Canadian Pacific Railway was employing at least six thousand and was looking for two thousand more.

Contemporary newspapers depicted the Chinese as "semi-slaves," preferred by employers not only because they worked for less but also because they were meek, docile men who worked uncomplainingly, however bad the conditions. It was said that six Chinese workers died for every mile of railway through the Fraser Canyon, and it may be true that the 58 miles from Yale to Lytton

claimed almost 350 lives, including those suffering from beri-beri when they arrived at the worksite. But far from being powerless victims, Chinese workers took an active role in promoting their own safety and well-being.

Railway workers were hired through Chinese labour contractors, to whom they owed their passage money and from whom they expected fair dealing. Organized into work crews of about thirty men, they were accompanied by a cook, supplied by the labour contractor, and a "bookman," a representative of the contractor who acted as translator and kept track of hours and wages. In addition, they were served by a "commissioner," a "distinguished-looking" Chinese who held himself ready to settle disputes as he rode up and down the line, mounted on a powerful horse, protected from the sun by a large umbrella and followed "at a respectful distance" by his servant.

Many railway workers' complaints revolved around food. In August 1880, a gang of Chinese workmen became irritated with being served so much "Siwash chicken" (salmon) that they laid down tools and refused to work until the commissioner arranged for the "chicken" rations to be reduced. An incident that became known as the "Chinese riot" occurred in May 1881 when work crews learned that an additional two cents a day would be deducted from their wages for food. Already unhappy with the provisions they were receiving, a body of 250 men marched into Yale determined to liberate from the warehouse all the supplies earmarked for their use. The windows were shattered, and the door was attacked with an axe and a crowbar, before the ringleaders were arrested and led away.

Chinese crews were bossed by a white foreman or "herder," but workers were not prepared to follow orders they considered dangerous. On several occasions, they attacked the foreman rather than put themselves in danger. In the summer of 1882, John

Kerrigan, who was "springing holes" with small charges of powder, became incensed when his crew insisted on retreating into the distance. "There was no danger," Kerrigan said. "There was no necessity of going away so far." When two men raised their shovels as if to strike him, Kerrigan marched back to camp and collected his pistol. At quitting time, he informed the bookman that he would sign the account for only twenty-eight workers. The men who had threatened him would not be paid. "You can't do that," the bookman warned.

"All at once someone from behind struck me on the left side of the head with a club and knocked me to my knees," Kerrigan said. "At the same time, Ah Chuck snatched my pistol from out of my pocket." As Kerrigan stumbled to his feet, Ah Him struck out, missing his head, but landing a heavy blow on his shoulder. "I saw that the whole crowd was armed with sticks and stones, and I ran up to the top of the grade, they at the same time pelting me with rocks."

Six months later, a foreman named Miller let off a blast that sent a large rock hurtling through the air. When the rock smashed

into a man's head and decapitated him, the rest of the crew launched an attack, showering Miller with rocks as he ran for the river.

WITH THE completion of the CPR, several thousand Chinese were thrown out of work. Some returned to China, others stayed where they were, settling in Ashcroft and Kamloops and Yale. Still others spread around the province. Some made their way to Quesnel and Barkerville. Several hundred found work in the Nanaimo coal mines or in the Fraser River canneries. Many took refuge in Victoria's Chinatown, the oldest in the province and the largest north of San Francisco, where they crowded into tenements and shacks. Some became labourers, or market gardeners or vegetable peddlers. Others worked in laundries or enlisted as cooks and gardeners in the small army of servants that permitted Victorians to enjoy the highest standard of domestic ease in the province.

The presence of so many single men gave rise to a sorry trade. Young women, many of whom had been sold in China when they were mere girls, were transported to the coast to work in Chinatown

brothels. To acquire their services, brothel-keepers paid as much as $1,000. In theory, the girls signed contracts to work as prostitutes only until they had earned back the price of their acquisition. In reality, they were slaves. They spoke no English, they were terrified of whites, and many were addicted to opium. There was no way out.

IN 1885, after several provincial bills designed to limit Chinese immigration were declared unconstitutional, the Dominion government imposed a $50 head tax. Intended to curb immigration, the head tax had little effect. By 1892, each sailing of the CPR Empress ships was carrying hundreds of steerage passengers from Shanghai and Hong Kong. By the turn of the century, it was estimated that fourteen thousand Chinese were resident in the province. In 1901, the head tax was raised to $100, in 1903 to $500. In 1923, a new federal act effectively prevented further immigration from China. Not until 1947 were the wives and children of resident Chinese permitted to emigrate. That same year, the right to vote, which had been taken away in 1872, was finally restored.

Sau Kam was about ten years old in 1887 when she was discovered in a brothel and taken to the rescue home run by the Methodists in Victoria.

Lepers, almost all of whom were Chinese, were sent into quarantine on D'Arcy Island near Victoria.

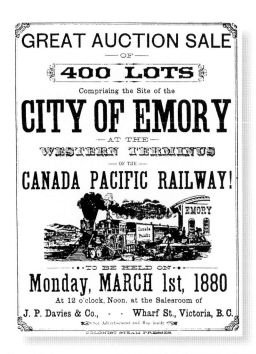

On 15 May 1880, a blast of dynamite echoed through the Fraser Canyon half a mile above Yale to mark the beginning of construction. Ahead lay five years of exhausting work. Men would be pushed almost beyond endurance to meet construction deadlines through some of the most difficult terrain on earth. The Yale-to-Lytton section of the line was particularly dangerous: fifteen major tunnels (one 1,600 feet long) to be drilled through solid granite, ledges to be carved out of sheer rock bluffs, trestles to be built where no other footing could be found.

No one will ever know how many men died. David McKay, who had taken a job on the railway to support his Chilliwack farm, was working beside "Rocky Mountain Jack" Corsen in the Big Tunnel when a section of the roof gave way, crushing them both. George Daig had left his new wife behind in San Francisco when he came north to take a job on the line. Only four days after his arrival, he was aboard a boat, ferrying a load of powder to a work site, when a blast was set off above the river. A rock flew through the air and struck Daig on the head, killing him instantly. A few days later, the boss of a Chinese work crew, ignoring a warning that all the charges had not gone off, walked forward and took a blast in his face. Surveyor Henry Cambie recorded four Chinese killed on the job from 13 August to 7 September 1880: one drowned in the Fraser, another was crushed by a falling log, and two were killed by rock slides.

Top: Speculators tried to promote Emory into a metropolis. Unfortunately for investors, it faded away after Andrew Onderdonk chose to establish his construction headquarters a few miles upriver at Yale.

Bottom: As railway construction headquarters, Yale revisited its gold-rush importance. "Men were coming in from everywhere by the hundreds—all kinds of good men—as well as roughnecks from San Francisco—Barbary Coast hoodlums. The streets were crowded—saloons doing a roaring business, and fights a daily occurrence."

Top: A cantilever bridge under construction at Cisco Flat south of Lytton.

Bottom: Built at Spuzzum during the winter of 1881–82, the sternwheeler *Skuzzy* was designed to ferry supplies to work camps on the upper Fraser River. With her safety valve screwed shut and a hundred men hauling on towlines, the *Skuzzy* steamed through Hells Gate, the only vessel to make the upstream passage.

No official tally was kept. Inquests were held only if the circumstances of death were not perfectly clear. When Patrick Kelley was found lying face down on the frosty ground one November morning, his death resulted in an inquest. So, too, did the death of Michael Shea, who had spent the night drinking his pay at Yale and died in a fall from a bluff on his way back to camp. Melchior Eberts became the subject of an official inquiry after his body was found crumpled between two stumps, 200 feet below the top of snow-covered Alexandra Bluff. But dying on the job was different. There was nothing mysterious about that at all.

Even while the canyon was being rocked by explosions, the people who had depended on the Fraser River for centuries managed to maintain their traditional fishery. The salmon-drying racks of the Stó:lō and Nlaka'pamux people lined the canyon to catch the hot August air pumping out of the Interior. In August 1881, the *Inland Sentinel* was moved to complain: "Quite a number of Indians are now drying salmon convenient to Yale. The stench near Number 2 Tunnel is very offensive."

Descendants of the Native men who had guided Simon Fraser through the canyon took jobs on the railway and dangled from ropes hanging from the top of steep bluffs to drill dynamite holes in the rock face. Annie York, a Nlaka'pamux from Spuzzum, recalled an uncle who had worked on the railway: "He was a powder man, and he always makes the holes where they are going to blast . . . he was hammering along and he never thought about if this thing would go off . . . He put the caps in, and he pound it . . . The blast went off, and he went off up in the air . . . He was lucky to get away . . . others died."

During railway construction, Native people from Yale and Spuzzum enjoyed a brief burst of prosperity. Some took jobs on the railway, others supplied the workers with salmon.

"It is generally believed that a few years more of such neglect will put an end to the Cariboo Road!" the *Inland Sentinel* worried in 1882. "The Railway Company will want a 'monopoly' of the freight business." That proved to be exactly what the CPR wanted.

By the time the railway was completed, more than 7 miles of the road between Yale and Lytton were completely destroyed.

By July 1885, when the tracks stretched from Port Moody to Savona's Ferry, contractor Andrew Onderdonk began to run excursion trains. The passengers must have been dedicated sightseers.

The view was awe-inspiring, but sitting at a standstill, in an open car, below an unstable bluff, seems rather foolhardy.

While thousands of men sweated to drive the railway line east, other crews were pushing the line west. The CPR had abandoned the Yellowhead in favour of Kicking Horse Pass. By November 1884, tracks had been laid through the Rockies and had reached the Columbia River, where the workers collected in First Crossing or Columbia Crossing (Donald), a tough little town, to wait out the worst of the winter.

Top: Columbia Crossing (Donald) was known as a "gambling, drinking, fighting little mountain town."

Bottom: Columbia Crossing's log-cabin saloons dispensed beer, whisky and the favours of "fallen angels." "There is a lamentable want of a sense of shame at Columbia Crossing," one resident admitted.

From the beginning, Sam Steele of the North West Mounted Police questioned the CPR's decision to route the tracks through Rogers Pass. In February 1885, he noted: "Avalanches of the most tremendous weight and power began to roar down the mountainsides. One avalanche which came at the summit of the pass descended 5,000 feet with such velocity that it went across the valley and up on the opposite side 800 feet." Despite an ambitious program of snowshed construction, Rogers Pass claimed more than two hundred lives in the first twenty-five years of the line's operation.

By 1910, the Canadian Pacific Railway would have good reason to question the choice of the route through Rogers Pass.

The year 1910 was a bad one for snow. On 4 March, the track was blocked by a large slide thundering down off Avalanche Mountain. While the eastbound train was held at Glacier House, the crew of a rotary snowplow was dispatched from Revelstoke. As they moved along the track, they picked up additional men, hooking up their sleeping and cooking cars as they went. By the time they

Top: Scenic in summer, the avalanche-prone Rogers Pass route through the Rockies could prove deadly in winter.

Bottom: Rotary snowplows, pushed by engines, buzzed through the deep snow left by avalanches.

reached the slide, there were over sixty men ready to get to work.

"We bucked right into the snowslide," Bill LaChance remembered. "It had run down and filled the cut . . . maybe 14 feet high. It was full of timber. The rotary would clean it out but then we'd come to logs. So then we'd back up and all these men there with shovels, they'd jump down in the tunnel we'd made and pull out the timber."

Near midnight, the men and the plow were working in the snow cut when a second avalanche crashed down from the opposite slope. "Well, it hit me—and how!" LaChance recalled. "It took me right out of the gangway and right up through the top of that tunnel we had made. Then the snow got hold of me . . . It pulled me out twice my length, the way it felt, and then it just doubled me all up and rolled me . . . Then the pressure came on, oh, just like as if there were tons on top of me."

Somehow LaChance managed to free himself. His mouth tasted of blood. His spit left "a great big dark spot on the snow." He was afraid to put his hands inside his overalls, afraid he'd find his "guts."

Nothing was moving. "The engine should have been blowing a lot of steam, but there was no sound there. Everything was just dead." Sixty-two men lost their lives. Of all the crewmen who had been in the path of the slide, Bill LaChance was the sole survivor.

The 1910 calamity convinced the CPR that something had to be done about Rogers Pass. In 1913, work began on the Connaught Tunnel—5 miles long and 2 miles below Mount Macdonald.

When the Connaught Tunnel opened in 1916, Rogers Pass and 10 miles of some of the most dangerous track in the world were abandoned.

In 1910, sixty-two men, working in a cut (similar to this one) created by a rotary plow, were buried alive when a second avalanche struck.

Superintendent Sam Steele (centre front) and a small contingent of North West Mounted Police maintained law and order along the railway belt from the Rockies to the Selkirks.

Superintendent Sam Steele (centre front) and a small contingent of North West Mounted Police maintained law and order along the railway belt from the Rockies to the Selkirks.

"In the evening the fun begun at dances to which the navvies and toughs went . . . The town being awake most of the night, we had to be likewise . . . We were rarely in bed before two or three a.m., and were up in the morning between six and seven."
—NWMP Commissioner Sam Steele

Major A. B. Rogers was assigned the task of finding a pass through the Selkirk Mountains. Wiry and tough, he lived on chewing tobacco, bacon and beans. "Give Rogers six plugs [of chewing tobacco] and five bacon rinds and he will travel for two weeks," men said.

Sam Steele of the North West Mounted Police, who was charged with maintaining law and order in the railway camps, had his hands full. In theory, the 20-mile-wide railway belt was alcohol-free. In practice, it was anything but. Columbia Crossing abounded with log-cabin saloons. The bartender at the Italian Saloon, a woman with "a loud coarse laugh," dispensed "beer, cigars, and something more fiery, in unlimited quantities." At the French Quarter saloon, men and boys lined the walls waiting for the opportunity to dance with "the usual type of fallen angels."

By the spring of 1885, work camps were strung out along Rogers Pass. William Cornelius Van Horne, general manager of the CPR, had had good reasons for choosing the pass. The Big Bend route, originally suggested by Moberly, was undeniably easier, but it would have added about 75 miles of track and at least two hours of travel time. So Van Horne had opted for Rogers Pass, but without appreciating the problems that the line would encounter. First, there was the snow—as much as 50 feet fell on the summit of the pass. Then, there were the snowslides and avalanches, tons and tons of snow hurtling down steep slopes to blanket the right-of-way. In February 1885, with work scarcely underway, snowslides buried seven men. Two did not survive.

"The men are frightened," the construction engineer warned Van Horne. "I find the snowslides on the Selkirks are much more serious than I anticipated and I think are quite beyond your ideas of their magnitude and danger to the line."

Van Horne ordered them to press on. By August, the tracks were at the summit. By September, they had reached the Columbia River at Golden. Men worked at a fever pitch to meet the crews pushing from the west before winter locked them in.

On 7 November 1885, the last spike on the transcontinental railway was driven at Craigellachie, a lonely spot on Eagle Pass. After a brief ceremony, the conductor called out, "All aboard for the Pacific." The train passed over the last spike and headed west.

CPR director Donald Smith had the honour of driving the last spike. Standing stoutly beside him is William Cornelius Van Horne, general manager of the CPR. Called upon to give a speech, Van Horne stated simply, "All I can say is that the work has been done well in every way." Peering over Smith's shoulder is seventeen-year-old Edward Mallandaine of Victoria.

*"The richest, the most sparsely populated
and most attractive Province of Canada"*
—Governor General Earl Grey

CHAPTER II

SEARCHING *for a* BETTER LIFE

THE CANADIAN PACIFIC RAILWAY produced change from the Rocky Mountains to Vancouver Island. Established towns declined, new communities bloomed, inaccessible areas were opened for settlement. The railway drew British Columbia closer to Europe (ten days from Liverpool to the Pacific coast), and the CPR's worldwide publicity attracted attention to the province. In 1880, when railway construction began, there were fewer than fifty thousand people (Native and others) in the province. Within ten years, the number doubled, and decisions made by the CPR influenced where the newcomers settled.

The Canadian Pacific Railway was part of a modern transportation system that spanned the globe. The return fare from Toronto to Victoria was $110; to Australia, $410; to China, $447.50. And an "around the world" ticket could be had for $610.

In 1884, when the CPR's William Cornelius Van Horne visited the coast on a tour of inspection, he realized at once that Port Moody would never do as the site of the western terminus. There was too little flat land for roundhouses and rail yards. Besides, Port Moody had little potential to become a great seaport; it lay far up Burrard Inlet, beyond the Second Narrows, a treacherous stretch of water where currents exceeding 6 knots sped through a narrow "fairway." Van Horne was much more pleased with the lay of the land to the west at Granville, the little town clustered around "Gassy" Jack Deighton's saloon near Hastings Mill.

THE CANADIAN PACIFIC

THE NEW HIGHWAY TO THE ORIENT

ACROSS THE Mountains, Prairies and Rivers of CANADA.

Stoney Creek Bridge
Selkirk Mountains

The cover of an 1890 promotional booklet featured the Stoney Creek bridge in the Selkirks but stressed that the passage through British Columbia was a short route to the Orient. Soon, the CPR would begin to woo tourists by emphasizing the spectacular scenery through which the line passed.

Locating the terminal at Granville would require laying an additional 12 miles of track. To offset the cost, the CPR approached the province to see if anything could be done about a land grant—something in the neighbourhood of 11,000 acres, the company suggested. The province congratulated itself on driving a hard bargain, extracting from the CPR a promise that it would build a large hotel and an opera house before handing over 6,000 acres of crown land straddling False Creek.

In January 1885, when the CPR's decision became public, Victoria's businessmen were aghast. Having resigned themselves to losing the railway, they had invested in Port Moody. Now, the CPR was calmly abandoning its original terminus. Then, to add insult to injury, Van Horne announced that he was changing the name of his new terminal from Granville to Vancouver.

Van Horne had "snatched" the name of their island, Victorians seethed. He seemed determined "to wipe Victoria off the face of the map." Actually, that was a fair description of what Van Horne had in mind. If he had his way, Vancouver would become "the metropolis of the west, the London of the Pacific."

"Lately we have changed our name from the pleasing one of Granville, for this bombastic swaggering title of Vancouver."
—Father Clinton

"It seems rather stupid to have called the new town, which is the terminus of the railway, by the same name as the island, as it must sometimes lead to confusion."
—Duchess of Sutherland

"One huge flame, a hundred feet long,
burst from the Deighton Hotel, leaped 'Maple Tree Square,'
and swallowed up the buildings; the fire
went down the old 'Hastings Road' faster than a man
could run. Two iron tires and some ashes were all
that was left of man, horse, and cart which perished
in the middle of Carrall street."
—William F. Findlay

"You cannot imagine any place rougher and
more disagreeable in appearance than Vancouver itself
as it is covered with burnt logs and stumps and
not a green thing to be seen."
—Henry Abbott

On 6 April 1886, the City of Vancouver was incorporated by an act of the provincial legislature. Two months later, the town went up in smoke. On the afternoon of 13 June, a sudden wind whipped up the slash fires smouldering on the western edge of the settlement. Fire swept through the brush, climbed still standing trees and engulfed the town. Buildings, with pitch from newly sawn lumber oozing from their walls, went up with a whoosh. "Vancouver did not burn—it exploded," an observer recalled.

Within half an hour, it was all over. At least twenty people were dead, including a mother and child whose bodies were found at the bottom of the well in which they had taken shelter. Survivors, standing waist-deep in the waters of Burrard Inlet and False Creek, had only the clothes on their backs and whatever they had managed to carry with them—for one man, it was a Bible; for a woman, her sewing machine. As one fellow mused, "He was a rich man who had his life and a blanket that night."

The embers had scarcely cooled when rebuilding began. "I never saw so much enterprise amidst so much desolation," an impressed visitor reported. Within four days, a three-storey hotel was welcoming guests; within a month, fourteen hotels and dozens of stores had thrown open their doors. "We cannot afford to stand still," the *Vancouver News* urged. "Progress is our watchword."

Top: In February 1886, lots were being sold near the corner of Hastings and Main Streets in Vancouver.

Bottom: Five weeks after the great fire in Vancouver, a printer's shop and a furniture store had opened on Cordova Street. By the end of the year, Cordova and nearby Carrall and Water Streets boasted twenty-three hotels, fourteen office buildings, fifty-one stores, two stables, nine saloons and one church.

On 23 May 1887, the first train from Montreal pulled into Vancouver. With regular service established, real estate agents gathered at the station to jostle competitors out of their way as they attempted to capture every man disembarking from the train. According to one rattled traveller, "Inside of an hour every real-estate man in the place would know him and his business in Vancouver." The city was alive with noise. "Blasting goes on daily in Vancouver, and few precautions are taken to warn passers-by," a lady visitor complained.

Land prices soared. By 1888, city lots "with only room for one small house" were changing hands for $5,000. The city boasted almost 6 miles of planked streets and 9 miles of wooden sidewalks. The streets were bathed in electric light, and telephones connected homes and businesses.

In 1891, the federal census revealed that 14 per cent of British Columbia's population now lived in Vancouver. Victorians did not warm to the news that the mainland city, with almost 14,000 residents, had zoomed into contention as the province's largest city. The census had counted 16,841 Victorians, and the city council, which had confidently predicted a total of 25,000, demanded a recount. The federal government refused. Victoria hired its own census takers. Indignant Victorians, eager to rectify the "serious blunder," co-operated so fully that 6,000 previously uncounted residents surfaced. The new result would be "gall and wormwood" to Vancouver, the *Colonist* crowed. But Vancouverites managed to shrug off Victoria's boasts with ease.

"When we arrived [in 1888], only two trees were still standing, and they were burning like a blast furnace inside their hollow trunks. They were nearly three hundred feet in height and measured between thirty and forty feet in circumference . . . they fell with a sweep, a rush, and a roar of sound."
—W. H. H. Murray

Facing page: In 1887, the CPR began construction on a one hundred–room hotel (visible in the distance), "away out on the hill" on the corner of Georgia and Granville Streets in Vancouver. William Cornelius Van Horne was not impressed with its design. Introduced to the architect Thomas Sorby, he growled, "So you're the damn fool who spoilt the building with all those little windows."

Below: Hastings Mill on Burrard Inlet, 1893. With the coming of the railway, "British Columbia Tooth Picks"— three feet square—were transported east along the Canadian Pacific Railway's main line.

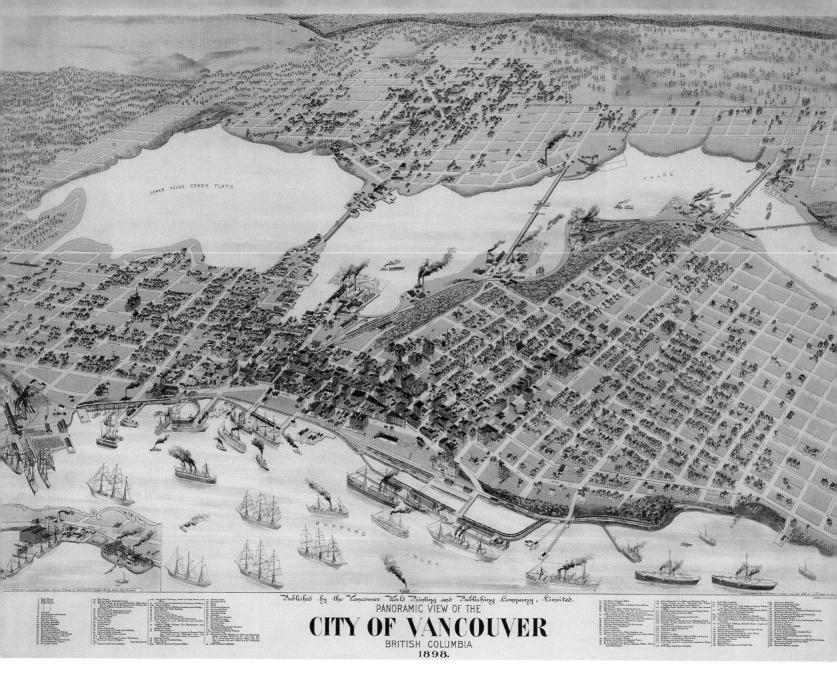

Published by the Vancouver World's Printing and Publishing Company, Limited.

PANORAMIC VIEW OF THE

CITY OF VANCOUVER

BRITISH COLUMBIA
1898.

A decade after the arrival of the Canadian Pacific Railway, Vancouver had been transformed from a village around a sawmill to a bustling city (as shown in this bird's-eye view graphic map).

"The extraordinary thing about Vancouver is that in the midst of all this wildness it is so absolutely modern; no one would think about putting up a house without a telephone and electric light."

—Douglas Sladen

The CPR's goal was to "span the world." The company's transcontinental railway connected the Atlantic and Pacific Oceans, with Canada acting as a land bridge between Asia and England. Even before the driving of the last spike, the CPR had chartered ships to sail to Vancouver from Hong Kong and Singapore, laden with tea and silk bound for England. In April 1891, the first of the CPR's Empress fleet, the *Empress of India*, steamed into Vancouver harbour to the sound of cheers and a brass band, and Victoria's jealousy grew. When an American, Benjamin Tingley Rogers, opened a sugar refinery in Vancouver, he found a market for his product as far away as Winnipeg, but none of his sugar reached Vancouver Island. Victoria merchants simply refused to patronize a Vancouver industry.

Victoria cherished its role as British Columbia's largest, most important city. During the 1880s, tired wooden gold-rush buildings had been replaced with stout business blocks of brick and stone. Telephones were introduced in 1878, and in 1883 Victoria became the first town in the province to light its streets with electricity. The social scene, centred on the lieutenant-governor and the admiral of the fleet, was unrivalled. During the 1870s and 1880s, men who had done well out of colonial appointments or who had made fortunes in industry began to build palatial homes, designed for entertaining and gracious living.

One of the three 160-foot light masts erected in Victoria in 1883 was located at the corner of Blanshard and Burdett Streets, overlooking the James Bay mud flats. By 1889, twenty-one additional masts had been erected. "The effect is most pleasing and pretty," the *Colonist* observed.

Built for coal baron Robert Dunsmuir, "Craigdarroch" stood on 28 acres. Costing half a million dollars, it was easily the most expensive private residence in the province. Dunsmuir died in 1889, a year before the monument to his success was completed.

A garden city, "one of the prettiest on the continent," Victoria was also the centre of business and commerce, home port of the sealing fleet and home to the largest ironworks on the Pacific coast outside of San Francisco. But Victorians knew their commercial pre-eminence was doomed. Because of the CPR, Vancouver would become *the* great west coast metropolis. Victoria would have to settle for second place, and even that depended on remaining the capital city.

In 1892, the island members of the legislature and their supporters from the Interior succeeded in "anchoring" the capital in Victoria by voting in favour of the construction of new parliament buildings. After an international competition, Francis Rattenbury, a young Englishman only recently arrived in Vancouver, was selected as the architect, and construction began in 1895.

Men at work on the deck of a sealing ship. Victoria was home to a fleet of sixty to **seventy schooners that pursued seals in the Bering Sea.**

Top: British Columbia's new parliament buildings were completed in 1898. Victorians were relieved that their construction had "anchored" the capital in the city.

Bottom: During the winter of 1897–98, Victoria and Vancouver received an unexpected boost from the Klondike gold rush. Both cities took to calling themselves "the Gateway to the Klondike," the best place to buy supplies before heading to the Yukon.

Not for nothing is the west coast of Vancouver Island known as the "Graveyard of the Pacific." A shore of uncommon beauty, of misty headlands and pristine golden beaches that seem to stretch forever, it is also desolate and dangerous—at times grey and wet and cloaked in fog, at times hammered by gales producing mountainous waves, which pound at the base of tall cliffs that rise almost vertically above narrow rocky ledges. Along that rugged coast, hundreds of vessels have come to grief. One stretch of shoreline, from Port Renfrew to Cape Beale, has claimed over fifty ships, "a ship a mile."

Some vessels ran into trouble at the entrance to Juan de Fuca Strait. To navigate the strait, a sailing ship required either a favourable wind or a tow. On 30 December 1895, the *Janet Cowan*, a four-masted barque, 109 days out of Capetown and bound for Hastings Mill, was standing off the entrance of the strait, waiting for the wind to shift, when the barometer plunged and a gale set in.

For several hours, the crew, lashed by snow and sleet, battled the 55-knot gusts screaming through the rigging. Then came the lookout's call, "Breakers ahead!" And the *Janet Cowan* crunched onto a reef near Pachena Point. Three men

drowned attempting to reach the shore. The survivors clambered up the cliffs. Some followed the telegraph line in the hope of finding help. The others camped on the rocky clifftop ledge, in case the sight of the wreck attracted rescuers. Ten days passed before help came. By then, the captain, three seamen and the cook had died of exposure.

Other shipwrecks resulted from navigational errors. When skippers navigated by dead reckoning (the calculation of position based on the speed of the hull through the water), they sometimes fell victim to the vagaries of the north-setting current off the American coast. During the win-

ter storm season, the current increases by several knots. Ships' captains, carried farther north than they believed themselves to be, steered toward the entrance of Juan de Fuca Strait and rammed their vessels onto Vancouver Island.

Captain Oscar Johnson of the *Valencia* was 20 miles off-course when he produced "a marine horror," a catastrophic shipwreck in which 117 people died. On 20 January 1906, the *Valencia* left San Francisco bound for Seattle. On the night of 22 January, Captain Johnson turned eastward for the entrance to Juan de Fuca Strait. Shortly before midnight, the *Valencia* rammed into a rocky

The barque *Colona* foundering off Cape Beale in 1913.

The original Tofino lifeboat, with August Arnet as skipper, in 1910.

ledge, pivoted around and came to rest stern-first, 60 feet from the base of a cliff, 3 miles from Pachena Point.

It was a filthy night—wind and driving rain. The ship was holed. Rising water shut down the generators, plunging the *Valencia* into darkness. No clear orders came from the bridge. Passengers groped their way to the lifeboats. The first three boats were improperly lowered and their occupants were catapulted into the sea. Two boats were successfully launched, but were caught broadside in the pounding surf and capsized. Only nine men made it safely to shore.

The following morning, the captain sent off a party of seamen aboard the last lifeboat. They were instructed to make their way up the cliff and to be ready to secure the line that the captain would fire from the ship so that the passengers could then be ferried ashore on a bosun's chair. Nothing went right. The men

rowed along the shore for hours before they found a landing place. Meanwhile, the *Valencia* was being swept by waves crashing over her bow. Her cabins were carried away. People huddled on the bare deck.

Eventually, the seamen stumbled into the lighthouse station at Cape Beale. Late on the afternoon of 23 January, the lightkeeper telegraphed for help. The following morning the first rescuer, the steamer *Queen City*, arrived on the scene. Soon, she was joined by another steamer and the salvage tug, *Salvor*. But the sea was running high, and none dared approach the *Valencia*.

By now, the passengers, including women and children, clad only in their nightclothes, were clinging to the rigging, climbing higher as the boat settled deeper in the water. With rescue boats standing by, the captain ordered the life rafts launched; however, most passengers felt safer aboard the ship, sure that

rescue was imminent. But it was not. Aboard the *Salvor*, a crewman shuddered, "It was terrible to stand there and watch the wreck break up, and see the people who were in the rigging drop off into the boiling sea."

When a party of three men, who had made their way along the narrow telegraph trail from the Carmanah light, reached the *Valencia* on the afternoon of 24 January, the surviving passengers let out a cheer. But the men had no way of reaching the ship. They stood and watched the *Valencia* break apart.

Thrown into the water, passengers grabbed hold of pieces of wreckage; the tide carried them out to sea, where the rescue vessels might have saved them had they not already sailed away. The *Valencia* carried 154 passengers and crew when she steamed out of San Francisco. Only thirty-seven survived, and that number included no women and none of the children.

The thought of chilled-to-the bone passengers clinging for forty hours to a wave-swept ship, combined with the knowledge that none need have died if adequate life-saving equipment had been available, prompted government action. In 1907, a lighthouse was built at Pachena Point, and the following year work began on the West Coast Life Saving Trail. The shoulder-width trail that ran under the telegraph line was widened and bridges were built across streams and gorges to allow access for horse-drawn wagons capable of carrying heavy equipment. And every few miles, shelters were built to provide shipwreck survivors with refuge.

No longer needed after the introduction of radar and other aids to navigation, the Life Saving Trail has become one of the most popular attractions in Pacific Rim National Park.

THE CPR HAD PROMISED that the Cariboo Road would remain open, but by the time tracks were laid through the Fraser Canyon, 7 miles of road between Yale and Lytton had been destroyed. The Barnard Express Company had been forced to transfer its headquarters from Yale to Ashcroft, and while Yale faded, a little town grew around the railway's Ashcroft station.

At first, the Canadian Pacific Railway was promoted as "The New Highway to the Orient," but soon it began to focus on the appeal of the spectacular scenery through which the line passed. Resort hotels were built on the Fraser Canyon at North Bend, in the Selkirks near the summit of Rogers Pass and in the Rockies at Field.

The presence of the transcontinental line stimulated the construction of branch lines, opening land to settlement. In 1890, work began on the Shuswap & Okanagan Railway, which connected with the CPR main line at

Top: Kamloops (shown here c. 1890) achieved a new importance when it was selected as a divisional point for the CPR. Originally, the train tracks ran straight down the middle of the main street.

Bottom: Decked out in elegant Edwardian style, Cassoro's butcher shop in Kelowna greeted Christmas in 1910. By then, Kelowna was home to almost sixteen hundred residents.

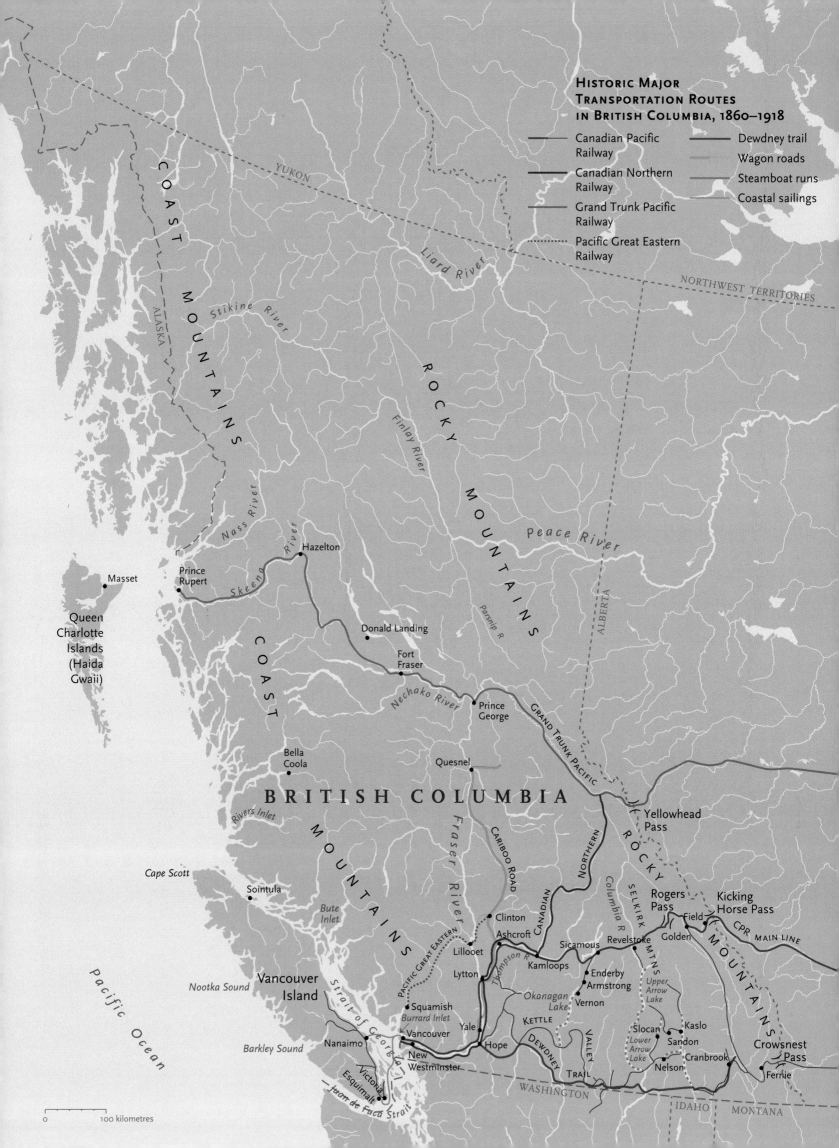

HISTORIC MAJOR
TRANSPORTATION ROUTES
IN BRITISH COLUMBIA, 1860–1918

——— Canadian Pacific
Railway
——— Canadian Northern
Railway
——— Grand Trunk Pacific
Railway
········ Pacific Great Eastern
Railway
——— Dewdney trail
——— Wagon roads
——— Steamboat runs
——— Coastal sailings

YUKON

NORTHWEST TERRITORIES

COAST MOUNTAINS

ALASKA

Stikine River

Liard River

ROCKY MOUNTAINS

Finlay River

Peace River

ALBERTA

Parsnip R

Nass River

Hazelton

Skeena River

Prince Rupert

Masset

Queen Charlotte Islands (Haida Gwaii)

COAST MOUNTAINS

Donald Landing

Fort Fraser

Nechako River

Prince George

GRAND TRUNK PACIFIC

Bella Coola

Quesnel

BRITISH COLUMBIA

Rivers Inlet

Yellowhead Pass

ROCKY

Cape Scott

Sointula

Bute Inlet

Fraser River

CARIBOO ROAD

NORTHERN

Columbia R

SELKIRK MTNS

Rogers Pass

Kicking Horse Pass

Field

Golden

CPR MAIN LINE

MOUNTAINS

Clinton

CANADIAN

Sicamous

Revelstoke

Ashcroft

Lillooet

PACIFIC GREAT EASTERN

Thompson R

Kamloops

Enderby

Armstrong

Upper Arrow Lake

Lytton

Vancouver Island

Nootka Sound

Strait of Georgia

Squamish

Burrard Inlet

Vernon

Okanagan Lake

KETTLE

Slocan

Kaslo

Sandon

VALLEY

Pacific Ocean

Barkley Sound

Nanaimo

Vancouver

Yale

New Westminster

Hope

DEWDNEY

Lower Arrow Lake

Cranbrook

Crowsnest Pass

Fernie

Esquimalt

Victoria

Juan de Fuca Strait

TRAIL

Nelson

WASHINGTON

IDAHO

MONTANA

0   100 kilometres

J. FRED. HUME & CO.
DEALERS IN
DRY GOODS, CLOTHING, BOOTS, SHOES, GROCERIES & PROVISIONS, CANNED GOODS, HARDWARE &c.
CROCKERY AND GLASSWARE, STATIONERY, CUTLERY, PAINTS, OILS, GLASS, PUTTY, LAMPS & LAMP FIXTURES, SPORTING GOODS.

This page: Hume's Store in Revelstoke, c. 1885. Originally known as Farwell, after a local landowner, and later as Second Crossing to mark the CPR's second crossing of the Columbia River, the town was renamed Revelstoke by the CPR in honour of the banker who had averted the railway's financial crisis.

Facing page: Sandon was one of the more successful towns in the "silvery Slocan." Most of the mine shafts in the Kootenays were located high on steep mountain hillsides. More miners lost their lives in avalanches than in mining accidents.

Sicamous and ran through Enderby, Armstrong and Vernon to Okanagan Lake. Once the CPR established steamboat service on the lake, the entire valley, which had been home to fewer than four hundred white settlers and more than twenty thousand cattle, became ripe for development.

In 1891, Governor General Lord Aberdeen purchased the 13,000-acre Coldstream Ranch and announced his intention "to plant orchards on a big scale." Following his lead, speculators purchased other ranches, including the O'Keefe rangeland near Vernon, subdivided the land into plots of 10 to 40 acres and promoted the valley as an orchard "Eden": beautiful, unspoiled, a "land of promise."

For years, prospectors and mining men had been poking about the Kootenays. They had found gold, but not placer gold—the "poor man's mine," the pure gold easily washed from river gravel by a man with a pan. Kootenay gold was bound with other metals. To bring heavy machinery to the mine site and then get the ore to a smelter required a transportation system. The Dewdney Trail, running from Hope to Rock Creek to Rossland to Fort Steele, was a pack trail, built for mules rather than heavy wagons. The Kootenays' gold and silver, its lead and zinc and coal, remained in place until the coming of the railway.

By the 1880s, two transcontinental railways were within reach of the Kootenays. To the north, the CPR passed through Revelstoke on the Columbia River, only a few miles from the head of Upper Arrow Lake. To the south, an American line, the Great Northern, crossed the Kootenay River in Utah and the Columbia River in Washington. Both the CPR and the Great Northern built short branch lines to connect the mines to lake and river steamers. Competition was intense. By 1898, the silver town of Sandon in the Slocan Mountains was being served by two branch

lines—the Great Northern to Kaslo on Kootenay Lake, and the CPR to Nakusp on Upper Arrow Lake.

The CPR also began to invest in the mining industry, purchasing the gold-rich Le Roi mine at Rossland and the Sullivan silver mine at Kimberley. In 1898, the railway, acting as the Consolidated Mining and Smelting Company, purchased the smelter built at Trail two years earlier.

The West Kootenay region boomed. By 1898, two thousand people were living in Sandon. Nelson, on an arm of Kootenay Lake near the Silver King Mine, bloomed into a city of almost seven thousand, the largest mainland town after Vancouver. Prospectors crawled over the country, and towns popped up wherever a promising claim was discovered: Slocan City at the south end of Slocan Lake, Riondel on Kootenay Lake near the Blue Bell Mine, Trout Lake City and Camborne in the Lardeau country high in the mountains above the north end of Arrow Lake.

Newspaperman Fred Smyth said of Slocan City: "The hotels were jammed full and everybody seemed to have plenty to spend. Those who could not get beds slept in chairs and on pool tables. Everyone was pepped up and overflowing with optimism." And the same could have been said about all the West Kootenay's instant "cities."

The East Kootenay, too, profited from the railway boom. In 1897, the CPR began building a line running from Lethbridge, Alberta, through the Crowsnest Pass to Cranbrook. With the promise of the railway, the Crow's Nest Pass Coal Company began to exploit the coal deposits at Coal Creek, and the town of Fernie was established to house the miners.

In 1903, Canada's oldest railway, the Grand Trunk, announced that it would compete with the CPR by building a railroad to the west coast. The Grand Trunk Pacific (GTP) would take the Yellowhead Pass through the

Facing page: The Kaslo and Slocan Railway (shown here at Payne's Bluff) was a narrow gauge line built by an American railroad company, the Great Northern, to connect the Slocan mines to Kaslo on Kootenay Lake, where ore was loaded onto barges for transport down the lake and on to Bonners Ferry on the GN main line. Later, the CPR purchased the Kaslo and Slocan and converted the tracks to standard gauge.

This page: A train crossing a wooden trestle bridge on the Great Northern line in the Kootenays.

Top: Miners at work in the Le Roi gold mine at Rossland, c. 1900.

Bottom: By the end of 1912, the tracks of the Grand Trunk Pacific had reached Tete Jaune Cache. The rule that railway workcamps were "dry" only tested the ingenuity of whisky smugglers.

Rockies and cross central British Columbia to emerge on the Pacific at the mouth of the Skeena River. There, on Kaien Island, the GTP would build its terminal city. Determined to outdo the CPR, the Grand Trunk announced that Prince Rupert would be designed by American landscape architects and become "the most perfectly laid out and most beautiful city in the Dominion." Optimism abounded. In May 1909, when the first Prince Rupert town lots were sold at auction in Vancouver, spirited bidding pushed prices up to $8,000 for a single lot.

When surveys revealed that the GTP would pass through Fort George, the old Hudson's Bay Company trading post shook itself awake. The post sat on a 97-acre fur trade reserve on the banks of the Fraser River. Immediately to the north was an Indian village of about a hundred inhabitants on a 1,500-acre reserve fronting on both the Fraser and Nechako Rivers. As early as 1906, outsiders began to pre-empt land south of the HBC property and west of the Indian reserve, hoping that their holdings would become the site chosen as the GTP station.

In 1909, the *Fort George Tribune* began publishing and announced: "There are no bakeries, laundries, milliners, tailors, blacksmiths, tinners, carpenters, stenographers, lawyers, doctors, preachers, constables or schoolteachers at Fort George." There was also very little social news: no births, deaths or marriages. The editor was forced to dig deep: "Born to Hamilton's cow, a bull calf."

Twenty-one-year-old Russell Walker was sent north with $1,000 and instructions from his employer, the North Coast Land Company, to open a real estate office. "We knew full well that we would have a million population between Yellowhead Pass and Prince Rupert," Walker recalled.

Prince Rupert (shown here in 1906) was selected as the western terminus of the Grand Trunk Pacific Railway. The GTP promoted Prince Rupert as the "Venice of the North," a carefully designed city of wide boulevards and magnificent buildings—and investors flooded in.

"Get in ahead of the railroads: you will make from $500 to $5000 per lot before the first railroad reaches Fort George."
—George Hammond, brochure

"Nobody could dispute that. That was inevitable. George Hammond sold 3 million dollars' worth of town lots in Central Fort George. Three million worth of town lots!"

Land speculators spent thousands of dollars promoting Fort George. In 1913, Dick Corless was lured from England. Deciding that the town looked promising, he sent for his wife and children. In the spring of 1914, Dick led Mary Ellen and their two small boys to a wooden-floored tent. They were still living in the tent the following autumn, when Mary Ellen gave birth to a baby girl. "It was forty below zero," she remembered. "We always took the baby and the potatoes to bed with us to keep them from freezing."

On 7 April 1913, the last spike on the Grand Trunk Pacific was driven at Fort Fraser. The following year, Fort George residents decided that Prince George would be a more fitting name for a town destined to be the "great city of the north," a city at the very hub of things in central British Columbia.

Land speculation became a growth industry. Okanagan apples were winning gold medals awarded by the Royal Horticultural Society, but since most Okanagan land accessible to irrigation was already spoken for, attention shifted to Kootenay Lake and then to the Windermere Valley in the East Kootenay. The Windermere Valley was 3,000 feet above sea level. Summers were short, winters long and cold. In pamphlets designed to appeal to middle-class Englishmen yearning for the country life, the Columbia Valley Irrigated Fruit Lands Ltd. promoted the valley as a lush, bucolic paradise, an English Eden, and settlers poured in.

Facing page: For the Native woman called "Six Mile Mary," who was believed to be over one hundred years old, the Fort George boom brought more customers for the fish she caught at Tabor Lake and then carried in baskets to the town site.

This page: A potlatch held near Victoria in the 1890s. Federal law banned the potlatch in 1884, but enforcement was desultory until 1922, when twenty-six people were jailed for having taken part in a Kwakwa̱ka'wakw potlatch and ceremonial masks, seized as part of the crackdown, were dispersed to museums in Ontario and New York.

In the federal census of 1911, almost 70 per cent of the province's residents described themselves as having British origins. Some had come to British Columbia as workingmen to take jobs in coal mines, on the railway or in lumber mills. Others belonged to what Lady Aberdeen called "a very good class."

"What a strange lot of people we were," Charles Holliday said of his fellow Okanagan settlers, "retired officers of the army and navy, retired Indian civil servants; men who had gone broke growing oranges or tea and thought apples and peaches might put them on their feet again; English schoolboys whose parents sent them to the 'colonies' with their blessings because they would not fit into anything at home; professional men, fed up with their profession, who with dreams of a life of ease longed to be farmers . . . and then sisters and cousins and aunts of men who had come out ahead of them."

Top: The clerks living in the Bank of Montreal's staff quarters in Vernon demonstrated a dedication to sport. Charles Holliday, a young Englishman who arrived in the Okanagan Valley in 1889, described himself and his fellows: "We were a pretty lively bunch and used to whoop her up considerably at times."

Bottom: After enjoying a picnic on Cowichan Bay, Mr. and Mrs. Bazett waited for the rising tide to refloat the *Flutterby*.

*"We used to play polo on Sunday morning
and rush back home and tie the ponies in the creek . . .
We'd go in and have a bite of lunch, rush up
and let the ponies go, change our clothes and go down
to the country club and play tennis all afternoon.
I played rugby, football, cricket and polo, all in one week."*
—Tommy Wilmot

*"We had an awfully good time here, you know.
People didn't work so hard as they do now."*
—Dorothea Walker

*"Masses of English magazines of every kind were
sent to us in great bundles from England—
the* Graphic *and the* Illustrated London News *and
The Sphere *and* Country Life *and the* Daily Mirror.*"*
—Dorothy Richardson

Propped up by money from home, most worked only as hard as they cared to and devoted themselves to the sporting life. In the Interior, they played polo and staged fox hunts, pursuing coyotes or a "drag." On the coast, they sailed in regattas and cruised to picnic sites. Everywhere, they played cricket, croquet and lawn tennis. And they built English-style homes, subscribed to English newspapers, sent their children to private schools and tried to create a close approximation of home.

*"We are of the opinion that
this province must be
a white man's country."*
—*Vancouver Province*

CHAPTER 12

PROGRESS *and*
PREJUDICE

IN THE TEN YEARS between 1901 and 1911, British Columbia's population rose from 178,657 to 392,480. Not all newcomers were welcomed. Many were greeted with resentment and hostility; others were simply turned away. Some immigrants found the "better life" elusive; others, who had chosen the province as the place to pursue their utopian dreams, would come to believe that the government was conspiring against them. And British Columbia's Native peoples, whose numbers declined from 28,949 to 20,174 over the decade, began to feel that their very existence was threatened.

As the pressure to prohibit further Chinese immigration grew, employers, forced to look elsewhere for cheap labour, turned to Europe and Japan as sources of supply. British Columbia's workingmen reacted with anger to the recruitment of men whose presence threatened their jobs by lowering the wage scale.

The children of the pioneer Dr. John C. Henderson family of the Chilliwack area pose with a donkey in 1903.

In Vancouver Island coal mines, Slavs, Croatians, Italians and Finns often arrived to discover that they had been hired as strikebreakers. Condemned as scabs, they earned the enmity of the old miners and were pursued by a simmering contempt that would endure for a generation and more. In the East Kootenay, the Crow's Nest Coal Company lured men to Morrissey, Natal, Michel and Fernie with advertisements in European newspapers, promising that in British Columbia "life was fair and work but a dream." But soon after the French, Slavic and Italian miners arrived, they realized that they had been enslaved by the mining company. The company paid their passage to British Columbia and then extracted a repayment instalment from every pay packet. Miners rented company-owned cottages and were required to make all their purchases from the company store. Some Coal Creek men would find that, after spending twenty years in the mines, they owed the company $600 and more.

On 22 May 1902, an explosion in Coal Creek's No. 2 colliery claimed 128 lives. Only four of the men pictured here survived.

Japanese workers were regarded as a threat not only because of their numbers, which increased dramatically after the turn of the century, but also because of their success. In the early 1890s, a few men had begun fishing on the Fraser River. By the turn of the century, Japanese fishermen and cannery workers dominated the industry. More than three thousand Japanese arrived in the first six months of 1907. The mood was already ugly when it was learned that the Vancouver-based Nippon Supply Company had been contracted by the CPR for twelve hundred Japanese workers and had been approached by the Grand Trunk Pacific for five thousand labourers to work on its line through British Columbia. Wild rumours spread. The province was being invaded by the "yellow men"—fifty thousand were on their way to work for the GTP! Huge barracks were being built at Prince Rupert for their arrival! The CPR was importing an additional twelve thousand!

Backed by the Trades and Labour Council, the Asiatic Exclusion League was formed in Vancouver. On 24 July 1907, when the *Kumeric* disembarked 1,189 Japanese at Vancouver, tensions rose. A bill to prohibit Japanese from entering the province was passed by the legislature, but Lieutenant-Governor James Dunsmuir, who had recently asked the Nippon Supply Company for five hundred men to work in his coal mines, refused to sign it on the grounds that it was unconstitutional.

On 7 September, a crowd, waving banners that read "Stand for a White Canada" and "A White Canada for Us," gathered at Vancouver city hall to hear impassioned speeches and to burn the lieutenant-governor in effigy. The crowd turned into a mob and marched through Chinatown, smashing windows and breaking into shops and stores. When they moved on to Powell Street and the Japanese quarter, they met with armed resistance. The Japanese showed fight, "a cause for rejoicing and anxiety," Prime Minister Wilfrid Laurier opined: rejoicing because "the rowdies got a well deserved licking," and anxiety because it might make the Japanese "very saucy and render an adjustment of the trouble more difficult." The adjustment to which Laurier referred was the settlement of damage claims, but another type of adjustment came as a result of the 1907 riot. In the interests of maintaining good relations, Japan volunteered to restrict emigration.

With Chinese immigration limited by the head tax (increased to $500 in 1903), and Japanese immigration restricted by a "gentlemen's agreement," the Asiatic Exclusion League and its supporters shifted their attention to the people of India. A federal Order-in-Council, produced to placate British Columbia, stipulated that immigrants must travel in one "continuous journey" from their home country. Since no direct steamship service existed from India to Canada, no one sailing from an Indian port would be allowed entry.

On 23 May 1914, the *Komagata Maru* entered Burrard Inlet, carrying 376 Indian immigrants. Because their ship had not sailed directly from India, they were not permitted to land. Telegrams flew between British Columbia and Ottawa, and from Ottawa to India and London. The passengers spent eight miserable weeks swinging at anchor in Vancouver harbour before all appeals were exhausted and the *Komagata Maru* was ordered away.

JAPANESE FANCY GOODS
J. M. NAGANO & CO.
BALMORAL BLOCK, VICTORIA, B.C.

In 1892, two immigrants from Japan, Manzo Nagano and his wife, settled in Victoria and opened a successful store specializing in Japanese novelties.

After spending six weeks in Vancouver harbour, the passengers from India on the *Komagata Maru* took over the ship. They held their position, repelling boarding attempts, until HMCS *Rainbow* took charge.

The Doukhobors, a Russian religious sect dedicated to hard work and communal living, began settling around Grand Forks and Nelson in 1908. The women shown here are taking the place of horses or oxen to pull a plow.

SOME IMMIGRANTS to the province had no interest in joining the wider community. Rather, they saw in British Columbia an opportunity to create their own private utopias. In 1908, Peter Verigin purchased two large blocks of land near Grand Forks and Nelson on behalf of the Doukhobors, a Russian religious sect dedicated to hard work, communal living and the simple life. By 1912, Doukhobor holdings had grown to almost 15,000 acres, and communities such as Castlegar, Brilliant and Grand Forks had developed distinct societies.

Other groups, with similar goals, were not nearly so successful. In 1900, Finnish coal miners, working in Dunsmuir mines and far from happy with their lot, decided to make a break for freedom. They invited to join them Matti Kurikka, a Finnish writer and philosopher who championed the formation of communal settlements based on socialist principles. In 1901, the government granted the company formed by Kurikka and his followers homestead rights to Malcolm Island, off the north coast of Vancouver Island. By the spring of 1903, more than two hundred people had settled at Sointula, "the place of Harmony." Two years later, the community was broke, and the company that held the colony's land was dissolved. About one hundred people remained, paying a dollar an acre to acquire their own land and managing to survive by trapping mink, working for logging companies or fishing for the cannery at Rivers Inlet. And so

Sointula survived—Finnish-speaking, staunchly socialist but, as its residents admitted, "no utopia."

A Danish colony at Cape Scott on the northwestern tip of Vancouver Island failed when the government refused to build a promised access road, but in the valley of the Bella Coola River, a "new Norway" managed to survive despite government indifference. Norwegian farmers who had settled on the American plains were looking for greener pastures. Some had lost their farms during the depression of 1893, others were encouraged to leave by the searing summer heat and frigid winters, and still others missed the sea. "Dad didn't like Minnesota," Annie Levelton recalled, "he wasn't used to the flat prairie country and he wanted to go where there was sea; he was used to that." Reverend Saugstad, a Lutheran minister who hoped to establish a colony of "morally perfect people in an ideal situation away from temptation," travelled around British Columbia in search of a site. He was impressed with the Bella Coola Valley, perhaps because of its isolation, perhaps because it reminded him of Norway.

Seventy-two colonists arrived in 1894. They agreed that land would be selected by lot, with each settler receiving one of the 160-acre plots strung out along the river. The centre of the community was Hagensborg, 12 miles from the sea. Despite the government's reneging on its promise to build a wagon road connecting the farms, the colony thrived. Men spent the summer at Rivers Inlet, fishing or working in the cannery, and then came

"We arrived [at Sointula] on June 3, 1902.
We arrived here late at night . . .
In this log cabin there were five double bunks
for all these families. Hay was piled on these bunks
for a mattress, and my husband and I and the
two children got one of these bunks for our own."
—Kaisa Riksman

Bella Coola's Norwegian colonists were strung out along the river, some as many as 25 miles from the sea. Because no wagon road connected the farms, settlers transported supplies in boats that they poled up the swift-flowing river or carried them on their backs over a trail through the woods.

Norwegian settler Ivar Fougner's Bella Coola farm. Everything Fougner needed, he packed in on his back, a 24-mile round trip over a rough trail. "They packed cookstoves on their backs," his son remembered. "They packed everything you need for your home."

home "with money in their pockets and courage in their hearts to return to clearing land." By the turn of the century, Bella Coola had more than two hundred residents, and the valley, warmed by the Japanese Current, was producing potatoes, carrots, turnips and apples, raspberries and cherries.

As more and more open land was enclosed by settlers' fences, Native people became increasingly concerned. In 1887, the Nisg̲a'a people of the Nass River met with a commission sent north to determine the reasons for their unrest. The Nisg̲a'a explained: "They [the government] have never bought it [the land] from us or our forefathers. They have never fought and conquered our people and taken the land that way, and yet they say now that they will give us so much land—our own land."

At Kamloops on 25 August 1910, chiefs of the Secwepemc, Nlaka'pamux and Okanagan people presented Prime Minister Wilfrid Laurier with a "memorial," a statement defining their plight. "For a time we did not feel the stealing of our lands very heavily. As the country was sparsely settled, we still had considerable liberty in the way of hunting, fishing and grazing over by far the most of it. However, owing to increased settlement, in late years this has become changed, and we are being more and more restricted to our reservations which in most places are unfit and inadequate to maintain us . . . Our old people ask, 'How are we to live?'"

On 3 March 1911, three chiefs (B. P. Kelly of Hartley Bay, John Chilheetsa of Douglas Lake and George Quakatston of Cowichan), representing all the Native peoples of the province, travelled to Victoria to meet with Premier Richard McBride and his executive council. Chief Kelly recounted earlier appeals for fair treatment: the 1887 approach by the people of the Nass River and Port Simpson, the 1891 petition of the Cowichan people, the 1906 visit to England of three chiefs to present their grievances to the king. Nothing had been done. Now, they wanted action.

A Stl'atl'imx man fishing for salmon in the traditional way at the turn of the century.

"We are here to appeal to you that our rights be recognized, to press before you our aboriginal title to this land of our forefathers still unextinguished . . . Our aim is to have this great issue determined in the courts of justice, and we promise to abide by its decision. Gentlemen, this is a great issue which you, as a governing body, must not ignore."

But Premier McBride found that there was no "great issue" to settle. To him, it was all very simple. The Indians had no title to the land; there was no question to submit to the courts.

Facing page: In 1913, a Royal Commission toured the province to determine the appropriate size of Indian reserves in British Columbia. Its visits were welcomed by Native people, who hoped that their grievances would be addressed. The final report recommended the creation of new reserves and the enlargement of others, but also removed land equal to about half the gains. Native people, noting that they would lose some of their best reserve land, objected.

This page: During his lifetime, a Nuu-chah-nulth man known as Old Jim built more than forty traditional canoes, including this one, which was 42 feet long. In 1924, it was presented to the lieutenant-governor and is now in the Royal British Columbia Museum.

O F ALL British Columbia's industries, coal mining produced the most labour strife. It was dirty, dangerous work, and it honed in men a fine sense of their rights. Mine owners and managers, on the alert for growing militancy and determined to defeat union activity, greeted complaints and protests as invitations to do battle.

In February 1877, one hundred Vancouver Island miners went on strike at Robert Dunsmuir's Wellington Colliery to protest a cut in wage rates and the inaccuracy of the scales used to weigh their coal. Dunsmuir served eviction notices for company-owned houses and recruited strikebreakers in San Francisco. After the sheriff was turned back

as he tried to effect the evictions, Dunsmuir applied to the government for assistance. When the sheriff returned, he was accompanied by 107 armed militiamen. Sixteen weeks after walking off the job, the men returned to work.

In May 1890, again at the Wellington Colliery, men who had joined the recently formed Miners' and Mine Labourers' Protective Association went on strike over the length of their working day. The Dunsmuir family refused to negotiate, and once again the militia arrived to evict striking miners. The strike and lockout lasted seventeen months, but that was nothing compared to the confrontation that occurred twenty years later.

In May 1912, Vancouver Island

miners, newly emboldened by their membership in America's biggest union, the United Mine Workers of America, went on strike against four coal companies over a variety of issues, including recognition of their union. The companies refused to talk and immediately set about recruiting strikebreakers.

A year into the strike, over three thousand men remained off the job. But a few miners had begun to straggle back, protected by a bevy of special constables. In addition, the companies had been so successful in hiring strikebreakers in Europe that some mines were achieving full production.

Serious trouble began at Nanaimo in August 1913, when union miners and their wives

gathered near the mine entrance to hurl stones and insults at the strikebreakers. The following day, the Nanaimo men marched to South Wellington, where they swelled the numbers of local miners who had gathered at the fence enclosing the company property in which the strikebreakers were housed. A mob of six hundred stormed the fence, and as the strikebreakers ran for the woods, men rampaged through the compound, smashing crockery and breaking windows.

In Ladysmith that same night, the Temperance Hotel, home to a group of imported strikebreakers, was wracked by an explosion. Someone in the group gathered in front of the hotel called out, "Hurrah! The balloon has gone

The Western Fuel Company's Number 1 mine at Nanaimo, c. 1900.

up!" An angry crowd, yelling and singing "Hurrah, hurrah. We'll drive the scabs away," began to move through the town. At the home of a man named McKenzie, a local miner who had returned to work, a stick of dynamite was lobbed through the window of the children's bedroom. When McKenzie picked up the dynamite to throw it out the window, it exploded, blowing his hand away.

Meanwhile, union men and their wives from South Wellington and Nanaimo were moving on the mining town of Extension. Wives and children of strikebreakers fled their homes and took refuge in the bush. Bullets flew as scabs and strikers exchanged gunfire. Homes were looted and set ablaze.

Attorney General William Bowser called in the army. Men from the 6th Regiment Duke of Connaught's Own Rifles were dispatched to Extension, and 450 Seaforth Highlanders were sent to Cumberland. Soon, more than a thousand soldiers were enforcing martial law in all Vancouver Island coal towns.

The army remained in place as the strike dragged on. Then, in August 1914, came the Great War.

The soldiers were called to active duty, and the union men decided to accept conditions they had earlier rejected. But bitter feelings between strikers and scabs lingered. Years later, a miner recalled: "To this day there's families in this area that don't talk to each other."

Top: Ladysmith coal miners, c. 1910.

Bottom: When the violence in Vancouver Island coal towns escalated beyond the control of the provincial police (pictured here in Nanaimo in 1913), the attorney general called in the army.

Top: By 1910, the Pacific Whaling Company was operating four stations on the coast, where whales were converted into oil, fertilizer and bone.

Bottom: The Union Steamship SS *Camosun* at Prince Rupert, c. 1912. Formed in 1889, the Union Steamship Company carried passengers and freight to small coastal communities, becoming a lifeline for sawmills, canneries and logging camps.

DURING THE FIRST DECADE of the new century, Victoria and Vancouver boomed. The island city welcomed a new industry. Fur seals had been decimated, and the sealing fleet was gone. But in 1904, former sealers formed the Pacific Whaling Company and ordered whaling ships from Norway. The following year, it established a whaling station at Sechart on Barkley Sound. By 1911, the company had expanded to ten vessels and built three additional processing stations: at Kyuquot on Vancouver Island, and at Rose Harbour and Naden Harbour in the Queen Charlotte Islands. That year, the four stations processed 1,624 whales. The season lasted from April until October, after which the whalers returned to Victoria to spend their profits. But other industries continued to slip away to the mainland, and Victoria was forced to rely on government and tourism for its prosperity.

The Canadian Pacific Railway fulfilled its promise to put Victoria on the tourist map. The company's coastal steamship service was running the elegantly appointed Princess boats from Victoria to Vancouver and Seattle, and its Empress liners were delivering the well-heeled world travellers on which Victoria's livelihood increasingly depended. To encourage wealthy tourists to dally in the city, the CPR agreed to build a tourist hotel. And once the Empress opened its doors, Victoria reaped the benefits of the

A panoramic postcard from 1908 shows the Empress Hotel (flying a flag), the CPR's *Princess Victoria* (right) and her rival the Puget Sound Navigation Company's *Indianapolis*.

Panoramic view of Victoria, British Columbia, showing the Provincial Parliament Buildings, the new Canadian Pacific Hotel "The Empress", The Dominion Post Office and Custom House, with the C. P. R. "Flyer" Princess S. S. Victoria lying at the wharf.

CPR's worldwide publicity. As one Victoria resident put it, "From London dock to Empress Hotel door was one uninterrupted slither of easy travel."

After visiting Victoria and the Empress, the popular British author Rudyard Kipling assured his readers: "On a thousand a year pension a man would be a millionaire in these parts, and for four hundred he could live very well." People flooded into the city. Some were wealthy retirees from Winnipeg; others came from colonial outposts in Asia, attracted by the city's Englishness. Still others were young men from England, looking for opportunities and adventure.

The Union Club, a gentlemen's club on the English model, welcomed five hundred new members. The Hudson's Bay Company began construction of a grand new department store. Open land around the city disappeared as cow yards and Chinese market gardens were divided into building lots. Speculators carved up the James Douglas estate, and stout Edwardian houses replaced Joseph Trutch's orchard. The 28-acre estate surrounding Robert Dunsmuir's castle was cut into 144 building lots. Tudor-style mansions, designed by Samuel Maclure, the province's most sought-after residential architect, marched along Rockland Avenue to Government House.

At the turn of the century, Victoria's population was 20,919. By 1911, it had risen to 31,660. To Victorians, growth seemed to be proceeding at a

"Real estate men recommend it as a little piece of England, but no England is set in any such seas. To realize Victoria you must take all the eye admires most in Bournemouth, Torquay, the Isle of Wight, the Happy Valley of Hong Kong, the Doon, Sorrento, and Camps Bay; add reminiscences of the Thousand Islands, and arrange the whole round the Bay of Naples, with some of the Himalayas for the background."
—Rudyard Kipling

Bill Miner, a notorious American stagecoach and train robber, made the news with the province's first train robbery in 1904, when he held up the CPR train near Mission. After robbing a second CPR train in 1906, he was captured by a posse near Douglas Lake and sentenced to life in prison. He escaped from the penitentiary in 1909 and fled to the United States.

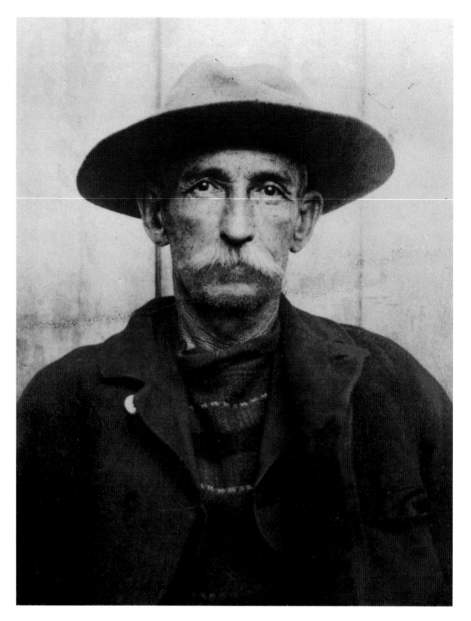

"One fishing season so many thousands [of salmon] were thrown back, and the bodies carried by the tides into Burrard Inlet, that the rotting fish littered the beaches and actually stopped bathing and walking on the sand at English Bay bathing beach for two or three weeks in hot mid-summer. A swimmer might bump his chin into a floating carcass, or step on putrid flesh concealed under the sand. Dead fish were everywhere."
—Major James S. Matthews

"In 1913, I only found one dead sockeye, a male, on the shore of Skwa-am Bay at Adams Lake where, after former big runs, the bar of dead, spawned out salmon used to go a wagon load to every five feet."
—David Mitchell

frantic pace. Compared to Vancouver, it was standing still. By 1911, almost 50 per cent of all British Columbians made their home in the Lower Mainland. Industries were concentrated along Burrard Inlet; and on the Fraser River, the fishing industry had turned into a giant.

Thousands of fishermen were operating on the river. Fishboats often caught more than canneries had time to process, and tons of dead fish were thrown back in the water. But the first serious threat to salmon stocks did not come from wasteful practices or overfishing. In 1913, the Canadian Northern Railway, a third transcontinental line, was laying tracks through the Fraser Canyon. Before work began, engineers with the Department of Indian Affairs had mapped the river to identify ancient fishing places, where no debris could be thrown into the river. Unfortunately, no family laid claim to Hells Gate, and during construction, all the rock hewed out for Hells Gate Tunnel was tumbled into the water. As the channel narrowed, the speed of the current increased, making it impossible for millions of salmon to make their way upriver to the spawning grounds. It happened that 1913 was a peak year in the sockeye's four-year cycle, and canneries packed 2,392,895 cases. In 1917, the catch was down almost 80 per cent, and the pack fell to 559,702 cases. Four years later, the pack was only 142,598.

Top: In 1905, gasoline engines had yet to be introduced to the salmon fleet. Instead, fishboats were propelled by sails or oars.

Middle: Cannery workers at Alert Bay near the turn of the century. Up and down the coast, Native people played an important role in the fishing industry. Men sailed with the fishing fleets; women worked in canneries and processing plants.

Bottom: A canned salmon label.

An early flight at Minorou racetrack on Lulu Island, possibly the Charles K. Hamilton pioneer flight of 25 March 1910.

Vancouver became "a magnificent metropolis" as European capital poured into the city. The businessmen who had formed the Hundred Thousand Club with the rallying cry, "In nineteen-ten, Vancouver then, will have one hundred thousand men," found their dreams coming true. By 1911, there were 100,401 Vancouverites, and that number did not include suburban municipalities such as Point Grey and South Vancouver, which had not yet come within the city limits. British Columbia's first skyscraper, the four-teen-storey Dominion Trust Building, boasted of being the tallest building in the British Empire—but only until work began on the Tower Building, designed to rise a dizzying seventeen storeys. The CPR contributed to the boom by clearing land for the exclusive Shaughnessy Heights subdivision and by planning a huge addition to the Hotel Vancouver.

But the good times proved too good to last. By 1912, a continent-wide depression was making itself felt in British Columbia. Over the next two years, savings and fortunes were swept away. Miners and mill workers were laid off. Labour relations soured. And the news from Europe became increasingly troubling.

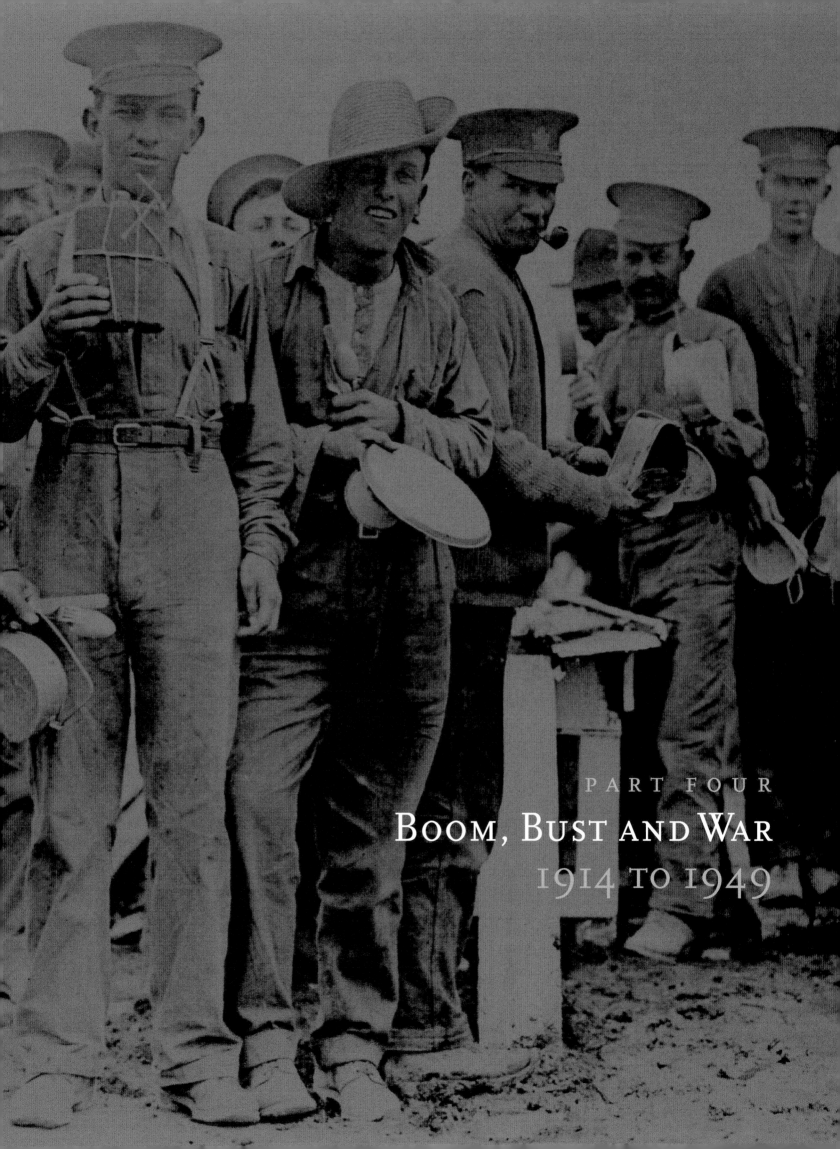

BOOM, BUST AND WAR

1914 TO 1949

CHAPTER 13

FIGHTING *for the* EMPIRE

Previous page: Volunteers from the Interior. Camp Vernon became their training and recruitment centre. By 1916, more than seven thousand men were training at the camp while the civilian population of Vernon was scarcely three thousand.

This page: Richard McBride became the premier of British Columbia in 1903, when he was thirty-two years old. In 1915, with his health failing and his popularity dimmed by rumours that he had personally profited from the purchase of the Chilean submarines, he resigned from office. One of British Columbia's most popular premiers, he remains the youngest man to hold the office.

ON 30 JULY 1914, the *Vancouver Province* gave voice to a growing concern: "If Great Britain and Germany are drawn into a European war, what is going to happen to British Columbia?"

It was known that the German cruiser *Leipzig* was patrolling the coast off California and that four other German warships were operating in the Pacific. "How will this defenceless province protect herself from raids by hostile cruisers?" the *Province* worried. "Vancouver could be bombarded, Nanaimo, Union Bay and Ladysmith lose their coal stocks, Prince Rupert wiped out and the small coastal villages raided and the Pacific coast would have no means of fighting back."

Many people on the coast were shaken. Some made plans to transfer money and valuables to American banks. One Victorian went so far as to equip his family vault at Ross Bay Cemetery as an emergency shelter.

But no one took British Columbia's vulnerability more seriously than the province's premier, Sir Richard McBride.

A Seattle shipyard had just completed construction of two submarines for the Chilean navy, but Chile was reluctant to pay its bills until its specifications had been met. On 3 August 1914, the shipyard offered the submarines to British Columbia: $1,150,000 for the pair. Premier McBride acted without hesitation. At dawn on the morning of 5 August, in

Juan de Fuca Strait, Seattle shipyard employees rendezvoused with British Columbia's representatives, took possession of the province's cheque and handed over the vessels.

Most British Columbians greeted the outbreak of war with enthusiasm. In Kamloops, an excited crowd gathered outside the newspaper office, eager for the latest telegram, and newsboys hovered, ready to snatch off the presses the "extra" reporting that the Empire was at war. When word reached Victoria, the throngs outside the *Colonist's* office burst into cheers, followed by heartfelt renditions of "God Save the Queen" and "Rule Britannia."

In Vancouver, an angry crowd attacked the German consulate, tore down the double-headed eagle above the door and then burned an effigy of the German kaiser. The sugar millionaire Benjamin Rogers, commodore of the Royal Vancouver Yacht Club, offered his yacht *Aquila* to the navy, and his fellow club members organized a flotilla to convoy their boats to Esquimalt. Likewise, a hundred Japanese fishermen in Steveston offered themselves and their boats for whatever service might be required.

Throughout the province, British army reservists scrambled to book passage to England to rejoin their regiments. Recruitment offices were swamped: in Rossland, 50 men enlisted; in Duncan, 147 Cowichan Valley men signed up, including 58 of the 60-member Cowichan Cricket Club. In Victoria, local regiments had more volunteers than they could handle.

Colin Campbell, superintendent of the provincial police, worried about sabotage. British Columbia's only overland links to the rest of Canada were the three transcontinental railways—three highly vulnerable lines of track, two of which funnelled through the Fraser Canyon on their way to the coast. He was also concerned about the coal ships loading at Union Bay on Vancouver Island and about the dynamite stored in the Canadian Explosives Company's magazines at Departure Bay, Bowen Island and Burrard Inlet, and in the Interior. But uppermost in Campbell's mind were the CPR trains carrying ammunition and explosives. On 5 August, he wired constables in Field, Revelstoke, Ashcroft, Lytton, North Bend and Kamloops, warning them to keep a close watch on the ammunition trains. Two days later, he advised his men to extend their vigilance to "suspicious characters." "See that all tramps and bums are kept moving," he ordered.

The Chilean submarines were not an unqualified success. As they made their way into the Esquimalt naval base, they narrowly escaped being blown out of the water by members of a shore battery who had not been warned of their arrival. Beset by operational problems, they were transferred to the east coast. "Both boats were towed a considerable portion of the voyage to Halifax," a naval officer recalled.

"I went over the fields to Dede's and heard there that war was declared . . . we all just looked blankly at one another. No one had any idea what the next move was going to be. Everyone wondered."
—Emily Carr

From the *British Columbian*, 6 August 1914.

"It was really quite surprising," Attorney General William Bowser mused, "the number of people who were suddenly seized with the delusion that German spies were about to perpetrate some heinous deed."

On 15 August 1914, Ottawa ordered the arrest of German reservists. Two months later, the order was expanded to include the registration and possible internment of all "enemy aliens." Aliens fell into two categories. The first included Germans who had received military training in their youth and were now on the list of long-term reservists. Most men in this group came from the vibrant German business community, men who were judged to be "educated, pushful and intelligent." A second group was termed "Austrians," but actually included Serbs, Croats, Hungarians and Ukrainians—in fact, men from any nation under the sway of the German Empire. The Austrians, who were mostly from the labouring class, were considered a danger because they could be found in coal mines and in work camps near bridges and railways.

Despite public demands that all aliens be imprisoned, the authorities preferred to impound individual suspects rather than indulge in mass arrests. Camps were established at Nanaimo and Vernon, and at first internments were few. But in 1915, when Harry Stevens, member of Parliament for Vancouver, suggested that all enemy aliens be interned "to relieve the local unemployment situation," Prime Minister Robert Borden agreed.

On 1 June 1915, 115 aliens were arrested at Nanaimo, and coal miners who had been without work since the 1912 strike found their services required once again. The Vernon camp, already home to 150 Germans and Austrians, braced itself to receive four hundred more.

The notion that the internees might have a soft life rankled Harry Stevens. "It is a shame that such men should be kept in idleness at the country's expense," he declared. "I strongly favour the idea of putting them to work on the roads." That idea met with immediate approval. Using internees as labourers meant the building of roads that otherwise would have been too expensive to contemplate. Work camps were established in remote locations, such as Tete Jaune Cache, Yoho National Park and Mara Lake. Only Austrian internees were sent to work camps. The principles of the 1907 Hague Convention were scrupulously applied. Officers were not expected to work. Germans, most of whom were well-off, and some of whom boasted aristocratic lineage, were considered to be in the officer class. They were interned together at Vernon and had a relatively comfortable war.

Gentlemen internees were allowed to be accompanied by their families. Freiherr Rochus von Luttwitz (Baron Sutturtz) had been picked up amid stories of noisy celebrations of German victories at his Point Grey home and was alleged to have declared upon his arrest in May 1915: "Why bother about interning me? The war will be over in October. We shall be on our way to Germany. You Canadians will be our prisoners." At Vernon, the baron enjoyed the company of his wife, Elfrieda, the former Countess of Einsiedel. Dr. Otto Grunert, one of the founders of the Bank of Vancouver, had the good fortune to be interned not only with his wife but also his family's maid. Carl von Mackensen, famous for the lavish parties he gave at his home in Port Kells, was interned with his cook and feasted on food specially ordered for him by Vernon grocers.

Top: As these motorists, bogged down in "Cariboo Sand," demonstrated in 1914, most roads in British Columbia remained more suited to horse-drawn wagons than automobiles. In 1911 and again in 1912, the number of cars in British Columbia doubled. By 1914, there were 6,668 registered vehicles on the road.

Bottom: In 1915, "enemy aliens" were put to work on the Monashee Road. By the end of 1917, most of the road-work camps had been closed. So many British Columbians were serving in the war that industries were experiencing a labour shortage and internees were released to work in mines and mills.

In Vernon, German internees, most of whom were monied and high-born, enjoyed a relatively comfortable war.

By 1915, most British Columbians had begun to realize that, rather than being a short, glorious adventure, the war would be long and punishing. In January, army purchasing agents began to scour ranches in the Cariboo, Chilcotin and Okanagan for replacement horses. "All the army requirements called for was for a horse to be ridden two or three times. He was then considered gentle enough for the troops," rancher Alex Bulman recalled. "Many old soldiers on their return from overseas said, 'Those damned remounts killed or wounded more men than did the German army.'"

But the German army was doing better than Bulman suggested. There were few towns and cities in the province that had not received bad news. From a hospital bed in England, Private Lionel Geldhart wrote to his home in Duncan: "Poor Hayward was mortally wounded at Ypres, in the stomach and the groin. He was in fearful agony and kept crying out all night, 'Shoot me, do please.' Young Anketell Jones was hit in the leg but his pal Guilsbride . . . is missing, killed, I think. Ted Southern is dead. Tommy Young, my pal, is also gone. Jimmy Law . . . was hit by shrapnel in the trench with two others and fearfully mangled, dying quickly. These are all Duncanites."

On 8 May 1915, British Columbians learned that a British passenger liner, the *Lusitania*, had been sunk by a German submarine. Early reports revealed that among the passengers were forty-four British Columbians from Kamloops, Penticton, Nelson, Prince Rupert, Nanaimo, Ashcroft, Fernie, Vancouver and Victoria.

Top: Bill Rochfort, a lieutenant in the 47th Battalion, sent this sketch home to his young son in Victoria.

Bottom: On 1 June 1915, Quesnel volunteers marched off to war along Front Street, with Alex Wendt playing the trumpet and Reg Booth beating the drum.

Victorians turned out to cheer as the *Princess Sophia* carried men to war.

"We old sailors decided we had stood for too much and we decided to stop it, once and for all. Our first objective was the German Club. Well, to make a long story short, all hell broke loose. All I heard from some of the soldiers was 'go to it, boys.'"
—Walter Roberts

On the day he learned that his wife and two children had gone down with the ship, David Lambie, a miner from Rossland, booked passage for England so that he could enlist in a British unit and take revenge on the enemy. When word reached Victoria that Jim "Boy" Dunsmuir was among the town's fifteen *Lusitania* victims, the city exploded.

The grandson of the Nanaimo coal baron, and son of the former premier and lieutenant-governor, Jim Dunsmuir had been on the way to England to join a British cavalry regiment. When soldiers drinking at Victoria's Kaiserhof Hotel heard the news of Dunsmuir's death, they leapt onto the bar and began to sing patriotic songs. A crowd gathered to roar approval as men climbed the hotel's fire escape to string Union Jacks from the roof. Someone shouted, "On to the German Club!" and three hundred people, singing and chanting, marched to the club's premises and ransacked the building. Soon, a mob of more than five hundred, followed by about three thousand spectators, was roaming through the streets to attack any business run by a man with a German-sounding name.

Peace was restored at midnight. Armed guards were posted all around the town, including Government House. Both the lieutenant-governor

Anti-German demonstrators
attacked Victoria's Kaiserhof
Hotel when news of the
Lusitania's sinking reached
the city on 8 May 1915.

and his wife were from old Victoria families. Francis Stilman Barnard's father had founded the Cariboo's lifeline, the Barnard Express. His wife, Martha, was the daughter of Joseph Loewen, the pioneer brewer; and her mother, Eva, was the sister of Frank Laumeister, who had introduced camels to the Cariboo during the gold rush. But rumours swirled through the city's barrooms that Loewen's brewery had provided free beer to the German Club and that the sinking of the *Lusitania* had been celebrated at Government House.

Volunteers continued to come forward during 1916, including men who had no obvious reason for defending the British Empire. Tow Inouye, born in Yokohama in 1883, married and with five small children, presented himself at the Kamloops recruitment office. At Douglas Lake, forty-two-year-old cowboy George McLean, whose uncle had been hanged at New Westminster for the murder of Johnny Ussher, saddled up his horse and rode into town to enlist. But as casualty lists grew, patriotic fervour dimmed. When the city of Armstrong asked Kelowna to endorse a proposal to recruit an Okanagan battalion, Kelowna refused on the grounds that the district had few enough men to work in the orchards and packing houses.

"She [Mrs. Duncan Reid] was a knitter of socks... With her own wrinkled fingers—she was about seventy then—this good friend knitted eight hundred single socks—four hundred pair—one half sock for each day of the war."
—Major J. S. Matthews

Top: Tow Inouye's military will.

Bottom: Social gatherings, like this garden party on Victoria's fashionable Rockland Avenue, became patriotic events held to raise funds for the war.

20

Perforated sheet for Will from Pay Book of Reg.

No. 688274

Name Tow Inouye

Unit 47th Battalion

Military Will

In The event of my death I Give The Whole of my Property and eff ests to my Wife Mikama Inouye PO Box 419 Kamloops B.C.

Signature Tow Inouye

Rank and Regt. Private 47th

Date 14:12:16

DURING the heady days of British Columbia's pre-war boom, Alvo von Alvensleben was the very model of what it took to rise to the top of Vancouver's business community. He was tall and handsome; he had impeccable connections to the German aristocracy; he was married to a local woman; and he was a self-made man.

Gustav Constantin Alvo von Alvensleben was born in Germany in 1880. His father, Count von Alvensleben, the former ambassador to the court of the tsar, insisted that his son embark on a military career. Alvo stuck it out for five years, then resigned his commission as a second lieutenant and struck out on his own. He arrived in Vancouver in 1904. "Drive me to a cheap hotel," he told the hack-driver and settled into a dollar-a-night establishment on Water Street. When his money ran out, he got a job first as a "boat puller" for a salmon cannery on the Fraser River and then as a night watchman at the cannery. The following year, he acquired a boat, and by the end of the run, had $1,500 in the bank. He went into real estate.

By 1914, he was at the peak of a financial empire. His company had become the conduit through which German money was funnelled into British Columbia investments. His clients were said to include General von Mackensen, Emma Mumm, Bertha Krupp and the kaiser himself. His investments stretched to the Standard Fish and Fertilizer Company, the Vancouver-Nanaimo Coal Mining Company, the Vancouver Timber and Trading Company, the Piercite Powder Company and the Queen Charlotte Islands Fisheries.

Von Alvensleben was the most prominent member of Vancouver's German community. In 1908, he married Mary Westcott, whose father owned the cannery at which he had worked. He built a huge rambling house (now Crofton House School) in Kerrisdale and entertained with abandon. At the head of Indian Arm on Burrard Inlet, one of his companies built Wigwam Inn. Designed as a *luftkurort*, a fresh-air resort for the wealthy German community, the inn welcomed other visitors. Among the first to register in 1911 were two millionaire Americans, John D. Rockefeller and John Jacob Astor.

When war was declared in 1914, von Alvensleben was on the Atlantic Ocean, returning to British Columbia after visiting his investors in Germany. Upon learning that some of his colleagues had been arrested, he hovered in Seattle to await developments.

When British Columbians discovered that von Alvensleben had escaped detention, they thought the worst. That he was the kaiser's secret agent. That on his Kerrisdale estate, overlooking the Fraser, there were huge gun emplacements. That he was visiting Vancouver twice a week, ferried to the city aboard a small motor launch to be picked up by a car on the Point Grey waterfront and swept secretly to his office.

Alvo von Alvensleben had achieved so much, he seemed capable of anything. Reports flooded in to the provincial police. The night porter on the train from Seattle to Vancouver swore that von Alvensleben was travelling the route dressed in women's clothes. "He used a stateroom—tipped well—porter usually found 2 silver dollars in basin in washroom," the police superintendent informed the immigration authorities. Tipping well—that actually sounded like Alvo. Far less likely was another story the police were called upon to investigate. In the case of a German setback, von Alvensleben had been heard to say that he would blow up the Parliament Buildings in Victoria, using timed explosives. He was seen as all-powerful and everywhere. When one of the stables at the Willows military camp caught fire—"strange to say, on a pouring wet night"—von Alvensleben was suspected.

The man himself, stripped of all his assets by the Custodian of Enemy Alien Property, remained in Seattle. In 1917, after the United States entered the war, he was interned with other enemy aliens at Fort Douglas, Utah, where, it was said, he led a tunnel committee in a near-successful bid for freedom.

After the war, he became an American citizen. During the Second World War, one of his sons was wounded landing with his American regiment on a Normandy beach. Alvo von Alvensleben died in Seattle in 1965.

Top: The famous Wigwam Inn at the head of Indian Arm on Burrard Inlet.

Bottom: German aristocrat Alvo von Alvensleben.

Top: The artist Emily Carr participated in Victoria's pre-war boom by constructing Hill House, a small apartment building near Beacon Hill Park. Her tenants, as described in her book *The House of All Sorts,* proved to be a burden. Later, Carr won a Governor General's Award for her writing, and recently one of her paintings sold for more than $1 million, but during her lifetime, she found it hard to make ends meet. To earn extra income, she raised English bob-tail sheepdogs—in total more than three hundred of them—in the backyard kennel at Hill House.

Bottom: Women joined the Red Cross, trained as nurses, worked in factories, knitted socks, raised money for patriotic causes and collected "soldiers' comforts." In short, they did whatever they could to support the war effort.

By 1917, voluntary enlistment had dropped dramatically all across Canada. With the army experiencing a manpower shortage, Ottawa passed the Military Service Act. On 29 August 1917, unmarried men aged twenty to thirty-four became subject to compulsory conscription.

To escape arrest, draft resisters melted into the bush. Provincial police-men, who knew the men they were sent to apprehend and sympathized with the circumstances that prompted their resistance, adopted a relaxed approach. A farmer outside Prince George avoided arrest simply by walking into the woods every Thursday, the day the policeman always called by to look for him. But the dominion police and the special constables—"bounty hunters," people called them—handled things differently, especially when it came to the well-known labour organizer Albert "Ginger" Goodwin.

Socialists and labour leaders believed that the war—"this delightful little ruling-class scrimmage"—was being fought to defend the capitalist system. To them, conscription was an abomination. Why should workingmen become cannon fodder while the bosses lined their pockets?

Ginger Goodwin was an outspoken opponent of the war. Placed on the blacklist after the 1912 coal miners' strike, he eventually found a job with the Consolidated Mining and Smelting Company at Trail, a town flush with wartime prosperity, thanks in part to the zinc it supplied to munitions makers. When compulsory conscription became law, Goodwin was organiz-ing local trade unionists—carpenters, plumbers, pipe-fitters—into a united

With almost a quarter of the Okanagan's workforce in the military, women were recruited to help with the harvest. "What kind of dress should be worn in the orchards?" one woman wondered. "This would be one time when women will be permitted to wear overalls," she was advised.

"Enforced military service is the complete and final denial of human freedom. What does Canada owe Europe? This can be answered in one word. Nothing!"
—British Columbia Federationist

Although he was an unprepossessing man, barely five feet six inches tall and with teeth "like spikes of rusty barbed wire," Albert "Ginger" Goodwin had the ability to sway crowds with his oratory.

front, the Trail Trades and Labour Council. In November 1917, the Labour Council called a strike against Consolidated Smelting.

Around the province, the strike was interpreted as a protest against conscription. "Terms of Military Service Act Flagrantly Disobeyed by 1,500 Smeltermen," a *Vancouver Province* headline declaimed. Goodwin was considered a dangerous agitator, a pacifist when it came to the European war but dedicated to the violent overthrow of capitalism. The strike collapsed on 20 December, after the smeltermen's international union, to which the Trail committee had written for support, branded the work stoppage unlawful.

Ginger Goodwin went home to Cumberland, with conscription looming over him. At first, his chronic lung problems had classified him as being unfit, but when he applied for an exemption based on his poor health, he was denied. After working his way through the appeals process, he was declared "fit for all service." When he was ordered to report, Goodwin and half a dozen other draft evaders took to the woods. In the rough country at the far end of Comox Lake, they lived off the land, hunting deer—"the king's beef"—and enjoying the support of sympathetic Cumberland residents.

On 27 July 1918, special constable Dan Campbell tracked down Ginger Goodwin and shot him dead. Campbell claimed that when confronted, Goodwin had raised his rifle, and that he had killed the fugitive in self-defence. That version of events was not contradicted at the coroner's inquest, and a grand jury found insufficient evidence to proceed with a charge of manslaughter against Campbell. But to the labour movement, Ginger Goodwin had been hunted down and murdered. He became a martyr to the workingman's cause. Thousands attended his funeral in Cumberland. In Vancouver, the Trades and Labour Council called for a general strike.

The twenty-four-hour strike began at noon on 2 August. Longshoremen walked off the job. Some members of the metal workers', electricians' and construction workers' unions laid down their tools. Also participating in the protest were the streetcar drivers, and their involvement went a long way to undermining public support.

At the time, Vancouver was full of convalescent soldiers. On the morning of the strike, they followed their usual practice of riding the streetcars from Langara and other military hospitals into the city. When they discovered that they could not return to their quarters, they were furious. Upon learning that the protest was due to the death of a draft dodger, they became enraged. Fights broke out all over town. After a protest meeting at a downtown theatre, at which Goodwin was described as "a despicable coward," citizens and veterans marched on the headquarters of the Labour Council. They burst inside, grappled with the council's secretary, Victor Midgey, forced him to kiss the flag and manhandled him down to the street, where he was enthusiastically beaten. At 10:30 that night, the streetcar drivers returned to work.

By 1918, nerves had worn thin. People were weary of the war and tired of shortages. Women were facing another autumn of sugar rationing, which made it difficult to preserve the summer's fruit. The war seemed to be creeping to a close, but still men continued to die. Surely things could not get any worse.

Then, in October 1918, the "Spanish flu" reached British Columbia. Believed to have been brought home by returning soldiers, the virus struck in an instant. One moment, a person felt fine. Suddenly, his head began to pound and his back to ache; his temperature soared and he began to tremble uncontrollably. Some sufferers experienced profuse nosebleeds and coughed up dark blood. Death was the result of "black pneumonia."

Spanish flu appeared first in Victoria. On 8 October, 50 sufferers were identified, and the schools were closed. Two days later, the count had risen to 105, and public gatherings were banned. By the middle of October, public assemblies had been banned in Duncan, Cumberland, Salmon Arm, Prince Rupert, Courtenay, Fernie, Nanaimo, New Westminster, Rossland, Nelson and Port Alberni. In Vancouver, health authorities put their faith in daily fumigation and disinfecting, one official recommending "the stronger smelling sorts such as creosote and Lysol, as these remind people that the influenza is in their midst." But as the number of victims climbed to over a thousand, Vancouver, too, banned public gatherings.

The call went out for more nurses. Doctors recommended fumigating homes with a formaldehyde lamp. Pharmacies sold out of disinfectants; groceries ran out of cinnamon and garlic. On their ranch near Westwold, Alex Bulman's mother did her best to protect her family: "She fed us raw onions and fumigated the house regularly with various powerful-smelling things. The one she used most was sulphur, which she placed in tin pans on top of the woodstove."

A quarantine was placed on the Queen Charlotte Islands to protect the spruce production considered essential to the war effort. Powell River escaped infection by quarantining the rest of the province and having a doctor examine every passenger aboard the Union Steamships who wished to disembark. But otherwise, the Spanish flu spread throughout the province. At Bella Bella, two hundred people fell ill and thirty-five died. At Anyox, twenty-eight miners died. At Lillooet, Frank Gott found temporary work making coffins. At Prince George, an inexperienced undertaker found himself overwhelmed; Dick Corless had just taken a job with the town's only undertaker when influenza broke out. "People were just dying, something awful," he remembered. His employer promptly retired to Victoria. While Dick and his wife learned on the job, as many as fourteen bodies piled up in the woodshed behind their house.

One of many war posters asking civilians to conserve and do without to support the war effort.

"A few months ago, we were fighting every day and night, and at times we had to dig out our comrades, buried alive, and we had to shoot down Germans, and I will say that I have more respect for fellows in grey than I have for these damned skulkers."
—"Returned Soldier" Devereaux

"I myself now take the kid gloves off. If the cars aren't running tomorrow, I'll board one myself as conductor, and let a soldier run it."
—Mrs. Levy

OF ALL the British Columbians who enlisted in 1916, Frank Gott was certainly the oldest. In fact, he was probably the oldest enlisted man in the Canadian Army. When he joined the 102nd Battalion in Lillooet, he was at least fifty-seven and may well have been five years older.

Gott was a small man. Compact and wiry, he weighed only 135 pounds, but he was incredibly strong. He worked as a guide and packer. According to his friend Archie Phair, "He carried packs his own weight for miles over rugged mountains and really enjoyed such hardships."

Another friend recalled that Gott was so tough, he "could sleep in a snowbank out in the hills." He was also a crack shot. For years, residents of Lillooet talked about the season that he and his brother brought in nineteen grizzlies, including the largest bear anyone had ever seen.

Major James Skitt Matthews developed a deep admiration for the "full blood Indian" under his command. When the 102nd was sent to Ypres, Matthews's company spent its first day in the trenches under "merciless" shelling.

"Gott sat erect, rifle between his legs, still as a monument and 'took it,'" Matthews recalled. "A splendid example of coolheadedness."

"How do you like this, Gott?" Matthews enquired.

"Fine, sir."

"Better than Lillooet, Gott?"

"Oh, yes. If I'd known it was like this I'd have come sooner."

"What an awful old bluffer," Matthews smiled as he walked away.

Sometime later, after the battle of Regina Trench, the army came to grips with Gott's age. During one inspection, a senior officer found his eyes wandering to Gott's white hair. "How old are you?" he demanded.

"Military age, sir," Gott sang out.

"Not your military age. Your real age."

"Sixty-three, sir," Gott admitted. And he was sent home to Lillooet with a smouldering case of tuberculosis and a khaki uni-

form of which he was enormously proud.

For a time, he went back to packing and guiding. But by 1929, he had become feeble, and he was broke. He was hunting only for food when he fell foul of game warden Albert Farey. Finding him with a deer shot out of season, Farey said, "Consider yourself under arrest, old boy," and he confiscated all the meat

Gott had put away for winter.

Three years later, Gott and two young friends were camped above Bridge River, when Farey rode up to their campfire and spotted the remains of a fresh deer. Gott later claimed, "I was tired and sick and hungry for fresh meat. I lay down in camp exhausted, for a sleep. When I woke up, I found fresh meat in the camp. My partner killed a doe. We had a feed. But I was sick. I was dying."

The game warden bent over the deer. "Where's your tag?" he growled. And Frank Gott raised his rifle and pumped two bullets into Albert Farey's back. He handed his gun to one friend, gave his horse to the other. "I'm done for," he said, and walked away.

A posse was organized to bring Gott in. He was spotted by two game wardens several days later on a sandy bank above the Bridge River. Called upon to surrender, Gott replied, "I'm a soldier. I never surrender," and he whirled away. Four shots were fired—warning shots, the wardens claimed. Gott fell. He was taken to the hospital at Lytton, where he died a few hours later.

News of the affair whizzed up and down the Fraser. A mass meeting at Lillooet demanded that the game wardens be charged with manslaughter. The inquest into Gott's death found that the bullet wound was superficial. He had died of tuberculosis and "privation."

But the residents of Lillooet were having none of it. "They shot eighteen bullets into Frank Gott," they were still telling each other forty years later.

Frank Gott's commanding officer described him as a "full blood Indian." Others believed Gott's father was a Frenchman drawn to British Columbia by the gold rush.

As newspapers filled with the obituaries of flu victims, the grim toll from the war continued. On 21 October 1918, the *Victoria Times* told readers that two Victoria brothers, Frank and Bob Miller, had been killed in France within three days of each other; that Major Roderick Bell-Irving had been blown apart by a shell; and that Lieutenant Bell, Private Carter and Private Day, all local men, had succumbed to their wounds.

But, finally, the war creaked to its close. At one minute past midnight on the morning of 11 November 1918, the *Vancouver Sun* received the news of the armistice. Within minutes, the city came alive with the sounds of church bells and factory whistles. Eight hours later, when the CPR telegraph office in Kelowna opened, the mayor climbed to the roof of the *Kelowna Courier* office and waved a Union Jack to the cheers of the crowd that had gathered below. As church bells rang, the mayor of Vernon declared a public holiday.

British Columbia, with the highest per capita enlistment of any Canadian province, paid a high price for its devotion to the Empire. Of the 55,750 volunteers who served with the Canadian Expeditionary Force, 6,255 were killed and 13,607 wounded.

Prince Rupert was dealt a severe blow by the war. The Grand Trunk Pacific Railway had had great plans for its terminal city, which was 500 miles closer to ports across the Pacific, to supercede Vancouver as the west coast's major port. Francis Rattenbury, architect of the provincial parliament buildings, had been asked to design an elegant and up-to-date transportation complex: a deluxe railway station, a marine terminal for the line of steamers that would compete with the CPR's Empresses and, on a slight rise above the docks and the station, the most imposing railway hotel in the west. But the GTP was bankrupted by the war, and work on Rattenbury's buildings was halted almost before it began. The Canadian National Railway, which took over the GTP line, concentrated its activities on Vancouver, and Prince Rupert's grand dreams came to nothing.

Walhachin, a "little England," a gentleman's utopia on the benchland above the Thompson River, did not recover from the war. Of the 107 Walhachin men of military age, 97 had volunteered—the highest enlistment rate of any town in the British Empire. The Walhachin men who returned from the war found a devastated settlement. Because it would have been far too expensive to raise water from the river to irrigate the benchlands, a long flume had been built to carry water from springs and lakes in the highlands. But when torrential rains washed out the irrigation flume, there had been too little manpower available to make repairs. The orchards withered and died. And Walhachin became a lost dream and a symbol of sacrifice.

"In 1918, when the flu started, we were living down in the Cache [Prince George] . . . All the families just about died right out. I can remember one man and one child being left in one family. People were just dying like flies in those days. We were very fortunate. Not one of us in our home got the flu, and Mother was handling these people all the time."
—Susan Dornbierer

"Town shut tight—schools, theatres, churches, meetings all prohibited."
—Isabella Rogers

"Then the 'flu came . . . It was when the soldier boys were coming home. My grandmother was old then, old and weak, I guess. It took her, yes . . . That 'flu finished her. I was sick with the 'flu. I couldn't get up and help nobody! I couldn't help granny. I raised up in my bed after they told me and I looked out the window. I saw my granny's coffin . . . They were hauling her down to the graveyard to bury her.
—Secwepemc elder Augusta Tappage

FIVE COMMANDMENTS OF INFLUENZA PREVENTION

1. An abundance of fresh air in sleeping apartments, windows open.
2. Living rooms should not be overheated.
3. Bowels should be free, at least one movement a day; for those constipated a teaspoonful of phosphate of soda should be taken each morning in two or three glasses of water.
4. A cold shower bath immediately upon rising I consider the most valuable method of increasing resistance known; for those unaccustomed to this a luke warm sponge bath, gradually using colder water each day until in the course of a week cold water can be used; avoid hot baths as you would rattlesnakes.
5. Drink from six to sixteen glasses of cold water each day. Keep cheerful and fear not. Job said, "Verily the thing I feared hath come upon me."

—Dr. Ernest A. Hall

"Rum-runners, gunmen, thugs,
        and all the parasites which thrive in the miasma
of the underworld of the Pacific Coast
            are fostered by the policy now in force."
                            —*Vancouver World*

CHAPTER 14

RUM-RUNNING *and* HOMESTEADING

BRITISH COLUMBIA'S ECONOMY slumped as industries geared down from full-speed-ahead war production. Returned soldiers pushed unemployment above 20 per cent. In Vancouver, several thousand out-of-work men kept busy building the Stanley Park seawall. "Things were flatter than flat. Nobody had a dollar," a Victoria resident mourned. "Everything was different after the war."

Prohibition only added to the gloom. In the 1916 election (the same election that extended the franchise to women), 36,490 voters had

answered yes to the question: "Are you in favour of bringing the B.C. Prohibition Act into force?" Among the 27,217 opposed were 80 per cent of the men serving overseas (who had also registered their displeasure at giving votes to women).

On 1 October 1917, Prohibition became law. Private whisky sellers were put out of business. Saloons managed to survive by serving a weak brew—watery beer with less than 1.5 per cent

Throughout British Columbia, barrooms, like this one in the Exchange Hotel in Sandon, were forced to close after the Prohibition Act became law.

alcohol, known disparagingly as "ferret's piss" or "beaver piss." Whisky, wine and regular beer were banned, the single exception being alcohol prescribed by a doctor for medicinal purposes, to be consumed only within the confines of private homes. In 1919, doctors found reason to write 315,177 prescriptions, and although they suggested that the lingering flu epidemic was responsible for the demand, it was uncanny how many people required "medicinal whisky" at Christmas.

Charged with enforcing the act, policemen faced innumerable problems, not the least of which involved definitions. A provincial policeman whose duties included patrolling floating logging and fishing camps wired his superintendent from Swanson Bay: "Does two room shack on a float occupied and owned by four men constitute a private dwelling house?" The superintendent wired back: "Shack on float is a boat or conveyance. It is not a dwelling house under the prohibition act."

An equally vexing problem was what to do with confiscated liquor. When the constable at Princeton took possession of five 50-gallon kegs of "very poor grade" rye whisky, he decided to store them in a jail cell, a choice that delighted the prisoners. "During the night they contrived to reach into the cell where the liquor is stored and, by aid of a screw, tapped one of the kegs and were all dead to the world this morning," the constable reported. "The sooner we get rid of the infernal stuff the better I will be pleased."

Few people were happy with Prohibition. Returned soldiers were quick to point out that a "dry" province was not on the list of things for which they had been fighting. Of one mind with the veterans was Bella Rogers, the grande dame of Vancouver society, whose home became a haven of hospitality.

"Yacht club smoker at the Vancouver club," she informed her diary in February 1918. "Several members came here afterwards to counteract the grape juice."

On 15 July 1920, a second referendum was held. A majority of voters, including women who were voting for the first time, opted for moderation. Public drinking continued to be banned, but alcohol could be purchased for private consumption from government-run liquor stores. Customers were required to visit their local government vendor to apply for a liquor-purchase permit. Unfortunately for consumers, there were only seventeen liquor stores in the entire province, and those that did exist put patrons through a time-consuming process that often led to lines a quarter mile long.

But at least liquor was available in British Columbia. And that was more than could be said of Washington, Oregon and California. The United States had embarked on a "noble experiment" of its own. In January 1920, beverages with an alcohol content above 1.5 per cent were banned.

More than a few British Columbia fortunes were enriched by organized rum-running. Distilleries and distributors in Vancouver and Victoria formed a rum-running co-operative known discreetly as Consolidated Exporters. Ocean-going schooners were equipped as floating warehouses. Lying off the coast of Washington, Oregon and California, carefully positioned outside the 3-mile limit, these "mother ships" serviced the fleets of small boats that darted out from shore. A bottle of Scotch that cost $1.40 in British Columbia brought $4 off the coast of California. With most mother ships capable of carrying up to thirty thousand cases, rum-running was an immensely profitable business.

R. P. Rithet & Co. described itself as "Wholesale Merchants, Shipping and Insurance Agents." Most Victorians knew that it was also the busiest bootlegger on Wharf Street, the city's "Rum Row."

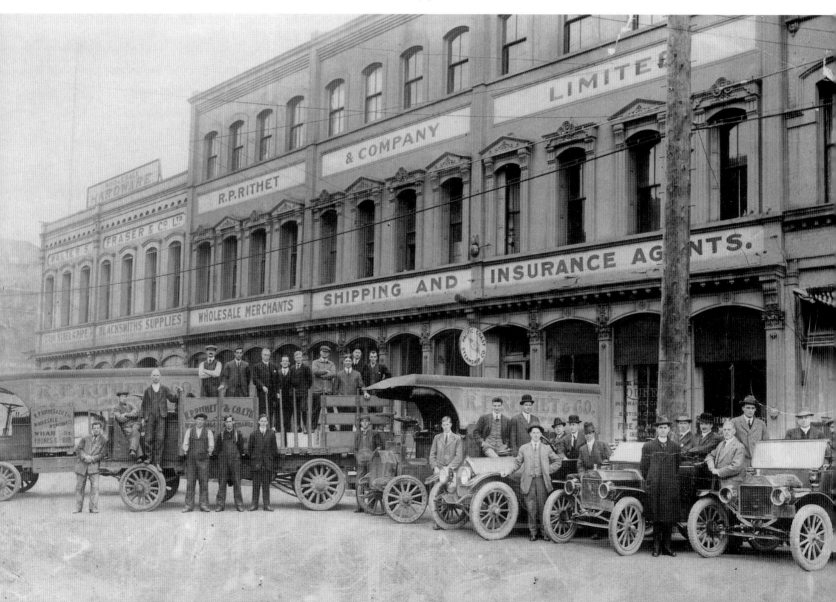

To supply customers around Puget Sound, Consolidated Exporters hired fishboats to chug innocently out of Victoria harbour, loaded to the waterline with cases of whisky, officially consigned to some town up the British Columbia coast but actually destined for an out-of-the-way rendezvous with American rum-runners. Billy Gilmour, who hauled for Rithet's, chose to cache his liquor at the former leper colony on D'Arcy Island. "Billy didn't believe in being half-safe," a provincial policeman said.

Baby Bottleman, a not very subtly named Seattle rum-runner, was a frequent visitor to Cadboro Bay near Victoria where, it was said, she gassed up at the Royal Victoria Yacht Club's dock.

The most popular meeting place was Discovery Island, the Canadian island closest to the international boundary and Puget Sound. And that proved a boon to Discovery's lighthouse keeper, Mary Ann Croft. Mary Ann had had a hard life. In 1885, at the age of twenty, she had married a man whom others found "worthless in every sense of the word." When her husband was sent to the insane asylum at New Westminster, she moved with her two small children to Discovery Island, where her father, Richard Brinn, was the lighthouse keeper. When Brinn died in 1901, Mary Ann wrote to the government asking for his job: "I am entirely depending on the earnings of this station for a living for myself and family." In 1902, she became the first female lightkeeper in Canada. On inquiring about a pension in 1919, Mary Ann was informed that there would be none. She was in the right place when the rum-runners began to call at Discovery Island. According to provincial policeman Cecil Clark, she feathered her retirement nest by relaying signals between American and Canadian boats. "We called her 'Queen of the Rum-runners,'" he grinned.

Bootlegging was not confined to the coast. Fernie, tucked into British Columbia's southeast corner, less than 100 miles north of Montana, became home to the Liquor Export House. Whisky and rum reached Fernie in huge oak barrels. At the Export House, their contents were doctored before being poured into bottles, labelled and wrapped into twelve-bottle sacks. The Export House ran a fleet of a dozen trucks, Oldsmobiles and Cadillacs equipped with special high-speed engines lovingly cared for by a former airplane mechanic. After a truck was loaded with fifty-four sacks, the driver, accompanied by a "shotgun guard," crept out of the warehouse and headed south.

While rum-running was lining more than a few pockets, prosperity was given an additional nudge by a variety of public works, some postponed by the war, others designed to meet the needs of returning soldiers and changing times. In 1921, the federal government began building the long-promised, war-postponed dry dock. Located at Skinner's Cove in Esquimalt, it was the largest dry dock in Canada and the second-largest in the world. Flooded, it held 43 million gallons of water, enough to float the largest ships.

"The drivers were all young men and the shotgun guards were old and tough. The trucks headed south to the border over the most hazardous of roads, but the drivers knew the routes, and very seldom wrecked a truck or broke a bottle. The only thing they had to worry about was hitting the ditch or getting highjacked by rival United States bootleggers."
—Sidney Hutcheson

Before the war, work had begun in Vancouver on a new campus for the University of British Columbia. By 1922, only the skeleton of the science building stood at the Point Grey site, while 1,176 students were crammed into a scattering of shingled buildings on the Fairview slope. In response to a student protest, commemorated as the "Great Trek," the

government voted $1.5 million for a building program, and in 1926 the university moved to its new campus.

To provide arable land for returning veterans, the British Columbia government launched itself into land reclamation schemes. In the lower Fraser Valley, Sumas Lake was drained, revealing 8,000 acres of some of the most

Masajiro Miyazaki, University of British Columbia Class of 1925, recalled the Great Trek: "We marched through downtown, carrying placards with such signs as 'Point Grey or Bust' and singing the campaign song 'We are through with tents and hovels, We are through with shingle stain,' and made a trek to the Point Grey university site. We all got on the building and had our picture taken."

"I chose a 12-acre lot close to the canal and about 3/4 of a mile north of Osoyoos. We used coal oil lamps, the old sad irons and for fuel the wood from the mountains. During the summer we used water from the canal for domestic purposes. Many a time there would be a dead animal in it which the Ditch Rider would have to remove."
—Adam Cumine

fertile land on earth. In the south Okanagan, the government purchased several thousand acres of rangeland and transformed the semi-desert into fertile fields by damming the Okanagan River and then redirecting the water through flumes, aqueducts and a 20-mile-long irrigation ditch. The towns of Osoyoos and Oliver flourished as returned soldiers settled into the valley. Near Osoyoos, Adam Cumine scraped the sagebrush off his land and planted cantaloupes: "Much to my surprise they came up beautifully."

Both the Grand Trunk Pacific and the Canadian Northern Railways were bankrupted by the war. In 1919, they became the property of the federal government and were combined as the Canadian National Railway (CNR). For the CNR, it became important to attract settlers along the GTP's line through central British Columbia. Cheap fares, combined with the heavily advertised settlement schemes, encouraged a new wave of immigrants. Few had a clear idea of the conditions they would encounter. In 1924, Joseph and Mary Galinis homesteaded at Sinkut Lake, outside Vanderhoof. "Coming from Chicago, we never saw snow like that—seven or eight feet that winter."

An apple box label.

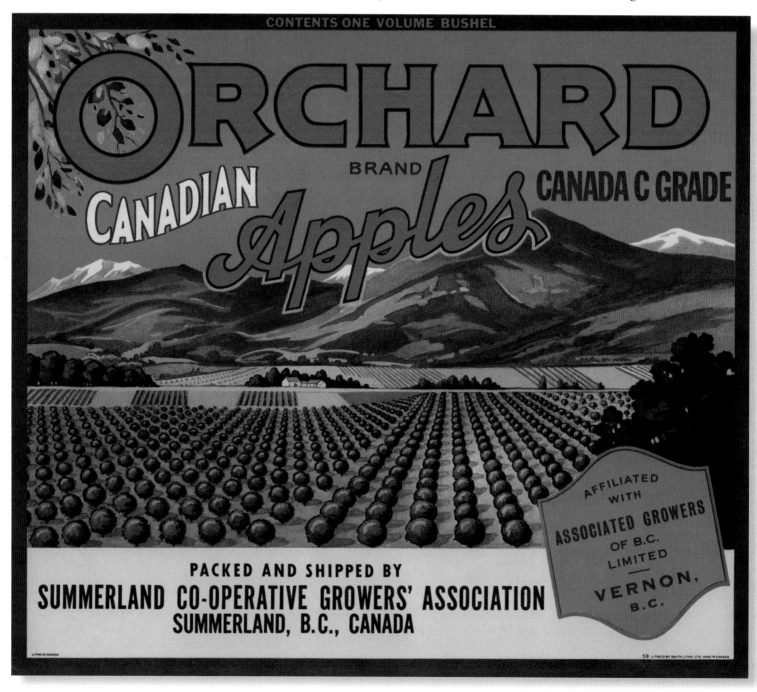

KARIEL LUCILL ADEMS was an unlikely homesteader. She was enjoying the glamorous life of an actress in San Francisco in 1913, when she married a Canadian, Jack Adems, and agreed to go to the Peace River country with him. They took up 160 acres at Finlay Forks "in a huge basin of a rich, fertile valley" near the meeting of the Parsnip, Finlay and Peace Rivers. "There are only about six white men in the country here and every one is a character for a book!" Lucill wrote in August 1913. "I am the only white girl in the country for 300 miles and I am a great curiosity to the Indians."

Soon, she found a female friend, Maggie Fox, the Native wife of the white man who operated a trading post nearby. "I have grown to love her and the days with her and her ... children in the woods, hunting grouse and learning the value of the different barks and herbs."

Lucill infused homesteading with a rosy glow. "I am writing this by the light of a huge log fire," she wrote. "There is an exquisite glory in sitting here under the sky with the trees all about me like sentinels of the night; and the love-man beside me smoking his pipe, and Nell, the dog, dreaming in the warmth of the fire's glow. Jack has just returned after a six weeks' trip up the river for our winter supplies. I stayed here with the Indians and the marvelous autumn."

As the marvellous autumn turned into winter, Lucill knew that she and Jack would be cut off until spring thaw. Because she was pregnant, Jack wanted her to leave, to go to McLeod Lake until the baby was born. But Lucill insisted on staying.

"I am closed away from the world and all its help, with only Maggie Fox to care for me—no doctors, no nurses—no one but Jack ... I felt that my place was here and Maggie Fox was here to help; so I stayed. I have grown to love the simplicity of this life and want my baby to be born naturally as the Indian babies are born."

In November, she fell on the ice. "I was taken terribly ill and nearly died. We are 300 miles from a doctor. Every old prospector for miles around brought me his box of pills and best advice." Soon afterwards, she went into labour. "All the Indians and Maggie Fox were away on their traplines. Jack and I were all alone. He had all the duties of doctor and nurse."

The baby they named Joy lived for only three days. "Now she is sleeping out under a big pine tree beside my cabin door. The ground is frozen so deep that they could not dig a grave for her, so they have laid her tiny box beneath the deep snow until the ground thaws out in the spring."

The Adems made great plans for the future, but then the war came, and they left the Peace River country. When they returned in 1919, they chose another parcel of land, at Gold Bar, 36 miles above Hudson's Hope (20 miles above the present-day Bennett Dam). There, they built "All's Well," a comfortable log cabin where they raised two boys.

Their advancing years forced the Adems to leave the Peace, but they continued to have faith in the future of the area, holding tight to their 1,000 acres along the river. Jack died in 1951. Lucill lived on for twenty years, dying in Victoria at the age of ninety-two, four years after "All's Well" was drowned by Williston Lake.

Top left: Kariel Lucill Adems, c. 1910.

Top right: Lucill and Jack Adems, c. 1921.

Bottom: Jack and Lucill Adems with their two boys near their Peace River home "All's Well" in the 1920s.

Mrs. Gibbins, a widow living in London with four little children, decided to take advantage of the cheap land being offered by a colonization scheme. She selected a few acres on Tabor Mountain near Prince George, with a vague idea of starting a chicken farm. She arrived in Prince George in April 1927. "It was snowing and blowing hard," her son George, who was then ten years old, remembered. The Gibbins were loaded into a horse-drawn wagon. "They just dropped us on this farm—five or six acres and a one-room farmhouse." In the morning, his mother pushed George and his seven-year-old brother out the door. "She said, 'All I know is there is a school about 3 miles that way.' And she pointed the two of us in that direction. And we just trudged off down the road."

Even for settlers who were better prepared, homesteading involved grindingly hard work. In 1924, a Swiss couple, Gustav and Caroline Buchi, chose a few acres north of Prince George. They cleared the land by hand, and then, too poor to afford a horse, attached themselves to a plough. "We pulled it around at 4:00 A.M. so that no one would see us," Caroline remembered.

In the southern part of the province, local economies were boosted by the growing popularity of the automobile. Galvanized into action by the missionary zeal of the Automobile Club of British Columbia, the provincial

The highway through the Fraser Canyon, two feet narrower than the old wagon road, opened in May 1927. (In 1906, two hundred motor vehicles were registered in British Columbia; by 1930, the number had risen to almost a hundred thousand.) Travelling the canyon highway remained an adventure in driving until the 1960s, when the roadway was upgraded to Trans-Canada Highway standards.

government began to improve existing wagon roads. In 1922, work started on a highway through the Fraser Canyon, a replacement for the old wagon road that the CPR had destroyed almost forty years earlier.

Old roads in British Columbia followed the dictates of geography and ran north and south; an east-west transprovincial highway became a priority for both the federal and provincial governments. By 1927, when the canyon highway opened, a road between Golden and Lake Louise had also been completed. Now, only the Selkirks stood in the way of a road running all the way from Vancouver to Calgary. After toying with the idea of following the CPR through Rogers Pass, the governments opted for the route along the Columbia River, and construction of the Big Bend highway got underway in 1929.

By the mid-1920s, British Columbia had shaken off the post-war gloom. The population was growing (the 1921 census counted 524,582 British Columbians; by 1931, the number would rise to 694,263); the economy was rolling, and the province was moving away from its pioneer past.

In 1922, Kootenai people donned their traditional dress to take part in a pageant at Windermere that recalled David Thompson's arrival in the Columbia River valley.

Dakelh chiefs in masks and ceremonial regalia gathered at Fort St. James in 1924 to commemorate the centennial of the visit of Sir George Simpson, governor of the Hudson's Bay Company. Happy enough to see Native peoples take part in historical re-enactments, both the federal and provincial governments were following policies that seriously affected indigenous cultures.

Pack trains and freight wagons pulled by teams of horses and oxen had been replaced by the boxcars of the Pacific Great Eastern Railway (PGE), completed in 1914 from Squamish to Quesnel. Two years later, the last "big outfit"—Tommy Harmon and his eight-horse team hauling 12 tons of drilling equipment—had left Ashcroft for Barkerville. By 1920, the Barnard Express was winding down.

Having lost its role as the supply centre for the north, Ashcroft might have withered on the vine had it not been for its Chinese residents, who developed a thriving new industry. On land leased from local ranchers, they planted potatoes and tomatoes. Ashcroft potatoes became famous for their quality, and Ashcroft tomatoes were even more extraordinary, ripening early on soil capable of producing more than 20 tons an acre. In 1925, the Barnard Express freight barn was converted into a cannery. The goal that first season was twenty thousand cases, each containing a dozen 28-ounce cans. The following year the pack rose to thirty-six thousand cases; in 1927, forty thousand. The cannery became the town's major employer. Women, in particular, found work as "peelers." Paid 5 cents for every 14 quarts of tomatoes they peeled, experienced workers could earn as much as $5 for a ten-hour day.

Unlike Ashcroft, Soda Creek had no luck in making itself over after the freight wagons left the road. There was some hope that the new Cariboo highway would bring tourists, but the road passed the town by. As Soda Creek faded away, Williams Lake came to life. The old wagon road had bypassed Williams Lake; the new highway ran right through it, and in 1920 the PGE arrived. Thanks to the road and the railway, it became the supply centre for ranchers and miners. By 1927, the Williams Lake rodeo, which had begun as a small gathering of local cowboys, had become a three-day celebration including a big dance at the Stampede Hall, featuring "the snappiest orchestra in the Interior."

Alberni Indian Residential School, c. 1930. When residential schools were introduced by the federal government in 1890, attendance was voluntary. In 1920, attendance was made compulsory. Instruction was in English and children were forbidden to speak their native tongues. "We were made to write on the board one hundred times, "I will not speak Indian any more," one student recalled.

"Twenty years ago, there were gay times in the old town, especially at night on steamer days. Hardly a soul in Soda Creek ever went to bed before the early hours of the morning. There was always a good sprinkling of teamsters in town, 'flush' with the receipts of their load of up-country freight. Soda Creek was, perhaps, the best 'poker' town on the road—which is saying a good deal."
—Louis Lebourdais

Williams Lake
B.C. 1924.
Stampede,
Charlie Trieserra steer riding

Charlie Trieserra, shown here steer riding in the 1924 Williams Lake Stampede, was descended from one of the Mexican packers who had come north during the gold rush.

"Overnight, almost it has been recognized that the Panama Canal makes Vancouver the port of Western Canada, the Montreal of the Pacific coast, with a vaster potential trade than Montreal ever knew rapidly developing. The word has gone abroad all over the continent, 'Watch Vancouver, B.C.'"

—*Vancouver Daily World*

During the 1920s, while Vancouver solidified its position as the major city in the province, Victoria became even more dependent on tourists and retirees. The post-war depression had hit Victoria hard. Its shipyards, working day and night during the war, had been scaled back, and hundreds had lost their jobs. Other industries left the island for the terminal city of Vancouver, and Victoria's workers followed them; school enrolments dropped as young families moved to the mainland. But Victoria had been discovered by well-heeled retirees from the prairies. As a "better class" of person replaced working men and women, the city began to age. By the end of the 1920s, Victoria's population would be the oldest in Canada, with 9 per cent of its residents over the age of sixty-five.

The city's tourist industry began to recover when the CPR's Empress liners were put back in service after having been requisitioned by the Admiralty during the war. In 1922, two new ships, the *Empress of Canada* and the *Empress of Australia*, were added to the fleet. To extend the tourist season into the winter, the CPR and Victoria city council brokered a deal: on city-owned land, the company built the Crystal Garden—"the largest, indoor, heated, saltwater swimming pool in the Empire." Encouraged by the results, the CPR embarked on a huge addition to the Empress Hotel, a magnificent new wing that cost $2.5 million and almost doubled the hotel's capacity.

Vancouver, meanwhile, was reaping the benefits of the Panama Canal. Completed in 1914, the canal linked the Atlantic and Pacific Oceans, enabling ships to avoid the long and treacherous route around Cape Horn. Vancouver grew into a major port loading grain from the prairies, apples from the Okanagan, salmon from coastal canneries and lumber from mills around the province. The Second Narrows Bridge, the first road-and-rail

Top: Having proven their worth during the war, airplanes began to play an increasingly important role in transportation in the province. In 1923, piloted by Squadron Leader Earl Godfrey, this Curtiss HS2L single-engine flying boat made the first flight up the British Columbia coast.

Bottom: Pilot Earl McLeod prepares a pigeon to carry the message being written by Howard Hines. There was no radio communication in the early 1920s, so aviators took along pigeons in their planes to send messages back to base in case of a forced landing or other emergency.

This page: During the 1920s, living conditions for men in logging camps improved due to the pressure applied by the British Columbia Loggers Union, formed in 1919. After loggers and sawmill workers joined together as the Lumber Workers Industrial Union, membership grew to fifteen thousand, and it became the largest union in the province.

Facing page: By 1929, Vancouver had become the hub of the province. One third of all British Columbians lived within its boundaries. In this view of Granville Street, the CPR's huge addi-tion to the Hotel Vancouver, completed during the war, appears on the left.

Percy Williams was credited with having put Vancouver on the world map when he won two gold medals, for the 100- and 200-metre sprints, at the 1928 Olympics in Amsterdam.

An injury put an end to the career of "one of the greatest runners in Canadian track and field history."

link across Burrard Inlet, opened to traffic in 1925. The CPR's Hotel Vancouver was doing so well that soon three new luxury hotels were under construction: the Devonshire in 1925, the Georgia the following year, and in 1928, the CNR's $7-million British Columbia. By 1929, Vancouver's population had grown to 228,193—one third of all British Columbians now lived within its boundaries.

Almost everyone was doing well. Property values were increasing. Wages for industrial workers had risen to their highest level, an average of $29.50 per week. And then, in October 1929, the stock market crashed.

*"It's the dreariness of life
that's my chief memory of the Depression,
the aching dullness of nothing to do."*
—Peter Stursberg

CHAPTER 15

DESPERATE TIMES

AT FIRST, the Wall Street debacle of October 1929 was interpreted as a temporary slump. "Recovery From Market Crash May Take A Year," a Vancouver newspaper cautioned. British Columbians responded with business-as-usual optimism. In Vancouver, voters supported bylaws that would raise their taxes to finance the construction of the Burrard Street Bridge and an airport on Sea Island.

But within a year, the province was staggering. Miners were laid off as the demand for coal fell. Smelter workers were forced to accept a cut in pay when the price of lead dropped. The building industry collapsed, throwing Burrard Inlet sawmills into a shambles. In Vancouver, work on the CNR's hotel came to a halt. In 1930, when the centre span of the Second Narrows Bridge was rammed by a log barge, there was no money for repairs. Meanwhile, the world experienced a glut of grain; sales of Canadian wheat plummeted, and the impact was felt all along the Vancouver waterfront. The city filled with unemployed men. By December 1930, breadlines were winding down the street in front of the City Relief Office.

On the eve of the Depression, Vancouver voters supported a bylaw to replace the Lulu Island airport (shown here) with a new facility on Sea Island.

Vancouver's Lions Gate Bridge was built by the Guinness brewery interests to provide access to their luxury sub-division, the British Pacific Properties, on the north shore of Burrard Inlet. In 1927, Vancouver voters had rejected a similar proposal because the approach road would divide Stanley Park in two. The Guinness bridge, which came forward during the worst year of the Depression, was accepted with scarcely a whimper of protest. It was completed in November 1938.

On a June morning in 1931, Colonel R. D. Williams, one of three Vancouver harbour commissioners, was gazing out the window of his office in one of the old Hastings Mill buildings when he saw a man disappear under a pile of rails stacked on the CPR right-of-way. "It was a shocking afternoon; the rain came down in sheets," Williams remembered. He went out to investigate, stooped down to look under the rails and found fourteen men taking shelter. Williams offered them the use of a couple of empty wooden sheds. "We had a stove down at La Pointe Pier, so I got that, and then went round and bought canned milk, tea, sugar and some bread and tobacco."

The hobo "jungle" at Ballantyne Pier grew and grew, from fourteen men in June to over two hundred by August. Unemployed men from across Canada made their way to Vancouver. The city's cost of living was the lowest of any major urban centre in the country, and the climate was certainly the most salubrious. Vancouver became "just a blamed summer resort for all the hoboes in Canada," Reverend Andrew Roddan observed.

Most men reached the city by "riding the rods," catching rides on freight trains. "Coming into Vancouver they'd try and jump off before they got in the yards, and run like heck," an east side resident recalled. If they waited until the train slowed, they faced arrest by the "bulls." If they put a foot on the ground too soon, they risked being dragged under the wheels. "That's when a lot of them got killed. They used to call it the 'bull horrors.'"

Fears grew that people who were homeless and unemployed would be swayed by communist rhetoric. Might they become a "Red army"? Could Vancouver soon have a revolution on its hands? In June 1931, police broke up a demonstration of five thousand unemployed. In August, a similar

"I came into Coquitlam on a freight and I started to walk along the street there when a policeman drove up. He asked me where I was going and I told him I had come off a freight. So he told me to keep on and I'd find the jungles."
—16-year-old Nova Scotian

"I visited the 'Jungle' below Georgia viaduct. There are about 250 men there. Grounds are filthy and covered with decaying garbage, with open toilets. Flies swarm over everything and on all open food. I consider that, with the rainy season approaching, we are in grave danger of an epidemic of typhoid or other diseases."
—Dr. McDonald

For most of the 1930s, the Canadian National Railway's hotel in Vancouver, the British Columbia, remained an empty shell. Completed in 1939, it was renamed the Hotel Vancouver and was operated jointly by the CNR and the CPR.

On 17 April 1935, Nelson's Opera House was destroyed by fire. A stately little city of brick and stone, including a courthouse designed by the architect of British Columbia's parliament buildings, Nelson fared better than other Kootenay towns during the Depression thanks to its role as the administrative centre for the region.

demonstration turned into a riot. Five policemen were injured and eight demonstrators were arrested: seven men (a Swiss, a Dane, a Yugoslav, a Swede, two Austrians, a Canadian) and one fourteen-year-old girl. The provincial government promised to take action to "curb 'Red' leaders."

The shapers of the Canadian constitution had not foreseen a nationwide depression. Social services were regarded as being under local, rather than national, purview, and therefore responsibility for relief fell to the provinces. By the summer of 1931, British Columbia was home to forty-two thousand unemployed, of whom seventy-five hundred were from outside the province. The federal government was prepared to assist, but just what form that assistance would take was subject to negotiation.

Trusting that federal money would be forthcoming, the province took action. Relief camps, in which jobless men would be put to work on roads, were established immediately. By September 1931, three thousand men had been shuffled off to the camps, and Vancouver was making plans to look after its own. City council voted to put twenty-five hundred married men to work improving Kitsilano Beach and Lost Lagoon, and developing Fraserview Golf Course; the costs were to be financed, in part, by cutting the work week of regular city employees.

Many jobless men avoided relief camps by riding the rods to follow the harvest, picking up odd jobs here and there. Most towns along the tracks encouraged them to keep moving by supplying one meal and no more. Kamloops was different. A divisional point for both major railways, the town became a focus for transients. Whereas other towns handed out a few hundred meals a day, Kamloops's soup kitchen provided for as many as two thousand. By the summer of 1931, a thriving jungle of tents and cardboard

RAIN BRINGING UNEMPLOYMENT CONDITIONS TO A CRISIS. MORE THAN 15,000 REGISTERED IN THE CITY. TWENTY-FIVE HUNDRED RELIEF FAMILIES NOW REQUIRING CLOTHING AND RENT. TWO THOUSAND HOMELESS SINGLE MEN INCREASING BY SEVENTY FLOATERS DAILY. ONE THOUSAND MEN IN JUNGLES. ONE MAN FOUND DEAD THIS MORNING AND ANOTHER NEW ARRIVAL SENT TO HOSPITAL WITH POSSIBLE TYPHOID. MEDICAL OFFICES STATES EPIDEMIC POSSIBLE. INERTNESS OF DOMINION GOVERNMENT IN FAILING TO CONTROL TRANSIENTS AND DELAYING DECISION [on relief policy] HAS PARALYZED MUNICIPALITIES. IMMEDIATE ACTION IMPERATIVE.

—Vancouver alderman Atherton, telegram to federal labour minister

There are those among us to whom camp life is too evidently a new experience and these are no doubt suffering a great deal more than many of us from blistered hands, sore wrists, and aching muscles.
—Jerry, "Late of the Jungles"

Many residents of hobo jungles were young men— some no more than boys. "I know boys that were given a $20 bill by their fathers and told to hit the road," George Gibbins of Prince George remembered. "There was just no work and their families couldn't afford to keep them and that was it."

"My family were very unhappy with my having a job on the [Victoria] Times. They were extremely unhappy. They didn't feel that either my sister or I should be working in the first place. My father got poison pen letters from people saying, 'What are bankers' daughters doing taking the bread out of the mouths of starving people?'"
—Elizabeth Ruggles Macdonnell

"We had to wait till one of two things happened— the boy got a job or the girl got pregnant. You hoped that the first came first: the boy got the job."
—George Gibbins

"Nearly all the children's clothes I made from flour bags, dyed and all our pillow slips were from flour bags too, as well as my tea towels and aprons."
—Caroline Buchi

shacks, each with a neat pile of firewood beside it, had been established near the CNR tracks across the river from the town.

As word spread that the people of Kamloops and their police chief, Charles Anderson, were tolerant and understanding, the jungle became home to more than a thousand residents. One of the largest hobo encampments in the country, it was also one of the best organized. When the Secwepemc people complained that their trees were being cut for firewood, the transients promised to collect only deadwood. The town was easily accessible across the CNR railway bridge, but there was very little thievery. "Special instructions were given out that no store in Kamloops was to be weeded and none were, as far as I know," Sydney Hutcheson recalled.

Direct assistance was available to heads of households ($17.50 a month for a family of four). Single men were expected to go to the relief camps. Married women were expected to depend on their husbands; single women were to rely on their families or take jobs as domestic servants. No woman should take a job that could be filled by a deserving man; instead, she should find a man to look after her. But just as women were being advised to take refuge in marriage, weddings were being postponed. "Vancouver's wedding bells are as silent as those of other cities and the issuer of marriage licences is finding business as slack as purveyors of other commodities," a newspaper reported.

A few women took to riding the rods. One July day in 1932, workers on the Vancouver waterfront were "surprised and interested" to see two young women climb down from a freight car that had just arrived from the east. "Dusty and grimy, they still retained something of their flapperish chic and explained laughingly that they had come from Winnipeg. And a very nice trip, too, thank you."

Some women turned up in the hobo jungles. Sydney Hutcheson met a few in the Kamloops encampment. "Some of the women were really rough," he remembered. "One woman lived in a tent with 'Overland Shorty' and his 'boy friend.' Every once in a while she would make the rounds of all the groups of men and try to buy stamps . . . She wrote a letter to six different boy friends and told each one that she was pregnant and needed help, or else."

The birth rate fell. Mothers, already sending their children to school with lard sandwiches, shuddered at the thought of having more mouths to feed. One Vancouver woman admitted to visiting an abortionist on the "seedy side" of town on four occasions. "There was simply no way we could afford to have a baby," she remembered.

For other British Columbians, the Depression was barely noticeable. Old people, who since 1927 had been receiving a means-based government pension, found that, as prices fell, their living conditions improved. And people with regular jobs had seldom done better. Like many others, Bruce Hutchison, who covered provincial politics for the *Vancouver Province*, was forced to take a cut in pay—in his case from $55 to $50 a week. "Our standard of living actually rose because prices fell faster than wages," he said. "Times were hard, but not for us. We always had a maid in the house, the best of food in our stomachs, two second-hand cars in the garage."

Hutchison's $50 a week looked very good compared to the wages of junior reporters. When Peter Stursberg joined the *Victoria Times* in 1934, he was paid only $15 a week, but still he lived well. Squiring girlfriends to Saturday night dances at the Empress Hotel fitted easily into his budget. "For two dollars a couple, a three-course dinner was served with the full silver service . . . at tables arranged cabaret style around the magnificent ballroom with its great domed ceiling and shimmering chandeliers."

Generally, people living outside the urban centres were better able to cope with the hard times. Homesteaders were accustomed to being self-reliant, and in small towns, people helped each other. There were always odd jobs to be done—a few hours' work in exchange for a chicken or a bag of potatoes. Trading and bartering replaced currency; doctors and lawyers and storekeepers accepted all manner of things as payment.

Union towns had the advantage of built-in solidarity. In Fernie, most of the unemployed were former members of the United Mine Workers union, and they pulled together with a will. To bolster spirits and line a few pockets, a monthly whist drive was held at the Union Hall. "If you were unemployed, you and your wife brought something to eat and paid 5 cents at the door. If you were working, you paid 10 cents and a few sandwiches to get in," a union man recalled. "Prizes for whist winners were $5 for first, $3 for second and $2 for third. After the games, eats were served and there was always plenty. A group of unemployed played for the dance."

Some unemployed men deserted the cities and jungles to wander the countryside to look for work. In the spring of 1933, Charlie Hartsell and Fred Rankin were operating an illegal trapline on Slim Lake in the McGregor country east of Prince George. Both felt that they were "getting on in years," so when they encountered a drifter, they were happy to hire him. They taught him how to set traps and then sent him off to T-Hell-N-Gone (Shady) Lake with five days' supply of food. Two days after he set off, it began to snow heavily. When he had not returned after nine days, the two trappers went to look for him. They found him, frozen to death, only half a mile from their cabin. He had told them that he was a Pole, thirty-five years old, and that his name was Onufry Lewoniak. Other than that, they knew nothing about him. They buried him beside the lake and wondered if anyone would miss him.

Other men took advantage of Unemployed Free Placer Licences and the Cariboo experienced a bit of a boom. "It is estimated that about 1000 men have left for the goldfields this spring," the *Province* noted in May 1932.

According to some, the men who suffered the most were those in relief camps, many of them no worse than forestry or mining camps. Men complained about the work, groaned about the food and grumbled about bunkhouse living. But in forestry and mining camps, they had been relatively well paid. In relief camps, they worked for 20 cents a day.

Struggling farmers had little sympathy with the complaints coming from the relief camps. A man near Enderby, who had spent the morning feeding his stock, cleaning the stable, milking eight cows, cutting wood for the house and driving into town to trade his eggs for sugar, shook his head as he watched another truck bump along his road, carrying coal to the relief camp on Mara Lake. "Those men, being fed by the government, could get out into the woods at their camp door and in half a day cut enough wood to keep the camp warm all winter," he exclaimed. "If they don't have the guts to get out and cut wood and pack it in to keep themselves warm, they ought to be allowed to freeze."

Jobless men from the hobo jungle under the Georgia Viaduct in Vancouver. Photographer W. J. Moore described them as "Men from everywhere, all sorts of ages, education, characters, attainments, and which a common want and some misery had banded together."

"The Durban's stopping place [near Lillooet] was full of prospectors coming and going in a steady stream, men seeking for gold . . . planning their lives when they would find the gold, and building airy castles for themselves . . . Some, not having the courage to face those at home who they bragged to, end it with a bullet. Others will come next year and the next. Others will stake unworthy claims and bamboozle some poor fool to buy them."
—Emily Carr

"SUNDAY IN A RELIEF CAMP—I wonder if I really can give you a picture of one. We eat three sickly meals— do a little clothes washing—play poker—sit around in our bunks and gossip. Clothes hanging all over—wood strewn on the floor—nothing to do and no place to do it . . . floors used as spittoons—eat one meal and then you come back and lie down and wait for the next call . . . we are truly a lost legion of youth—rotting away."
—anonymous young man

BRITISH COLUMBIANS took to moving pictures with almost unseemly enthusiasm. In 1897, when the first "flickers" were screened at the Trilby Music Hall in Victoria, they proved so popular that the Delmonico Theatre, known for the "hottest burlesque shows in town," rushed to add films to its repertoire. Moving pictures reached Hazelton in 1910, when a travelling showman arrived in town with a projector and screen; he set up an impromptu theatre in an unused root cellar, where the audience sat on barrels and boxes or sprawled on the dirt floor.

By 1913, eight theatres were screening films in Vancouver, and the government was taking notice. The legislature passed an Act to Regulate Theatres and Kinematographs, which created the office of Censor of Moving Pictures and remained in effect, virtually unchanged, until 1970.

The censor was given the power to ban any film that portrayed lewdness, unfaithfulness or indecency, or that glorified crime or could be considered obscene. Without his approval, no film could be screened in British Columbia. Sometimes the censor simply threw up his hands. He deemed *Hot Pepper*, a little number submitted by Fox in 1933, to be "not suitable for British Columbia" on the grounds that it was "suggestive and offensive throughout." Sometimes he demanded changes. In 1937, he refused to accept Greta Garbo's *Camille* unless the scene showing "Garbo and Taylor in loving embrace" was shortened by cutting almost 16 feet of film. As for *My Little Chickadee*, starring

Top: The Dreamland in Vernon instructed patrons on proper conduct: "It is requested that ladies remove their hats when visiting this place of entertainment, and that men refrain from spitting on the floor."

Bottom: Hollywood came to Victoria in December 1933, when *The Crimson Paradise* premiered at the Capitol Theatre.

W. C. Fields, he demanded the elimination of the "suggestive dialogue in bedroom scenes with Fields and goat."

Not knowing what they were missing, British Columbians continued to be avid filmgoers. When the Rex, the first permanent theatre in the Cariboo, opened in 1920 in Quesnel, it proved to be particularly successful with old prospectors, like eighty-five-year-old Paddy Hodnutt from Barkerville, who jumped up and down in excitement while exclaiming loudly over the antics of "them lassies."

Filmmaking was perceived as a glamorous business, and more than a few British Columbians were eager to get in on the act. In 1917, Dominion Films was formed in Victoria and announced that it would purchase a block of land on the outskirts of the city and establish a studio to be known as Cinema City or Maple Leaf City. Five years later, Canadian Historic Features was formed in Vancouver with the intention of producing "moving pictures portraying the historical life of the Dominion of Canada." Both companies sank without a trace. Local investors kept their chequebooks closed, and in any

case, the industry was falling under the control of American distributors, who had no interest in handling either locally made or British films. (By 1929, two American companies controlled 95 per cent of film distribution in Canada.)

In 1927, the British government, alarmed by increasing American control of the film industry, instituted a quota system: within a few years, one out of every five films screened in Britain must be a product of that nation or its Empire. This gave hope to would-be producers in British Columbia and prompted a flurry of activity. The most successful promoter was Kenneth Bishop, who formed Commonwealth Productions in Victoria in 1932. What experience he had, Bishop had gained in Hollywood; but because he had been born in England, he could qualify for the quota as a British producer. His money problems were solved by Kathleen Dunsmuir. The granddaughter of coal baron Robert Dunsmuir, she had access to one of the largest fortunes generated in British Columbia, and she was movie-mad, determined to be a star.

Commonwealth's first feature, *The Crimson Paradise*, with Kathleen Dunsmuir appearing in a supporting role, premiered in Victoria in 1933. Bishop's next production, *Secrets of Chinatown*, a "lurid tale of a secret Oriental society," was released in 1934.

Neither film was a success. Commonwealth Productions declared bankruptcy, Kathleen Dunsmuir lost her $50,000 investment, and Kenneth Bishop scampered back to Hollywood. There, he closed a deal with Columbia Pictures to produce a number of "quota quickies," B-grade films financed by Columbia but with sufficient British contribution to allow them to meet the quota requirements. Bishop returned to Victoria, formed Central Films and rolled up his sleeves. By the end of 1937, Central Films had churned out a dozen features with titles such as *Secret Patrol*, *Manhattan Shakedown* (in which Victoria's Bastion Square masqueraded as New York), *Death Goes North*, *Tugboat Princess* (starring Valerie Hobson), *What Price Vengeance*, *Stampede*, *Women Against the World* and *Convicted* (starring nineteen-year-old Rita Hayworth).

While Central Films was making "quota quickies" in Victoria, Revelstoke became the scene of a more ambitious project. Produced by Gaumont British Pictures Association, *Silent Barriers* (also known as *The Great Barrier* and *The Great Divide*) was a fictional story centred on the building of the Canadian Pacific Railway, starring Richard Arlen and Lilli Palmer and featuring Engine 374, the locomotive that had pulled the first train to the Pacific.

By 1938, Kenneth Bishop was in trouble. The British had introduced a quality clause to their quota system. Most of his films were scarcely an hour long, and all were unremittingly second-rate. Central Films went out of business, locally based production ceased, and the studio at the Willows Fairground gathered dust. Bishop's productions had little artistic merit, but they provided jobs for many Victorians, and they added a frisson of Hollywood excitement to the dull Depression years.

Filming of the movie *Silent Barriers*, a fictionalized account of the building of the Canadian Pacific Railway, on location at Revelstoke.

In 1933, the federal government assumed responsibility for relief camps and gave the job of managing them to the Department of National Defence. Although Ottawa insisted that the decision had been simply an administrative one, the men in the camps now felt that they were under military control and "prisoners of the class war."

The following year, with a federal election looming, the government of Prime Minister R. B. Bennett took the vote away from camp workers. To register to vote, a citizen needed a "domicile," and relief camps would not be classed as domiciles. "The Mailed Fist of Dictator Bennett has descended once again upon the Relief Camp workers!" a newsletter circulated to all the camps roared.

The Relief Camp Workers Union urged men to go on strike and march on Vancouver. On 5 April 1935, two thousand men walked away from the camps, and within a week, more than fifteen hundred had congregated in the city. Vancouver's mayor, Gerry McGeer, convinced that the union was a communist front, was determined to maintain control. When he heard that demonstrators marching up and down the aisles of the Hudson's Bay Company store had smashed display cases, he hurried to Victory Square to read the Riot Act.

"We were trying to get some reaction from the city," Red Walsh, an unemployed steelworker, recalled. "Gerry McGeer, the mayor, we drove him up the wall! The question was, how long could we stay in town. There were men leaving individually on freights and going east and we didn't want the organization to fall apart. So, we suggested a trek to Ottawa." The "On-to-Ottawa Trek" was stopped cold when it reached Regina. However, as a result of election promises, the relief camps were abolished and replaced by a different system, in which men worked in railway, forestry and farm camps and were paid $15 a month. The following year, the federal government found it could do away with the work camps.

By 1936, the Depression was lifting: in August, 68,690 jobless were on relief in British Columbia, 11,000 fewer than in August of the preceding year. And there were other signs of better times. In Victoria, filmmakers were busy churning out "quota quickies" for the British market. In Vancouver, a new city hall opened its doors; in New Westminster, construction of the Pattullo Bridge over the Fraser River was getting underway.

Jobless men continued to congregate in Vancouver, however. Their number was boosted by boys who had been classed as "single unemployed" and whose parents could no longer claim them as dependants, even though they were living at home. Members of communist-led organizations, convinced that the economy was picking up only because of the war talk coming out of Europe, were determined to make a stand against an economic system that victimized the jobless. In May 1938, several hundred men marched into and occupied three Vancouver buildings: the Georgia Hotel, the post office and the art gallery. The idea was to focus attention on their grievances by forcing authorities to make mass arrests, but the authorities did not co-operate.

Two days later, the men left the Georgia Hotel, partly because they were paid $600 to do so and partly because the presence of the hotel beer parlour threatened to undermine discipline. The other two buildings they held for thirty days, during which time their leader, Steve Brodie, often suggested that the police need only arrest them and the occupation would end. Early on 18 June, "Bloody Sunday," the police made their move. Tear gas forced the men outside, where the police waited to club them into submission.

"It is now perfectly clear that Vancouver is being victimized by an organized attempt to capitalize, for revolutionary purposes, the conditions of depression that now exist. "
—Vancouver mayor Gerald McGeer

"Young Mike joined us at age 17, when the relief department in Nelson district told him his share of the family relief was now cut off, in order to have the entire $13.50 per month go to his widowed mother and two kid sisters."
—Steve Brodie

At Kamloops, unemployed
men who had walked away
from relief camps to protest
conditions, boarded an
eastbound train to join the
"On-to-Ottawa Trek."

Top: "Bloody Sunday," 19 June 1938. After unemployed men occupied the Vancouver Post Office and the Vancouver Art Gallery for thirty days, the police used tear gas to force them out of the post office and then attacked the men with batons as they stumbled onto the street. The police swore no unnecessary force was used.

Bottom: Following the "Bloody Sunday" evictions, demonstrators rampaged through Vancouver's downtown streets and fifteen thousand people assembled at the Powell Street grounds to demand the resignation of the Liberal premier, Duff Pattullo, who had been elected on the platform "Work and Wages." The premier, who had attempted a variety of programs, including public works projects such as the Pattullo Bridge, blamed his lack of success on Ottawa's reluctance to provide financial assistance.

In 1938, towards the end of the Depression years, the Trail Smoke Eaters reached the pinnacle of amateur hockey in Canada when they won the Allan Cup. The following year, the team won the world championship.

Bottom: In the early years of the Depression, many sawmills and logging camps closed. In mills that remained in operation, wages fell from 40 cents an hour to 25 cents for white workers, and to 10 cents for Chinese, Japanese and East Indians. In 1932, Britain's decision to give preferential treatment to products from Commonwealth nations prompted a recovery in the province's forests.

Top: A painting by Orville Fisher in the socialist realist style of the time, depicting idealized workers against a Vancouver background, c. 1939.

"The reluctance of the majority to demand better treatment amazes me yet," Steve Brodie wrote more than thirty years later. Journalist Bruce Hutchison agreed. "It never occurred to me that we were well off, that a revolution was silently underway on our doorstep," he wrote in 1976. "For a reporter, may God forgive him, the Depression was just another news story."

"Only a few minor riots flared up against a system which had no defence in morals and could not have defended against general violence if the hungry had rebelled. We can be sure of one thing—the hungry would never take another Depression as they took the last one, and no system, whatever its name and methods, could survive it."
—Bruce Hutchison

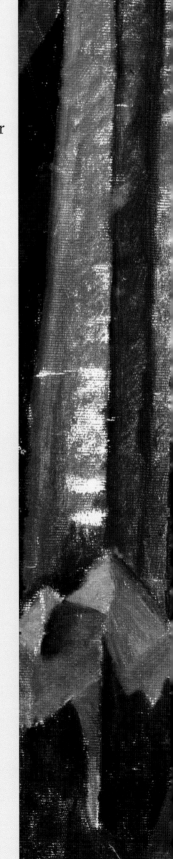

> "We have come to the end of 1940,
> and goodbye to it.
> I fear we are a long way from the worst yet.
> Mercifully we can't see ahead."
> —Emily Carr

CHAPTER 16

PREPARING *for* INVASION

"I noted with shame that Kamloops carried on its regular baseball game with all its noise and disturbance last Sunday [3 September]. Surely that godless thing will be stopped during these trying days."
—Dr. G. A. Wells, Bishop of the Cariboo

"Every war has its tune, a song to make forever sad the hearts of those who have listened. 'Roll Out the Barrel' was the enlistment tune in Victoria, played by the Canadian Scottish on every street corner. It followed us everywhere—into the Canadian Pacific steamship office, standing on the streets looking up to read the news bulletins above our heads, news which made our hearts stand still."
—Agnes Newton Keith

WHEN BRITAIN, and then Canada, declared war on Germany, British Columbians were enjoying the last weekend of summer. Some turned their attention to preparing for the worst. Hundreds of "far-seeing Vancouver housewives" flocked to city stores to lay in a supply of sugar. Others tried to put the looming conflict out of their minds. Members of the Royal Victoria Yacht Club sailed to Cowichan Bay for the annual regatta. "It was all very tense," Ruth Sherman remembered. "All the men were sure that a war was coming. They raced and I suppose they had fun. But all the time, they were waiting for the news, ready to leave for Victoria at a moment's notice."

During the first years of the conflict, British Columbia was considered so far removed from the scenes of battle that it became a "bolt hole," a safe place to sit out the war. The Empress Hotel welcomed new permanent residents, such as the English couple who had retired to the Riviera, escaped from France when war broke out, made their way to Victoria and settled into the hotel "for the duration."

When the war began, Thor Heyerdahl, who later achieved fame with his book *Kon-Tiki*, was in Bella Coola researching his theory that there was a link between the coastal people and the Polynesians. After Norway was invaded and his funds from home were cut off, he took a job in Rossland, where he enjoyed the skiing and entertained the townspeople with lantern shows detailing the year he had spent living with South Pacific islanders. Relaxing in a more luxurious "bolt hole" was the Swedish armament manufacturer Axel Wenner-Gren, who spent much of 1940 sailing along the coast in his steam yacht *Southern Cross*.

The province's status as a haven of safety ended abruptly on 7 December 1941, when Japan attacked the American naval base at Pearl Harbor in the

Untitled painting by Emily Carr, 1942. By 1942, Carr's paintings were earning critical acclaim. Her painting expeditions were disrupted by the war. She was forced to abandon a sketching trip to Mount Douglas near Victoria when the area was overrun by troops on training manoeuvres.

Hawaiian Islands. Suddenly, coastal British Columbia seemed to be on the front line. People believed, quite incorrectly as it turned out, that a Japanese task force was steaming across the Pacific to launch an attack on Vancouver Island. On the night of Pearl Harbor, Bruce Hutchison remembered, "Vancouver and Victoria were blacked out and the pathetic little air force at Patricia Bay prepared to commit suicide against overpowering odds."

Hong Kong fell on Christmas Day; Singapore in February 1942. Vancouver Island braced for attack. Forestry workers were placed on alert for incendiary bombs, carried across the Pacific by balloons to set British Columbia's forests aflame. The Department of Munitions and Supply made plans for the mass evacuation of the civilian population to the mainland. A small army of volunteers inventoried and indexed all commercial motor vehicles and all shipping, including every pleasure boat capable of carrying

This page: Under the direction of Rollie Halls (centre), pleasure boats were organized into Power Boat Squadrons based at Victoria, Sidney, Cowichan, Ladysmith, Nanaimo and Courtenay. Members painted their boats the approved colour (Bapco MSD Dark Grey) and donned Cowichan sweaters, their unofficial uniform.

Facing page: The pride of the Cunard fleet, the *Queen Elizabeth* was launched in 1939. Capable of carrying twelve thousand troops and fast enough to outrun submarines and anything afloat, the enormous liner presented an admirable target during the twelve days she spent motionless at the Esquimalt dry dock.

at least ten people. Civilians were organized into Air Raid Precaution units. Blackout orders were applied to homes and businesses. Car headlights were dimmed. The CPR Princess boats sailed under blackout restrictions.

On 25 February 1942, residents of Esquimalt awoke to an extraordinary sight. The world's largest ocean liner, the *Queen Elizabeth* had arrived at the Esquimalt graving dock for a refit. For twelve days, a thousand workers swarmed over the ship, scraping, painting and adding bunks for twelve thousand troops. Eight decks tall and higher than almost every building in Esquimalt or Victoria, the *Queen Elizabeth* was impossible to miss. That the graving dock was "lit up like a Christmas tree" and that the ship was so tempting a target only added to the nervousness of islanders. The Brown family of Esquimalt made an air raid shelter out of the old, disused septic tank buried in their garden. "Of course, it feels like going into your coffin," Mrs. Brown confessed. "But then I guess you'd be glad to get into a nice safe coffin when those bombs start falling."

In June 1942, as British Columbia's coastal cities braced for invasion, the students at St. Margaret's School in North Vancouver rehearsed for a gas attack.

War jitters were not confined to Victoria and Esquimalt. In Vancouver, Stanley Park was set aside as an evacuation area in case the city was bombed, and ten thousand volunteers registered at the Air Raid Precaution office. A few miles north of Oliver, Hirozo Fujita and his three sons were clearing their land. Neighbouring farmers surveyed the heaps of brush piled here and there and jumped to the conclusion that they were designed to become "flaming beacons" pointing Japanese bombers to the smelter at Trail.

Kamloops, where two railways and the highway met, was thought to be especially vulnerable to Japanese bombers. Calculating it would have forty minutes' warning of an attack by enemy planes, the city staged a full–scale drill in March 1942. Schools and other public buildings were evacuated, full blackout restrictions were put into effect, and citizens pored over publications such as "Incendiary Bombs, and How to Deal with Them" and "Blackout for Your Home."

On 13 June 1942, the *Victoria Colonist* went to press with the alarming news that Japan had captured two Aleutian Islands. Japanese submarines were believed to be lurking along the coast. Members of the Power Boat Squadron patrolled the shoreline, cruising along the Victoria and Esquimalt waterfront, searching for submarines and keeping an eye on the shore for signals from land-based operatives.

On the evening of 20 June 1942, the Japanese forces made their presence felt. Edward Redford, the wireless operator at the Estevan Point lighthouse station, heard an explosion and rushed out the door, thinking that one of his fuel tanks had gone up. Then, he "saw the sub quite clearly about a mile offshore."

Lightkeeper Mike Lally yelled at his wife, "Get the hell out of here! It's a Jap sub and they are shelling the lighthouse!" And as shells whistled past and exploded in the distance, he ran up the stairs to douse the light.

Minoru Hasegawa, commander of the Japanese submarine I-26, recalled his attack on the Estevan Point lighthouse: "It was evening when I shelled the area with about seventeen shots. Because of the dark, our gun-crew had difficulty in making our shots effective . . . There was not a single effective shot that night."

A few hours later, off Cape Flattery, Commander Meiji Tagami of the Japanese submarine *I-25* encountered the *Fort Camosun*, a Victoria-built freighter on her maiden voyage, loaded with zinc, lead and plywood for the British Ministry of War Transport. Just after midnight, a torpedo from the *I-25* smashed into the *Fort Camosun*'s port side. When she refused to sink, the submarine surfaced and strafed the deck. "Two Japanese Subs Off Coast!" a headline in the *Victoria Times* blared. "Jap West Coast Invasion termed 'Quite Possible,'" the *Vancouver News Herald* warned.

Most military experts in Ottawa believed that a full-scale invasion was logistically improbable; the west coast might experience small nuisance raids, but nothing more. Japanese residents of the coast presented little potential danger, either as saboteurs or fifth columnists. "From the Army point of view, I cannot see that they constitute the slightest menace to national security," Lieutenant-General Ken Stuart asserted. In British Columbia, that opinion went unheeded; to many politicians, the present alarm was a "heaven-sent opportunity" to disperse the province's Japanese residents. Of the 23,149 Japanese people in Canada, 22,096 lived in British Columbia, where it was believed that their concentration had enhanced their economic power. Of the province's Japanese population, 13,309 were Canadian-born and 2,903 were naturalized citizens. But their citizenship was regarded as irrelevant. On the day of Pearl Harbor, Ottawa had decreed that all fishboats owned by Japanese be impounded, in spite of the fact that Canadian citizenship was required for a licence to fish. "As long as you had black hair on your head and a Japanese face, you were an enemy alien," George Nitta recalled.

The confiscation of Japanese-owned fishboats did little to quiet the clamour in British Columbia. Members of Parliament, city councils, labour unions and veterans' associations were united in their demand that all Japanese be moved "east of the Rockies." On 14 January 1942, the federal government responded. All male Japanese nationals between the ages of eighteen and forty-five were ordered evacuated from the coast.

Takeo Nakano was working at the pulp mill at Woodfibre on Howe Sound when the orders came. Nakano had been in British Columbia for twenty-six of his forty years, but he had no intention of staying. He and his wife sent their savings home and dreamed of the day when there would be money enough for them to return to Japan. Admitting he was "not given to sophisticated political thinking," Nakano had "blind faith in Japan's eventual victory." In the meantime, he would be obedient to the orders of the Canadian authorities.

Nakano and fifty other Japanese nationals were put aboard the ferry for Vancouver and relocation to road work camps far from the coast. "The Woodfibre dockside was crowded with our wives and children seeing us off," Nakano recalled. "It was great confusion. My wife's white handkerchief fluttered." That night, he and his fellow internees were housed in the Livestock Building in the Hastings Park Exhibition grounds. "Our nostrils were immediately offended by a strong stench of cows and horses," Nakano remembered. "The bare concrete floors were lined with beds of straw-filled mattresses . . . The air was thick with tobacco smoke. I started to make up my bed but was overcome with nausea."

On the day Pearl Harbor was attacked, twelve hundred fishboats owned by Japanese Canadians were impounded. The Fishermen's Reserve was sent to round them up. "I think as fishermen ourselves we felt sorry for them," a reservist commented, "but there was a war on and rumours were rife of subs off the coast and so on."

"Our job was to round up all the Japanese-owned boats . . .
It was heartbreaking. I remember seeing Japanese
there and, you know, they were crying. There were men
in their old World War One uniforms, wearing the
Scottish tam . . . It was pretty tough. Those who were
Canadian-born were the same as you and I.
They'd never seen Japan."
—Trygve Arnet

O N 29 April 1942, the *New Canadian*, a Japanese-English newspaper published in Vancouver, printed orders from the British Columbia Security Commission:

> Persons of Japanese origin residing in Vancouver should terminate, not later than the 30th April, 1942, all leases or rental arrangements they may be working under. They must also be prepared to move either to Hastings Park or to work camps or to places under the Interior Housing Scheme at twenty-four hours notice.

When total evacuation from the coast had been ordered a month

The first evacuees—male Japanese nationals, aged from eighteen to forty-five, waved good-bye to their friends from the trains that would carry them to work camps in the Interior.

earlier, most Japanese residents had reacted with shock and disbelief. Now, they chose to accept their exile with patience. "Most of us didn't put up a fuss," an internee recalled. "It is part of our upbringing. *Shikata-ga-nai*—it can't be helped." The *New Canadian* urged compliance, suggesting that obedience to the orders would be seen as proof of loyalty to Canada.

Each adult was allowed to take only 150 pounds of baggage. But what to take? One family opted for "clothes, clothes, clothes—it will be cold there." A Vancouver dressmaker travelled with her sewing machine and a box of patterns; another woman considered her best dishes and sake cups essential.

For the thousands of people removed from the coast, the first glimpse of their new "homes" was dispiriting. A fourteen-year-old

boy recalled arriving at a Kootenay ghost town: "My mother was crying when she got off the train. Such a little pokey place and the mountains everywhere and I think it was raining." A woman, tired and travelling alone, stepped off the train at Kaslo and "went berserk." The first people sent to Sandon gazed about them and then sat on their suitcases and wailed, "O God, what a hole! What a hole, O God!"

At Greenwood, each family, even those with five or six children, was allotted a single room in one of the long-vacant mining boom hotels. A communal kitchen was located in the hallway of each floor. "It was terribly crowded. It was hard for the women to cook. So many pots and pans on one stove at the same time." At Tashme, people were crowded into tarpaper shacks, uninsulated and designed to

house two families—one room for each family with a shared kitchen in between.

The winter of 1942–43 was bitterly cold. Greenwood's hallway stoves could not begin to heat the living quarters. "In the morning, the wet shoes the kids had had the night before were frozen to the floors." A man interned at Sandon recalled: "No matter how furiously we burned our stoves, it was cold . . . Unless we hit the door with a hammer to loosen the ice, it would not open. The moisture dripped in every room, among the shelves, inside the boxes and beneath the bed. The bottom of the mattresses became green."

The first year was the worst. People asked each other, "Why? Why? What is all this?" Men found it difficult to cope with idleness; women suffered from the cramped quarters and the lack of privacy. But by the second year,

when it had become apparent that the war would not end soon, people began to settle in. Some turned their hands to vegetable gardening. In Greenwood, they built small houses to get their families out of the crowded hotels, and at New Denver, they winterized their cottages. As labour shortages grew, some men were allowed to take jobs in sawmills and with railway section gangs.

"We couldn't leave the camps. Not without a police permit," a Vancouver-born doctor, interned at New Denver, mused. "But there was no barbed wire."

"After one year we are becoming settled," a Sandon exile reported. "This has become our home."

Gradually, host towns came to accept their unwilling guests. Greenwood, once home to several thousand people, had shrunk to fewer than two hundred before the arrival of 1,701 internees brought the town to life. A Japanese resident of New Denver summed it up: "At first they didn't like us . . . But they start to make money from us—from 2,500 new people—and then they like us."

In 1949, when Japanese residents were finally allowed to return to the coast, a few chose to stay on in the Kootenays. Eighteen years later, the government deeded the title of eighty-eight homes to former internees, including almost two hundred old people who continued to reside in New Denver.

In 1988, the federal government agreed to pay each surviving internee $21,000 compensation and issued an apology, acknowledging that "the treatment of Japanese during and after World War II was unjust and violated principles of human rights as they are understood today."

Top: Interned in a near-derelict mining-boom hotel in Greenwood, women prepared meals for their families in a communal kitchen.

Bottom: Purpose-built for the families of the five hundred men employed on the Hope-Princeton Highway, the internment camp Tashme took its name from the first two letters in the names of the members of the Security Commission (Taylor, Shirras and Mead).

On 24 February 1942, the federal government toughened its stance. A coastal strip 100 miles wide was declared off limits to all people of Japanese ancestry, whatever their age, sex or citizenship. On 4 March, the British Columbia Security Commission, under the chairmanship of the Vancouver industrialist Austin C. Taylor, was established to organize the evacuation.

Subject to the commission's approval, evacuees could remove themselves "voluntarily" from the restricted coastal area. Fred Kozuki was among the fortunate few who were able to follow that route. A native of Hiroshima, Kozuki had arrived in British Columbia when he was thirteen. He attended school in Victoria, became a naturalized Canadian citizen, and in 1942 was operating a shop in Vancouver with his Canadian-born wife, Lily. Kozuki wrote to an old school friend, a former provincial policeman who was living at Williams Lake. After his friend vouched for him, Fred and Lily, together with their three children and Fred's father and brother, received permission to go to the Cariboo.

Some three thousand Japanese chose to relocate to eastern Canada or Alberta, where they worked in sugar-beet fields. An additional thousand people moved to self-supporting communities in British Columbia. Established at Christina Lake, Minto, Bridge River and East Lillooet, these settlements received no government funding. They were populated by people who had money enough to see them through the war, but they were far from pleasure resorts. The three hundred people who settled at East Lillooet lived in tarpaper shacks. "It got very hot in summer," Dr. Masajiro Miyazaki recalled. "In winter, since there was no insulation, the moisture on the walls would freeze when the temperature went down to 20 to 35 below zero."

The majority of the evacuees found themselves at the mercy of the Security Commission. Faced with the problem of finding living places for upwards of twelve thousand men, women and children, the commission came up with a solution: the near-deserted Kootenay mining towns of Kaslo, Slocan, New Denver, Roseberry, Sandon, Lemon Creek and Greenwood. Some people received a week's notice to prepare for evacuation; others were told to be ready in a few hours. All were permitted to take with them only what they could carry.

Tadaichi Nagao was one of Vancouver's oldest residents, having arrived in the city in 1886 to take a job at Hastings Mill. He was well known in his adopted home; for many years, he had acted as a court interpreter. "I don't want to leave Vancouver," Nagao said. "If we have to go, I suppose we shall have to go, but I hope not." But the orders came. Seventy-five-year-old Tadaichi Nagao and his ailing wife, Fumiko, were relocated to New Denver.

Vancouver's "Little Tokyo" (Powell and Cordova Streets) became a ghost town of empty roads, boarded-up cafes, and shop windows with their displays "dust-covered and topsy-turvy." "The big clock of the Furuya Co. is still hanging over the street, stopped at five past five," the *Vancouver Sun* reported. "Below, there is a large Japanese restaurant empty, unlocked and the electric lights still on."

Internees, who expected to return to find everything as they had left it, had not the slightest idea that the commission would soon begin to auction off all their possessions. In December, a housewife, who had asked a neighbour to look after her house when she and her family were sent to Tashme, wrote asking him to send her Christmas decorations and was devastated to learn that the house and all its contents had been sold.

At Kaslo, Sandon and Greenwood, families were crowded into old mining-boom hotels. At Tashme and New Denver, they were ushered into hurriedly built tarpaper shacks. For people accustomed to the mild coastal climate, the first winter in the mountain valleys was brutal. Adding to their misery was the knowledge that they were not welcome. While Greenwood's mayor had pleaded with the commission to send evacuees to save his town from extinction, other communities had voiced loud objections to the relocation. But gradually, living conditions improved, at least marginally, and acceptance grew, as towns came to depend on the spending power of their Japanese guests.

Just as the presence of thousands of internees brought Kootenay towns to life, other communities profited from the presence of the military. Terrace was, quite simply, transformed. Located by the Skeena River, on the CNR tracks between Prince Rupert and Prince George, the little lumber town of about five hundred residents suddenly achieved a strategic importance after the bombing of Pearl Harbor. If an attack was launched against Prince Rupert, it seemed logical to presume that the enemy would move inland along the railway line. To halt that advance, it was decided to station an infantry brigade in Terrace. On the outskirts of town, shops and stores, a drill hall, a hospital and barracks to house four thousand men were built. By 1943, the military outnumbered civilians by a ratio of eight to one.

The Peace River country also experienced a friendly invasion. For several years, the American and Canadian governments had been talking about building a road through British Columbia and the Yukon to Alaska. The war with Japan brought discussions to a head. On 11 February 1942, President Franklin D. Roosevelt authorized construction of the Alaska-Canada Military Highway. In exchange for a right-of-way through Canadian territory, the Americans would bear all construction costs (an estimated $150 million) and, after the war's end, would turn the road over to Canada.

From mile zero at Dawson Creek, the route ran to Fort St. John and Fort Nelson, then on to Watson Lake in the Yukon and to Fairbanks, Alaska.

"We went to Lillooet. When we were planning to go there, we heard that the people of the town were going to meet the train and shoot us with their rifles. It was scary and a lot of people were afraid."
—anonymous internee

"The average soldier, regardless of the entertainments and past-times provided in the camp area, hates Terrace and everything about it. This is due to the lack of entertainment in the village as the troops are forced to spend their off-hours wandering and congregating in crowds along the small streets and the few public places. This fact is most noticeable during the weekends. Saturday nights especially."
—Sergeant J. Chaharyn

By October 1942, after eight months of relentless effort, the Alaska-Canada Military Highway was through—a narrow, brute-force road with 90-degree turns and grades as steep as 25 per cent. The following year, private contractors, working under the direction of the U.S. Public Roads Administration, would begin to bring the highway up to civilian standards.

"The Road to Tokyo" would stretch 1,500 miles through muskeg and mud, through "up-standing bristling bush," through clouds of mosquitoes and "no-see-ums." It was an enormous undertaking, and it was also a race against time. The road must be through before winter. Thousands of soldiers and thousands of tons of supplies streamed through Dawson Creek and moved over the old winter road to Fort St. John, where the American engineers established a headquarters. "It was just a scratchin'," an old–timer said of Fort St. John. "Then, overnight, you might say, it come alive—with five thousand U.S. soldiers and other folks pilin' in here and seemed like as many trucks."

Among the newcomers were George and Margaret "Ma" Murray, proprietors of the *Bridge River–Lillooet News*. In 1933, one of the Depression's darker years, George Murray had been elected to the provincial legislature on a campaign that championed the north. About the Alaska Highway he was so passionate that his wife was moved to complain: "Seven thousand miles he's travelled in six months this year so far—doing what? Promoting a highway that only the Americans care a damn about."

Now that the highway was about to become a reality, George Murray felt he had to be there. He and Margaret pulled up stakes, moved to Fort St. John and established the *Alaska Highway News*, "the only paper in the world that gives a tinker's damn about the North Peace."

AS THE WAR DRAGGED ON, it became more and more apparent that British Columbia was not in danger of attack, but precautions continued just the same. Dimout regulations remained in effect, air raid wardens continued their patrols, and the *Vancouver Sun* was pleased to announce the arrival of a shipment of "Mickey Mouse" gas masks, sized for small children. Fear of invasion had long since been replaced by the irritation of coping with shortages. Sugar and gasoline were rationed. New tires were impossible to obtain. Liquor could be purchased, but only in small quantities. In August 1943, when meat was added to the ration list, housewives looked for meat-extending recipes and restaurants introduced "meatless Tuesdays."

The first ration books were distributed in 1942. The following year, when beef and pork were added to the list of rationed items, housewives were advised to experiment with "meatless Victory casseroles."

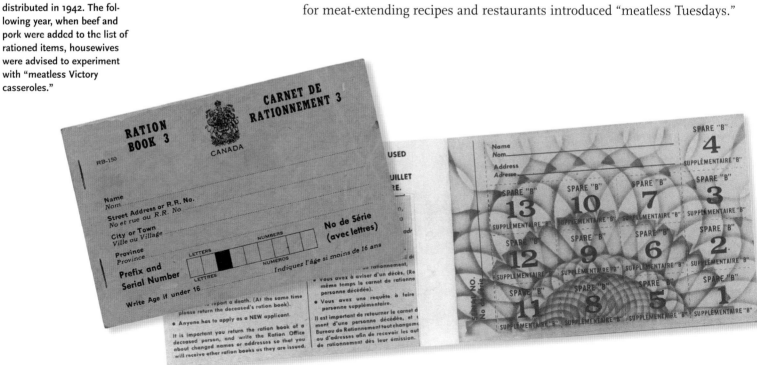

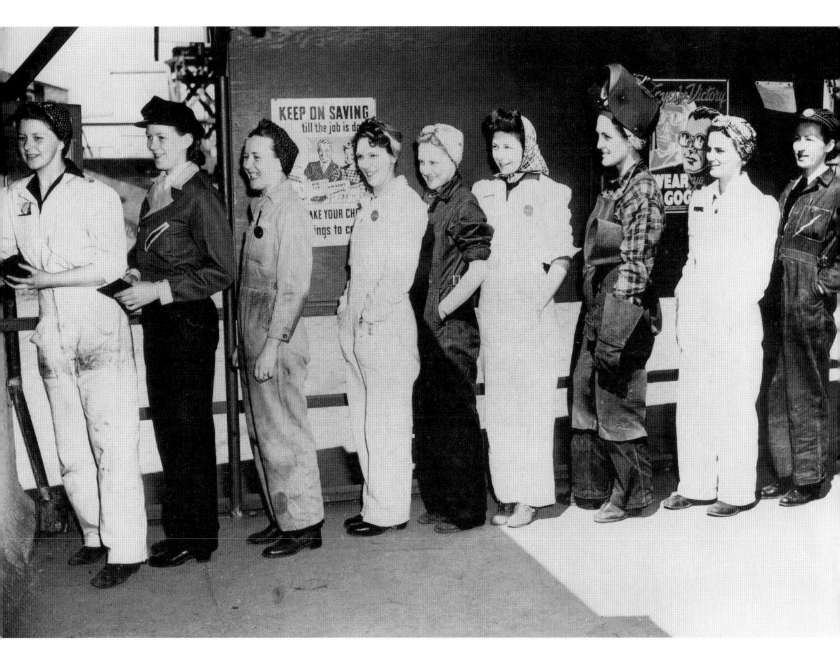

By 1943, women were
making up a large part of the
workforce at the Victoria
Machinery Depot in Victoria.

And just when there was nothing to buy, British Columbians were enjoying full employment. In Esquimalt, Yarrows shipyards worked day and night producing five corvettes, seventeen frigates and four minesweepers. Shipyards in Vancouver employed twenty-five thousand men and women. Another seventy-eight hundred worked at the expanded Boeing Aircraft plants on Sea Island, producing more than four hundred PBYs (Canso and Catalina flying boat bombers) and the midsections of the B29 Flying Fortress.

In Trail, employment was provided by the Consolidated Mining and Smelting Company, which was involved in the province's most secret wartime project—the manufacture of "heavy water," an essential ingredient in the process of nuclear fission. In November 1942, the company signed a contract with the United States government: the Americans agreed to invest $2 million for the construction of a new plant, and the smelter agreed to manufacture heavy water, disguised as Product No. 9, for use in the Manhattan Project and the development of the atomic bomb.

Almost as secret as the activity at the Trail smelter was the establishment of a base for the training of Chinese-Canadian commandos. Britain's Special Operations Executive (SOE) had experience in sending trained volunteers for secret operations behind enemy lines in Europe. When the time came to do the same thing in Japanese-occupied Malaya, the SOE had difficulty finding men who could blend in with the resident population, until they turned their attention to British Columbia's Chinese.

In May 1944, twelve men were selected from scores of volunteers and sent to Dunrobin's Bay on Okanagan Lake near Penticton for intensive training. They were taught the arts of survival, sabotage and silent killing. And to the surprise of the SOE, eight of the twelve also required a crash course in Chinese languages, which they had never learned to speak. The duty for which they had volunteered was extremely dangerous; the casualty rate was expected to be 80 per cent. But, they reasoned, if they were prepared to die in the nation's service, then surely they could no longer be denied the full privileges of citizenship. After the war, Chinese-Canadian veterans pressed their case, and in 1947, the right to vote was reinstated, and the Chinese Exclusion Act was repealed.

THE END OF THE WAR did not bring a return to normal life as far as British Columbia's Japanese were concerned. Several thousand chose to go to Japan, after having been encouraged—"coerced," some people said—to accept "repatriation." Of those who chose to remain in Canada, some opted to stay where they were. Takeo Nakano remained in Ontario and later wrote a book about his wartime experiences. Fred Kozuki and his family stayed in Williams Lake, where they built a motel and joined the ranks of the town's most respected citizens. Tadaichi Nagao, whose wife had died in New Denver in 1943, chose to live nearby until his own death in 1950. Dr. Miyazaki stayed in Lillooet, where he purchased one of the town's oldest and grandest houses.

But those who wanted to return to the coast had a long wait. Anti-Japanese sentiment remained high, fuelled by stories of atrocities coming out of prisoner-of-war camps, some of which had a British Columbia connection. Men who had been held at camps near Kowloon and Hong Kong spoke of Kanao Inouye, the "Kamloops Kid." Born in Kamloops in 1916,

This page: Louie King, Jim Shiu and Edward Chow (left to right) volunteered for "Operation Oblivion" and underwent commando training at Dunrobin's Bay on Okanagan Lake. In 1957, a member of the commando group, Douglas Jung, became the first Chinese Canadian to be elected as a Member of Parliament.

Facing page: With the coming of peace, Vancouver would experience a post-war boom.

DON'T KILL HER DADDY
WITH CARELESS TALK

People were encouraged to support the war by buying Victory Loans and War Savings certificates. During a 1944 campaign, the Chinese community in Kamloops subscribed an average of $202, the highest per capita participation in Canada.

Kanao was two months old when his father, Tow Inouye, had enlisted in the Canadian Expeditionary Force. He was ten when his father died, perhaps from the effects of the war wound he received in 1918. Kanao was studying in Japan when the war broke out. Called to military service, he was posted to prisoner-of-war camps, where he became known for his perfect English and his hatred of whites.

Prisoner-of-war Anatole Zaitzeff of Vancouver remembered Kanao Inouye: "He told me that he had been at the University of British Columbia in 1933 . . . that at university they had called him a yellow bastard and that he hated all of us and would see that we suffered for it." When the war ended, the "Kamloops Kid" was arrested. Tried by a British war crimes court and sentenced to hang, he appealed on the grounds that he was a Canadian citizen. The charges were changed to treason and he was hanged in August 1947.

By then, only six thousand Japanese residents remained in British Columbia (sixteen thousand fewer than the pre-war total), and politicians who had campaigned for their removal congratulated themselves for having achieved "redistribution" across Canada. Still, there was a reluctance to allow them to return to the coast where, it was feared, they would reassert their dominance of the fishing and logging industries. The mood started to change only when a royal commission began to investigate claims for confiscated property.

Japanese internees had suffered substantial losses. The Imada family had received $3,563 for a house and 16 acres of Fraser Valley farmland calculated to have been worth $7,935. Fukujiro Koyama's trawler had been sold for $400, less than half its real value. George Yasuzo Shoji, a former sergeant in the Princess Pats and a wounded veteran of the First World War, had refused to accept a cheque for $39.32, the amount he was offered, after deductions for taxes and commissions, for 19 acres of farmland, a two-storey house and 2,500 chickens. Other claims involved personal effects, "from Japanese dolls and English encyclopedias to chesterfields and sewing machines," items for which the Custodian of Enemy Property had no record at all.

As the hearings continued and more and more personal stories emerged, public attitudes began to change. In 1948, when the province banned the employment of Japanese workers on crown land, the International Woodworkers of America came to their defence, and the *Vancouver Sun*, in an editorial headlined, "These Japanese Are Ours," insisted that "British Columbia has long since outgrown this kind of racism." The following year, all restrictions were lifted: Japanese Canadians received the right to vote and to live and work wherever they pleased.

PART FIVE

TIDES OF CHANGE

1950 TO 2000

CHAPTER 17

POLITICS *in* PARADISE

Previous page: In 1958, the top of Ripple Rock, a menace to navigation in Seymour Narrows, was blasted away by the largest non-nuclear explosion the world had seen.

This page: By 1951, British Columbia's population had exceeded one million. Among the newcomers were war brides, some of whom must have found the transition to the British Columbia frontier rather trying.

IN 1952, British Columbians went to the polls in the most unusual election the province had ever seen, one that would set the course of the province for the next twenty years. Since 1903, when official political parties had been introduced, the Liberals and Conservatives had taken turns leading the province. After the 1941 election, in which Harold Winch's Co-operative Commonwealth Federation (CCF) received more votes than either of the old-line parties, Liberals and Conservatives joined forces to form a coalition government, "to win the war" and to deny the socialists the opportunity to govern. By 1952, the coalition had unravelled. The premier was "Boss" Johnson, a Liberal; the leader of the opposition was Herbert Anscomb, a Conservative and Johnson's recent finance minister. Two members of the legislature, Tilly Rolston and William Andrew Cecil Bennett, had left the Conservatives to sit as independents.

Despite his non-aligned status, Bennett was a committed member of the Social Credit League. A hardware merchant from Kelowna and a Conservative member of the house for ten years before he crossed the floor, Bennett found the traditional parties to be chronically indifferent to the Interior's potential. He sensed that people were ready for a post-war, fresh-start crusade. To Bennett, the Social Credit League represented "a new hope to tens of thousands of people in British Columbia."

When the election was called for 12 June 1952, Social Credit entered the campaign without an official leader. But that mattered hardly at all. A great many British Columbians were disillusioned with the old-line parties, whose interests seemed focussed on the cities while people in the hinterland continued to live in near-primitive conditions. When Cyril Shelford returned to the Ootsa Valley after six years of war, he found it as he had left it: "The roads in our area were impassable in the spring and fall; there was no electric power and very little running water." When George and "Ma" Murray gazed out their window at Fort St. John, they had a view of twelve outhouses.

Residents of the 70,000 square miles of British Columbia that lay east of the Rockies felt they had been forgotten by the "dead and distant hand of officialdom." When "Ma" Murray inserted a ballot in the *Alaska Highway News*, asking her 800 subscribers if they supported the idea of seceding from British Columbia and joining Alberta, she got 210 responses—all voting yes.

"Northern British Columbia has closer ties with Edmonton than with Victoria."
—*Alaska Highway News*

An early television set with a very small circular screen. In 1953, CBC Television began to broadcast out of Vancouver.

Rooftop aerials became a feature of the skyline, and viewers struggled with set-top antennas known as "rabbit ears."

THE SPRING of 1894 was unseasonably cool, the mountain snowpack unusually high. Then, in May, temperatures began to climb. Melting snow fed rivers and lakes. The Fraser River boiled through the canyon and rose to the deck of the Alexandra Suspension Bridge. In the valley, it burst its banks and tore out the CPR tracks at Agassiz and Dewdney and several other places along the line. As the waters spread across the valley floor, the bloated carcasses of drowned farm animals began to drift into Vancouver's False Creek. For three weeks, until the railway was repaired, British Columbia was isolated from the rest of Canada.

The 1894 flood was the worst in living memory, and weather conditions were eerily similar in the spring of 1948. But now residents of the Fraser Valley felt confident that the dykes along the river would save them. Then came a May heat wave, and the trickle of melting snow turned into cascades of water streaming down mountainsides. The Skeena, the Nechako, the Columbia, the Thompson, the Fraser, the Kootenay: every major river in the province was affected. The Bulkley River covered Telkwa's main street with 18 inches of water. At Hazelton, the Skeena River rose 2 inches an hour. In the Kootenays, Kimberley became a tent city after a fast-rising creek left five hundred people homeless. In the Okanagan, Vernon was pleading for sandbags, and low-lying land from Keremeos to Oliver was under water. At Prince George, thirty homes were evacuated, and trucks with loudspeakers patrolled the streets urging people to flee.

Over the next few days, the situation became worse. Near Grand Forks, a small boy was swept away by a swollen stream. Refugees from outlying farms poured into Prince George. Terrace was cut off when its road and rail links disappeared under water. Farmers near Kamloops shot their livestock before fleeing to the safety of the town. At Trail, the raging Columbia River threatened to sweep away waterfront homes as hundreds of volunteers struggled to raise the dyke protecting the town.

This page: In 1894, the waters of the Fraser River rose to the deck of the Alexandra Suspension Bridge.

Facing page: The Fraser River in flood at Hatzic in 1948.

In the Fraser Valley, the height of the river was measured at Mission. In 1894, it had risen to 25 feet 8 inches, but anything above 20 feet was considered dangerous. On 27 May 1948, the Fraser measured 21 feet 5 inches. On 29 May, it reached 23 feet 4 inches and continued to rise, washing out the highway and the tracks of both the CPR and CNR. The dyke at Agassiz gave way. Hatzic Prairie, Chilliwack, Pitt Meadows and Lulu Island were in danger. The premier declared a state of emergency. All the troops in the province—twelve hundred regulars and fourteen hundred reservists—were called to duty. The Royal Canadian Air Force airlifted supplies to marooned farms, and the navy manned a fleet of small boats, ferrying hundreds of people to higher ground.

On 1 June 1948, the Fraser River rose above 24 feet and peaked nine days later at 24 feet 11 inches. More than 50,000 acres were under water. At Mission, the Fraser was a 10-mile-wide lake. Thousands of people were homeless. To one observer, the valley was "eighty miles of misery."

More than a million sandbags had been flown in from Quebec. Some thirty-five thousand exhausted volunteers had worked night and day—piling sandbags, rowing over submerged fences to pluck people from rooftops, preparing coffee and sandwiches for other volunteers. Public health nurses began vaccinating evacuees against typhoid, and plans were being made to spray the entire valley with DDT. Damage was estimated at $20 million (1948 dollars). And it could have been far worse, had the river reached its 1894 level.

Young women vied for the title "Lady of the Lake" at the 1955 Kelowna Regatta.

After the war, the coalition government of John Hart had ordered some highway construction. In 1945, attention had been directed to completing the Hope-Princeton Highway, and orders had gone forward for the construction of the highway from Prince George through the Rockies to Dawson Creek. But it was not until 1952, when the Hart Highway opened to traffic, that residents of the Peace River country could drive to the rest of British Columbia without going through Alberta.

People in Prince George had almost despaired of ever seeing the Pacific Great Eastern (PGE) completed. A railway connection to the coast had been promised in 1912, and the PGE had become known as "Prince George Eventually" and "Past God's Endurance." The line finally reached Prince George forty years later, in 1952.

But while settlers in Prince George and the Peace River country had grumbled about being ignored, the people of Ootsa Lake felt betrayed. In 1950, the British Columbia government had signed an agreement with the Aluminum Company of Canada (Alcan). The company would build an aluminum smelter on the coast at the head of Douglas Channel, where the "instant" town of Kitimat would house its workers. To provide the smelter with hydroelectric power, Alcan received permission to dam the Nechako River, creating a reservoir of 350 square miles. Water from the reservoir would flow through a tunnel under the Coast Mountains, emerging at Kemano to drive the turbines that would provide energy for the smelter.

The people of the Ootsa Valley would be flooded out. The communities of Ootsa, Streatham, Wistaria and Marilla would be drowned. By the terms of the Water Act, settlers had no choice but to sell their land. Alcan began the bargaining process by offering $3,000 for a house and half-section— 320 acres of "land that had been cleared mostly by hand with pick and axe." Cyril Shelford led a delegation to Victoria, not to oppose the dam but to insist on a fair price for their land. They got nowhere with Premier Johnson. They got nowhere with Harold Winch, leader of the CCF opposition. But they received a sympathetic hearing from W. A. C. Bennett, who took their concerns to the legislature. "What kind of government do we have that wouldn't help a group seeking fair treatment?" he demanded. Cyril Shelford was so impressed that he joined the Social Credit League, ran in the 1952 election in the Omineca riding and won a seat in the provincial house. "People all over B.C. were looking for change," he said.

The CCF ran as the only alternative to the capitalist parties. The Conservatives and Liberals ran as alternatives to the socialists. The Social Crediters ran right up the middle, achieving a narrow victory thanks in no small part to the "transferable ballot."

Instead of marking an X beside one candidate, voters were asked to rank their choices: first, second, third and so on. In each riding, a candidate would be declared the winner only if he or she received over half of the first choices. If no winner emerged, the candidate receiving the fewest first choices would be dropped from consideration and all the second choices on his or her ballots would take effect. If those votes did not produce a winner, the next-lowest candidate would be dropped and his or her second choices distributed—and so on.

The day after the polls closed, only five of the province's forty-eight ridings were able to declare a winner. Then came the second count and, in some cases, the third count and the fourth count. It took weeks to sort

The Pacific Great Eastern Railway was a long time building, but by 1971 it ran from North Vancouver to Fort Nelson. In 1972, it was renamed B.C. Rail.

"Very few people—and no lawyers—recognize that when you force a farmer to relocate, you have to take into account that you're buying a piece of a man's life. It's not like the city where no one has real roots to the soil."
—Cyril Shelford

things out. The final results were chaos. The Socreds held nineteen seats, the CCF eighteen, the Liberals six, the Conservatives four, and there was one independent. No party had the twenty-five members needed for a majority, and the Socreds did not even have a leader. The latter problem was corrected on 15 July, when the successful Social Credit candidates selected W. A. C. Bennett. It was up to the lieutenant-governor to decide which minority party should be invited to form a government.

Lieutenant-Governor Clarence Wallace was racked by indecision, wavering between the CCF, which at least boasted members with legislative experience, and Social Credit, which represented the great unknown. Wallace stalled until 1 August—seven weeks after the election—before summoning W. A. C. Bennett to Government House. Power had been transferred to the hinterland.

"Here in British Columbia are to be seen the wealth of mineral, forest, oil and natural gas and potential hydroelectric resources which constitute perhaps the last economic frontier of North America," Bennett declared. Others could look out over the Peace River country and see "a winding, muddy river" and a near-empty land. But not Bennett. "I see dams," he exclaimed. "And I see power. And I see development. I see roads, highways, bridges and growing communities. I see cities—prosperous cities with schools, hospitals, universities."

Bennett had big plans. To implement them, he needed a majority government. In March 1953, his government was defeated and an election was called. Bennett achieved his majority, but because the transferable ballot remained in effect, he lost two ridings in which Social Crediters had held the lead on the first count. When the legislature met that fall, he did away with the transferable ballot.

Premier Bennett was determined to exploit the province's resources: its minerals, its coal, and its potential to produce hydroelectric power. He was also determined that every region should profit from industrial expansion. To achieve those goals, he practised the politics of pragmatism.

Although he was a committed teetotaller who celebrated election victories with Ovaltine, he allowed a new Liquor Act to go forward after the people had made it clear that they were in favour of a more liberal policy. For the first time since Prohibition, dining rooms could serve whisky, wine

In 1958, the time had come to do something about Ripple Rock. All shipping using the Inside Passage had to pass through Seymour Narrows between Maud Island and Vancouver Island. Near the southern end of the narrows lay Ripple Rock, just below the surface, reducing the 700-yard fairway to 400 yards, through which the current boiled at 10 to 12 knots. Over the years, Ripple Rock had sunk one ship and damaged many others. The mariners' bible, the *B.C. Pilot,* described it as "one of the most dreaded menaces to navigation on the Pacific rim." To engineers, the solution was simple: blast it out of the water.

Some people worried that the huge amount of explosives might trigger an earthquake or a tidal wave, but the explosion went off without a hitch, and Ripple Rock became a symbol of provincial progress.

and beer with meals, and licensed "cocktail lounges" came into existence.

And although he was an ardent free-enterpriser, Bennett was quite prepared to increase social services and to raise taxes on big business. He also supported public ownership if it suited his ends. Motor traffic to Vancouver Island depended on two privately run ferry systems: the Black Ball service, operated out of Seattle, and the CPR's Princess line. The CPR had no interest in improving its own service and even less in working with Black Ball ferries to produce a rational system. In 1958, after a seamen's strike threatened to sever connections to the mainland, Bennett took action. After presenting Black Ball with an offer it could not refuse, the province took over the American ships and created the British Columbia Ferry Corporation.

Acting on his promise to open up the province, Bennett announced that the PGE railway would be extended from Squamish to North Vancouver, and from Prince George to Dawson Creek. And he launched a road-building program such as British Columbia had never seen. Within six years of achieving his majority government, Bennett had invested more money in highways than had been spent in the entire history of the province, an achievement he characterized as "the greatest highway building program, not just in British Columbia's history, but per capita in the entire Western world."

Bennett believed that hydroelectric power would provide the impetus to province-wide development. For years, the Canadian and United States governments had been discussing the potential of the Columbia River, which rose in British Columbia but flowed to the sea through Washington and Oregon. Bennett was becoming impatient with the endless talk when Axel Wenner-Gren appeared on the scene. Another politician might have recoiled from doing business with the Swedish industrialist, who was believed to have been a Nazi sympathizer and a personal friend of Hermann Goering. But more important to W. A. C. Bennett than the rumours was the fact that Wenner-Gren's industrial empire stretched from Europe to South Africa and that he was showing an interest in northern British Columbia. In 1956, Bennett agreed, in principle, to the idea of granting Wenner-Gren rights to 40,000 acres, in return for the development of mines and pulp mills, and the construction of a 160-mile-an-hour monorail that would whiz up the Rocky Mountain Trench to the Yukon.

When Wenner-Gren's men began a careful survey of the area, they quickly realized that its greatest potential lay in the narrow walls of the Peace River Canyon—a perfect site for a massive hydroelectric dam. On 8 October 1957, the premier held a news conference. This day was "the most important that B.C. has experienced in its whole history," he enthused. A Peace River dam was feasible. Wenner-Gren's people would build "the greatest hydroelectric power project in the world." Northern British Columbia would become an industrial empire.

The Peace River Dam (renamed the Bennett Dam in 1967) became the linchpin in what became known as the "Two River" policy. To be cost-effective, hydroelectric projects required consumers who were ready and waiting for electric power. That two projects would produce an overabundance of power was clear. At first, it was supposed that Bennett was promoting the Peace only to galvanize Washington and Ottawa into action on the Columbia. But, from the beginning, he seems to have had something else in mind.

The planned dams on the Columbia would store water, delivering a consistent supply downriver so that the Americans could generate power on their side of the boundary. For building the dams and for permitting the flooding of provincial land, British Columbia would receive half the generated power. But, Bennett figured, if the Peace River produced sufficient energy for the province, then British Columbia could sell its share of Columbia power—the "downstream benefits"—to the Americans and use the money to build the dams. That way, the Columbia dams would cost British Columbia nothing. "Nothing's freer than free, my friend," Bennett beamed.

Before putting his plan into effect, Bennett needed a guaranteed purchaser of the power produced by the Peace, but the privately owned B.C. Electric Company would not commit. In 1961, the premier settled the matter by expropriating the company. Bill 5, which allowed for the "provincialization" of B.C. Electric, also provided for the expropriation of Peace River Power Development. "It answers, once and for all, charges that the Social Credit government had been controlled by the Wenner-Gren organization," Bennett pointed out.

The CCF, which had campaigned for the nationalization of the electric company, crowed "Well done, comrade" and "Hail Castro" as they voted in support of the bill. "Canada is rapidly acquiring the financial reputation of one of the most unstable South American republics," London's *Sunday Telegraph* commented. At home, B.C. Electric had few friends among its customers. For dragging its heels in the electrification of rural areas and charging high rates to urban customers, it had become known as "Beastly Electric."

Bennett's activities had the desired effect. Ottawa and Washington finally turned their attention to the Columbia. After months of negotiations, the Columbia River Treaty was signed. On 16 September 1964, President Lyndon Johnson and Prime Minister Lester B. Pearson met with Premier Bennett at the Peace Arch and, as the rain poured down, Johnson handed Bennett a cheque for $273 million, the purchase price of the province's share of Columbia River power for thirty years.

The Columbia River Treaty had its critics, but they were concerned mostly with the terms of the agreement. The words "ecology" and "environment" had not yet entered the public's vocabulary. When construction of

"I knew very well the way to get the Columbia was to get the Peace, then they'd know that British Columbia had lots of power and we wouldn't have to develop the Columbia. Everywhere I went and had meetings, people would show up in the audience, strangers. I did not know then, but I know now that they were CIA . . . As we went on, called tenders and let contracts, and they could see that we were beyond the point of no return, then the Americans talked business."

—Premier W. A. C. Bennett

Facing page: The Peace River Dam in 1966. In 1793, Alexander Mackenzie looked down the narrow walls of the Peace River Canyon and described "high, foaming, half-formed billows as far as the eye could follow." In 1966, the view had become a huge, earth-filled dam 600 feet high and more than a mile long.

"While I was head of the Canadian government and Mr. Johnson was head of the American government, in British Columbia Mr. Bennett was head of all he surveyed."

—Prime Minister Lester B. Pearson

A MacMillan Bloedel worker felling a tree, 1959. Harvey Reginald MacMillan, who had served as the province's chief forester and organized the airplane spruce program during the First World War, became the largest private timber operator in western Canada when he merged H. R. MacMillan Export Company with Bloedel, Stewart & Welch in 1951 and the Powell River Company in 1959.

"Have confidence in your organization and your country . . .
The lumber industry grew around me and I grew around it."
—H. R. MacMillan

the Peace River Dam began at Portage Mountain, most British Columbians, if they gave the matter any thought at all, were simply impressed by the sheer magnitude of the project: an earth-filled dam rising 400 feet and creating a lake of 640 square miles. The little town of Finlay Forks would disappear under hundreds of feet of water. There was a possibility that the huge new lake would change the local climate.

Work crews descended on Hudson's Hope. As helicopters buzzed up and down the river and the night air filled with the whine of heavy machinery,

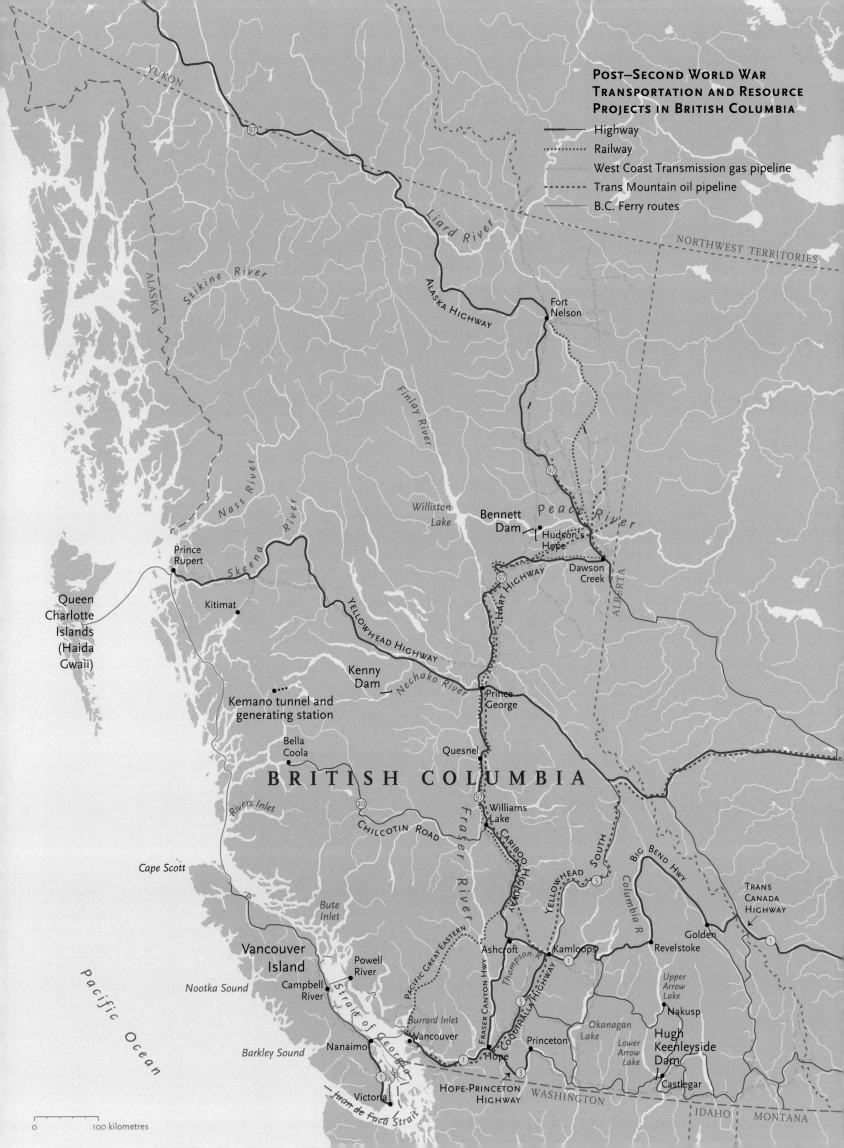

Post–Second World War
Transportation and Resource
Projects in British Columbia

Highway
Railway
West Coast Transmission gas pipeline
Trans Mountain oil pipeline
B.C. Ferry routes

YUKON

Liard River

Stikine River

ALASKA

Finlay River

Alaska Highway

NORTHWEST TERRITORIES

Fort Nelson

97

Nass River

Skeena River

Williston Lake

Peace River

Bennett Dam

Hudson's Hope

Prince Rupert

Kitimat

Yellowhead Highway

Hart Highway

97

Dawson Creek

ALBERTA

Queen Charlotte Islands (Haida Gwaii)

Kenny Dam

Nechako River

Kemano tunnel and generating station

Bella Coola

Quesnel

Prince George

BRITISH COLUMBIA

Rivers Inlet

20

CHILCOTIN ROAD

Fraser River

97

Williams Lake

CARIBOO HIGHWAY

YELLOWHEAD SOUTH

BIG BEND HWY

Columbia R

TRANS CANADA HIGHWAY

Cape Scott

Bute Inlet

5

Golden

1

Vancouver Island

Powell River

Campbell River

Nootka Sound

Strait of Georgia

PACIFIC GREAT EASTERN

Ashcroft

Thompson R

Kamloops

1

Revelstoke

Upper Arrow Lake

Nakusp

Pacific Ocean

Barkley Sound

Burrard Inlet

Vancouver

FRASER CANYON HWY

COQUIHALLA HIGHWAY

5

Princeton

Okanagan Lake

Lower Arrow Lake

Hugh Keenleyside Dam

Nanaimo

1

Hope

3

Castlegar

Victoria

Juan de Fuca Strait

Hope-Princeton Highway

WASHINGTON

IDAHO   MONTANA

0   100 kilometres

Top: In September 1967, Premier Bennett dumped the last 80 tons of earth on the Peace River Dam. To mark the occasion, the dam was renamed the Bennett Dam, prompting the premier to quip: "For years, some people have been saying, 'Damn Bennett.' It's nice to see it reversed for a change."

Bottom: Arrowhead, a once-thriving community at the head of Upper Arrow Lake, where the CPR branch line met the lake steamers, was submerged by the water rising behind the Arrow Dam.

residents hoped that the changes would be "for the best." Earl Pollon, a long-time resident of the Peace, found his thoughts turning to the upper river, the land that would soon be under water. What would happen to the trappers, the old bachelors who lived in the bush and scrabbled together a living by trapping and prospecting? And what about the beaver, lynx, marten and silver fox upon which they depended? What would become of men like "Two Mile" Bob Clark, who had come to look for gold thirty years earlier and had stayed and stayed, and who would soon be flooded out? But then Pollon thought of all the well-paid jobs at the dam site and the prosperity the dam promised to bring. "The past is dead," he told himself.

The dam was completed in 1967. In September of the following year, three thousand people crowded into the underground powerhouse at the Bennett Dam to watch the premier "turn on" Peace power. Meanwhile, work was nearing completion on the Arrow Dam, the first of three to be built under the terms of the Columbia River Treaty. The Arrow Dam (later renamed the Hugh Keenleyside Dam) would have a more modest impact on the land, as the level of the Upper and Lower Arrow Lakes was expected to rise a maximum of 30 feet. But the project would affect many more people, for the Arrow Lakes had a long history of settlement.

In the years before the First World War, there had been more than thirty lakeside communities. Some, like Beaton and Arrowhead, had sprung to life during the Kootenay mining boom. Others, like Renata, were the creation of speculators who had subdivided raw land into "orchards." Back then, the Arrow Lakes had seemed at the hub of things, well-served by stern-wheelers that connected with railway branch lines at either end.

By 1964, when B.C. Hydro began buying up the land, some of the old mining towns had already faded away. Ten years earlier, the CPR had withdrawn from service the *Minto*, the last of the Arrow Lakes paddlewheelers, leaving some communities connected to the outside world only by cross-lake ferries and barely passable roads. Still, residents clung to their lakeside homes, and B.C. Hydro was faced with the problem of relocating over two

"I served my hitch in the First World War and that bloody well cured me of so-called civilization. I came here to get away, and I'm bloody well going to stay. They're not going to drive me out! I bloody well intend to get up in the mornings and see those mountains as long as I live. But bloody Jesus, you can't argue with rising water, can you? I guess I'll have to move up onto another bench."
—"Two Mile" Bob Clark

"Renata was much more than a climate and cherries; it was a way of life, idyllic and irreplaceable."
—James Wood Wilson

The Hugh Keenleyside Dam on the Columbia backed up the river to form a 200-square-mile lake extending 145 miles to Revelstoke.

thousand people before the water began to rise. Some were happy enough to sell up and move to Revelstoke and Castlegar. But for most people, this was a sad time, made even more poignant by B.C. Hydro's practice of burning down the homes it had acquired even before neighbours negotiated their own sale.

Ed Gates and the tiny settlement of St. Leon became the symbol of dozens of personal tragedies. St. Leon's history went back to 1902, when Mike Grady had used the returns from his mineral claim near Silverton to build a luxury resort hotel. The resort fell on hard times when Prohibition

Facing page: Lights blazed from the new B.C. Hydro Building (built in 1953) twenty-four hours a day. Accused of wasteful practices, Hydro doused the nighttime illumination. It was a symbolic gesture: the building had been designed with the heat generated by the lights in mind, and subsidiary heating cut in on only the coldest days. When the lights went out, the subsidiary heaters in the basement had to come on and chug away.

This page: The luxury resort Gates of St. Leon was among the properties expropriated by the provincial government to make way for the rising waters of the Hugh Keenleyside Dam. Forlorn and deserted, it burned to the ground in 1968.

removed the appeal of the hotel's bar, but he hung on, a reclusive, shaggy-haired old man rambling around an empty building. After Grady's death, the hotel was purchased by Edwin Gates, an American who had worked at Trail's heavy-water plant during the Second World War. Gates restored and reopened the hotel and by the 1960s was doing well. When B.C. Hydro came calling, he refused to negotiate. His property was expropriated, the hotel burned to the ground, and a "heartbroken" Ed Gates moved to Nakusp.

CHAPTER 18

TWISTS *and* TURNS

THE 1950S WERE years of progress and growing prosperity. Drive-in movies and drive-in restaurants were introduced to cater to an increasingly mobile population. In 1953, the *Vancouver Sun* made a bold prediction: "Tall apartment buildings, of ten storeys or more, will start rising over English Bay within the next five years."

During the decade, British Columbians celebrated the defeat of two dreaded diseases, tuberculosis and poliomyelitis. Tuberculosis, a bacterial infection that usually attacked the lungs but could also settle in the bones or the brain, had been treated with complete bed rest, combined with plenty of fresh air. As early as 1895, when William Fortune began to take in patients at his ranch on Tranquille Creek, Kamloops, with its clear, dry air, had been singled out as one of the best locations in the province at which to effect a cure. Fortune's ranch grew into Tranquille Sanitorium, a huge government-run research and teaching centre, with a staff of 450, at which nurses from all over the province were trained. Then, it was discovered that antibiotics, developed during the last years of the war, provided a cure more effective than masses of fresh air, and in 1958, Tranquille Sanitorium was closed.

By then, polio also had been defeated. Polio was not a new disease in British Columbia. Every summer, a few scattered cases had cropped up here and there. But 1947 was different. By August, 135 cases had been registered—enough

Facing page: Polio vaccinations became available in 1955, much to the relief of parents who had lived in dread of the disease. According to one doctor, "There was a virtual crush to receive protection—with prompt and spectacular effectiveness."

to suggest the onset of an epidemic. And that was very worrying, for no one knew how polio was transmitted. One Vancouver pediatrician was convinced the cause was cyanide, found in unripe fruit; other experts laid the blame on hens' eggs. The death rate was not alarmingly high, but polio had devastating side effects. Young people were particularly vulnerable to the disease, and parents were haunted by thoughts of their children on crutches, in a wheelchair or confined in an "iron lung." Then, in 1955, the province began to vaccinate children with the newly available Salk vaccine. The number of new cases dropped dramatically, and polio soon became a disease of the past.

While medical science was improving life, nuclear science was threatening to end it. In Nevada, which did not seem very far away, the Americans were conducting above-ground tests of hydrogen bombs, and with the Cold War always threatening to become hot, the image of a looming mushroom cloud became a symbol of the decade. The first backyard atomic-bomb shelter in Canada was built in Vancouver's Shaughnessy neighbourhood in the summer of 1950. In 1957, a civil defence "survival plan" warned Lower Mainlanders: "You live in a target area. A hydrogen bomb dropped in the area would cause complete destruction for a radius of 4 miles, major damage for a radius of 7 miles, moderate damage for 10 miles. You must get beyond this 20-mile limit to be reasonably safe." Well-intentioned though those plans might have been, most people recognized them as pointless.

Signs of modernity were everywhere, and that only made the news coming out of the Kootenays seem all the more surprising. The Doukhobors, members of a religious sect who had settled in the province in 1908,

rejected the authority of the state. They did not register births, deaths and marriages, and they refused to send their children to school. By the 1950s, the Doukhobors had divided into two groups. The larger community was becoming more inclined to make compromises to comply with provincial and federal laws; but the Sons of Freedom, determined fundamentalists, were prepared to go to almost any lengths to defy authority.

In the past, attempts to force Doukhobor children to attend school had failed: parents paid fines for refusing to enrol their children and several Kootenay schools were destroyed in mysterious fires. In 1953, the province's attorney general decided to use the terms of the Public Schools Act and the Protection of Children Act to apprehend all Doukhobor children between the ages of seven and fifteen who were not receiving an approved form of education. At Perry's Siding, as their parents paraded naked in protest, more than a hundred children were taken into custody. The RCMP were sent to search other villages, where they seized children hidden in attics and crawl spaces, in cow barns and chicken houses. Among the children apprehended was Fred Conkin: "You don't speak English. You don't know why it's happening. Kids are screaming. You're crying." The children were taken to a dormitory in New Denver and held there until their parents consented to acceptable schooling.

By 1960, most Doukhobors had agreed to comply with the government, and the New Denver facility was closed. But the Sons of Freedom fought back. Homes were burned. Power lines and railway bridges were bombed. An attempt was made to blow up the Nelson courthouse, the site of the trials of those accused of various acts of terrorism. Protests petered out as the passing years reduced the power and passion of the older generation of leaders.

THE YEAR 1958 MARKED British Columbia's centennial, at least as far as mainlanders were concerned. Vancouver Islanders argued that the province of British Columbia had begun with the establishment of the

Mungo Martin, a Kwak-waka'wakw chief and carver, holds a ceremonial "copper" (a symbol of wealth and rank) to be presented, along with the totem pole he carved, as a gift to Her Majesty Queen Elizabeth II, to mark British Columbia's centennial in 1958.

Doukhobor parents were permitted to visit their children, housed at the New Denver School Dormitory, every other Sunday—but only through the chain-link fence.

Colony of Vancouver Island in 1849. Alternatively, the beginning might be traced to the union of the two colonies in 1866. Pegging the centennial to the establishment of the junior colony made very little sense. But the celebrations went ahead, and, in the public mind, it became a historical fact that British Columbia began with the gold rush.

As it happened, a very different event in 1958, more memorable than any centennial celebrations, seared itself into the public memory. In 1956, work had begun in Vancouver on a new, $19-million Second Narrows Bridge—a massive structure of concrete and steel, 4,180 feet long and carrying six lanes of traffic—the second-largest cantilever span in Canada. On 17 June 1958, seventy-nine men were working on the span, the weight of which was supported by a series of temporary structures. Suddenly, without warning, the bridge collapsed. Ironworker Bill Stroud dropped "like a cannonball" into the waters of the inlet 100 feet below. Painter Anthony Romaniuk found himself underwater, strapped to a girder. Another workman rode down with a girder, came to rest a few feet above the water and

Eighteen men died when the Second Narrows Bridge collapsed in June 1958. The bridge opened to traffic in 1960, a year behind schedule. In 1994, it was renamed the Ironworkers Memorial Bridge.

then looked down to discover that one of his legs had been severed above the knee. Eighteen men were killed: some crushed by mangled steel, others drowned in the fast-moving current. One man's body was never found. An investigation determined that an engineer had miscalculated the load the temporary structure could support. He had made a simple mathematical mistake, and his supervisor had not caught it. Both men were on the bridge when it collapsed. Neither survived.

During the 1960s, some British Columbians began to question the headlong development and urbanization of the post-war years. The Bennett Dam, for instance, had not brought the hoped-for prosperity to the north. During its construction, local workers had been told that they lacked the required experience and then watched as the best jobs went to imported workmen. And Williston Lake, rather than providing a new recreational resource, was a mass of dangerous stumps and floating logs.

The province's resources, once perceived as limitless and inexhaustible, were beginning to be seen as finite and threatened. In the Fraser Valley and the Okanagan, farmland was being paved over by urban sprawl. In the Cariboo and the Chilcotin, rangeland was suffering from overgrazing. Logging companies were moving into sensitive wilderness areas. Mining companies were ravaging the landscape and fouling rivers but leaving little compensatory profit behind.

By the end of the decade, there were other signs that the times were changing. "Ban the Bomb" marches had given way to anti–Vietnam War protests. American draft dodgers became the province's newest immigrants. Young people were rejecting their parents' standards. Marijuana

"To try to convince him [W. A. C. Bennett] that there was something beyond highways, beyond power megaprojects, beyond the physical things you can build with bulldozers, was impossible . . . There was no human face on the government."
—Jack Webster

Cool-Aid in Vancouver, 1970. When young people began to travel across the country, some communities reacted with alarm. After Victoria's mayor suggested that long-haired hippies be prevented from disembarking from B.C. Ferries, less excitable citizens formed Cool-Aid to provide shelter and other care for young travellers.

and LSD seemed to be shouldering aside nicotine and alcohol as the social drugs of choice. For the first time, people were becoming aware of the effects of pollution.

By 1972, W. A. C. Bennett had been in office for twenty years, the longest term of any British Columbia premier. He had lost touch with the public mood. Criticism of the government's megaprojects and its apparent lack of interest in environmental matters was mounting. In the past, Bennett had greeted complaints about pulp mill pollution with a jovial "That's the smell of money, my friend." Now, such a response had lost its charm. It was time for a change.

Traditionally, Bennett had fought elections by stirring up fear of the "godless socialists" and their alliance with organized labour, official since 1961, when the CCF was restructured as the New Democratic Party (NDP). But in 1972, he faced an unusual adversary: Dave Barrett, a beaming, bouncy, former social worker, did not seem threatening at all. "Little fat Dave" met Bennett's bluster with humour. When the premier accused him of being a follower of Marx, Barrett grinned: "Which Marx would that be? Groucho? Harpo? Zeppo?" It was hard to equate Barrett's good-natured teasing with Bennett's warning, "The socialist hordes are at the gates!"

The NDP won the election and became the first socialist government in British Columbia's history. Soon, Dave Barrett demonstrated just how much the times had changed. In the summer of 1973, the new premier attended the Williams Lake Stampede and entered the "bull throwing" contest, in which contestants hurled dried cow dung into the distance; he smiled broadly when he was named the "Number One B.S. Thrower" in the province.

From 1972 to 1975, the NDP government released a flood of legislation. The labour code was revamped, civil servants were given the right to strike, seniors were given a guaranteed income. The hourly minimum wage was raised from $2 to $2.50 and then $2.75. Liquor laws were liberalized to allow for neighbourhood pubs. Pharmacare was introduced. Logging companies and sawmills were purchased and operated by Crown corporations. Farmland was protected by the Agricultural Land Reserve. A Rentalsman's office was created to protect tenants. And the Insurance Corporation of British Columbia was formed to do away with the inequities of private insurance. Ambitious new programs resulted in a 28 per cent increase in the number of civil servants. The provincial budget soared, from $1.2 billion in Bennett's 1972 budget to $3.2 billion in 1975.

"It seemed to happen very quickly that environmental groups like SPEC and Greenpeace became forces to be reckoned with . . . The euphoria of the megaprojects was ending . . . Public critics were questioning the need for new generation and transmission projects and their impact on the environment. They were also asking about the increasing use of energy."
—Jim McCarthy, B.C. Hydro

Facing page: Now an international environmental organization, Greenpeace was formed in Vancouver in 1970 to protest American nuclear weapons tests under Amchitka Island in the Aleutians by sailing *Phyllis Cormack* into the test range. Later, Greenpeace launched an anti-whaling campaign, using *Phyllis Cormack* to harass whaling fleets.

This page: Dave Barrett (right), premier of British Columbia from 1972 to 1975, was known for his good humour and for his determination to put working people before corporations. Broadcaster Jack Webster claimed, "It was the first human government in B.C."

THE POST-WAR "can-do" energy, so apparent in the province's politicians and engineers, also infused its artists and writers. More and more of them began finding their inspiration in British Columbia, challenging the notion of art or literature or theatre or dance as being strictly rooted in European conventions. Over the next decades, the arts scene grew with the opening of galleries, art schools, theatres and publishing houses. The province is now home to talented and acclaimed artists in every field, but the ones mentioned here are those whose key works explore themes of place and identity in British Columbia.

Visual Artists

In 1951, the ban on the potlatch was finally lifted, and First Nations artistic traditions associated with the potlatch, such as the carving of ceremonial poles and masks, surfaced again. Under the aegis of the Museum of Anthropology at the University of British Columbia (and later at the provincial museum), Kwakwaka'wakw carver Mungo Martin headed an ambitious program to carve more than a dozen replica poles. He also created his own original poles and masks. Working with him was a group of apprentices that included Bill Reid and Henry Hunt, two artists who would also play leading roles in the growth of aboriginal art

that followed. Today, there is a large and growing body of Native artists, some traditional, others working in more fusion-driven or conceptual forms; many of them have achieved international reputations. These include Freda Diesing, Robert Davidson and Reg Davidson (Haida); Norman Tait (Nisga'a); Richard Hunt and Tony Hunt (Kwakwaka'wakw); Joe David and Art Thompson (Nuu-chah-nulth), Dempsey Bob (Tahltan-Tlingit), Walter Harris (Gitxsan) and Don Yeomans (Haida-Cree). Recently, they have been joined by Susan A. Point (Coast Salish), Jim Hart (Haida), Tim Paul (Nuu-chah-nulth) and Lawrence Paul Yuxweluptun

(Coast Salish–Okanagan), who are continuing with tradition as well as pushing its boundaries.

Also in the 1950s, a number of non-Native artists were inspired to take up uniquely British Columbia themes. Most notable are Jack Shadbolt and Gordon Smith, many of whose abstract works are based on themes of nature; B. C. Binning and E. J. Hughes, whose works express a love of boats and the seascape; Takao Tanabe, who is known as "the poet of the ocean shore"; and Sybil Andrews, whose modernist prints drew on life in Campbell River. Artists Toni Onley and Robert Bateman continued to make paintings with natural and environmental themes.

The 1960s and 1970s saw the emergence of conceptual artists such as Iain and Ingrid Baxter, whose photos of the Pacific National Exhibition and family picnics in Vancouver set a new ironic tone; and Gathie Falk, a painter and installation artist whose work also reflected a new way of perceiving the West Coast. The past two decades have been marked by the growth of a group of internationally celebrated conceptual photographers. Working with specifically British Columbia settings are Jeff Wall's posed tableaux set in Vancouver, Stan Douglas's multimedia piece on the town of Ruskin, B.C., Ian Wallace's piece on the Clayoquot Sound anti-logging protests; and Rodney Graham, Roy Arden and Ken Lum's various works on local themes.

Writers of Fiction

In 1947, Ethel Wilson published her first novel, *Hetty Dorval*; all of her works were set either in Vancouver or remote regions of the province. In the 1950s, Hubert Evans produced *Mist on the River*, on the theme of Native people in conflict with white society; Howard O'Hagan published short stories about wilderness characters and Rocky Mountain settings; and Sheila Watson wrote *The Double Hook*, set in the Cariboo and heralded as "the first truly modern Canadian novel."

The Raven and the First Men by Bill Reid at the University of British Columbia Museum of Anthropology.

Butterfly Transformation Theme by Jack Shadbolt, in the collection of Laing and Kathleen Brown.

In the 1960s and 1970s, the establishment of local publishing firms encouraged many writers. Paul St. Pierre wrote *The Breaking of Smith's Quarter Horse*, which took place in the Cariboo-Chilcotin; Robert Harlow began his trilogy set in a fictional town modelled on Prince George; the prolific George Bowering wrote poetry and fiction based on the province's history; Keith Maillard debuted with his provocative novel *Two Strand River*, set in Vancouver; and Jack Hodgins published *The Invention of the World*, the first of his remarkable novels about Vancouver Island life.

In the 1980s, Jane Rule turned her attention to writing novels that took place in Vancouver; Audrey Thomas published *Intertidal Life*, a novel set on the Gulf Islands; George McWhirter wrote *Paula Lake*, a novel about an errant lifeguard in Vancouver; L. R. Wright produced *The Suspect*, the first of her mysteries set on the Sunshine Coast and featuring an RCMP officer; and Lawrence Gough also began a crime series, his being set in Vancouver. In the 1990s, there was Marilyn Bowering's novel, *To All Appearances a Lady*, about the British and Chinese on the West Coast; Linda Svendsen's dark short stories in *Marine Life* were informed by the coast; Keath Fraser's novel *Popular Anatomy* treated Vancouver as "a slightly decadent place"; and Vi Plotnikoff's *Head Cook at Weddings and Funerals"*

explored Doukhobor culture in the 1950s; Douglas Coupland's short story collection *Polaroids from the Dead* included one titled "Lions Gate Bridge," set in Vancouver; and Michael Turner's novel *The Pornographer's Poem* is set in 1970s Vancouver.

Asian-Canadian novelists rose to the fore in the 1980s and 1990s: Joy Kogawa's *Obasan* was about the Japanese in internment camps during the Second World War, SKY Lee's *Disappearing Moon Cafe* and Wayson Choy's *The Jade Peony* were both set in Vancouver's Chinatown, and Larissa Lai's *When Fox Is a Thousand* linked a ninth-century poet/nun with a modern young Chinese-Canadian woman in Vancouver.

At the same time, Aboriginal writers and books came to public attention. These include Jeannette Armstrong's *Slash*, the realistic, gritty story of an Okanagan Native youth; and Lee Maracle's *Ravensong*, chronicling a flu epidemic in a coastal Native village. More recently, Richard Van Camp published *The Lesser Blessed* about the friendship of two boys, one Native, the other white; and Eden Robinson wrote about modern Haisla life in *Traplines* (short stories) and *Monkey Beach* (a novel).

Writers of Literary Non-Fiction
In the post-war years, Roderick Haig-Brown continued to produce books about the joys of angling

and the importance of nature in British Columbia; the prolific George Woodcock wrote a travel book about the province, *Ravens and Prophets*. In the 1960s, Native artist George Clutesi wrote *Son of Raven, Son of Deer* (myths of the Tseshaht) and *Potlatch*; and M. Wylie Blanchet published her classic *The Curve of Time,* about sailing the coast with her children. More recently, anthropologist Hugh Brody wrote about the dream maps, land use and hunting traditions of the Dunne-za in *Maps and Dreams*; Edith Iglauer described life with her commercial fisherman husband in *Fishing with John*; Denise Chong (*The Concubine's Children*) and Wayson Choy (*Paper Shadows*) both published memoirs of Vancouver's Chinatown; Evelyn Lau chronicled her experiences as a young prostitute in Vancouver in *Runaway: Diary of a Street Kid,* launching a career as a poet and fiction writer; Robert Bringhurst completed *A Story as Sharp as a Knife: The Classical Haida Mythtellers and Their World*; Gregory Scofield wrote *Thunder through My Veins: Memoirs of a Metis Childhood*; and Terry Glavin published *The Last Great Sea: A Voyage through the Human and Natural History of the North Pacific Ocean*.

Poets
In the 1950s, Earle Birney began his career with many long poems about place, including *The*

Damnation of Vancouver (he later founded the Department of Creative writing at the University of British Columbia); and Robin Skelton published *Patmos and Other Poems*. In the 1960s, Patrick Lane began publishing his poems about logging, Native people and hunting, particularly *Mountain Oysters*; Lionel Kearns made his debut, later making his mark with *Convergences*, on the impact of Captain Cook on the Native people of Nootka Sound; and George Bowering launched his prolific career, including *Rocky Mountain Foot, George Vancouver* and *Kerrisdale Elegies*. The 1970s saw the debuts of Susan Musgrave, whose writing is permeated by West Coast themes, with *Songs of the Sea-witch*; Peter Trower, the "logger-poet," whose books include *Between the Sky and the Splinters*; Tom Wayman, whose *Waiting for Wayman* was the first of his many collections on work and workers' lives; Daphne Marlatt, whose works include *Steveston* (based on the oral history of that town); Florence McNeil, whose collections such as *Walhachin* and *Barkerville* are about historical figures and places; and George McWhirter, whose later *The Island Man* is set on Vancouver Island, charged with motifs on the early Spanish explorers. In 1982, Phyllis Webb won the Governor General's Award for her collection *The Vision Tree*. More recent are Charles Lillard's "intensely local"

Shadow Weather; the debut of métis poet Gregory Scofield with *The Gathering: Stones for the Medicine Wheel*; Kate Braid's two collections about Emily Carr, *To This Cedar Fountain* and *Inward to the Bones*; and Michael Turner's *Company Town,* about a fictitious salmon cannery, and *Kingsway,* about a street in Vancouver.

Writers of Books for Children

In the 1950s and 1960s, Catherine Anthony Clark and Christie Harris presented Native history or themes in a number of their popular novels for children. In 1986, Sarah Ellis began her career writing fiction set in Vancouver (*Pick-up Sticks* won the 1991 Governor General's Award); also in 1986, Joy Kogawa published *Naomi's Road* about a Japanese-Canadian child in a wartime internment camp. In the 1990s, Paul Yee began publishing books set in Vancouver's Chinatown and stories about the Chinese immigrant experience in British Columbia; and Native writer Shirley Sterling wrote *My Name Is Seepeetza*, a novel exploring the hardships of life in a residential school.

Dramatists

In 1967, playwright George Ryga's *The Ecstasy of Rita Joe* dared to confront British Columbians with a gritty local theme about Native-White relations. That same year saw the staging of Gwen Ringwood's musical play *The Road Runs North*, based on the Cariboo gold rush, written for the Williams Lake centennial. Plays produced in the 1970s and 1980s include Sharon Pollock's *The Komagata Maru*, inspired by the historical incident, and *One Tiger to a Hill*, based on a New Westminster prison hostage-taking; and Margaret Hollingsworth's *Mother Country*, about the Britishness of people on an island off the coast. Headlines Theatre has long been involved in issued-based theatre, beginning with *Buy, Buy Vancouver* (in 1981, on the crisis in affordable housing); they have gone on to work with a number of Native groups to produce plays such as *No'xya'—Our Footprints* (in 1987, on land claims) and

Sheer Drop—Mountain Goats by Robert Bateman.

Reclaiming Our Spirits (in 1995, about residential schools), as well as *Mamu: The Currency of Life* (in 1994, on biodiversity and logging). In the 1990s, Joan McLeod won acclaim for her plays—including *Amigo's Blue Guitar* (a Governor General's Award winner in 1991)—which incorporate regional material. *The River—Home*, Native actor/director Margo

Kane's interdisciplinary performance piece, explored the relationship between Native peoples and rivers.

Filmmakers

The 1980s finally saw the creation of strongly regional films, including Phil Borsos's ground-breaking *The Grey Fox*, about outlaw Bill Miner's activities in southern

British Columbia, and Sandy Wilson's *My American Cousin*, which took place in the Okanagan. Building on the success of independent local films and filmmakers in the 1990s were: *The Lotus Eaters* (director Paul Shapiro, screenplay Peggy Thompson), set in the Gulf Islands; Mina Shum's *Double Happiness,* which took place in the alternate and Chinese communities in Vancouver; Bruce McDonald's *Hard Core Logo,* based on Michael Turner's book of poetry about a Vancouver punk band; *Rupert's Land* (director Jonathan Tammuz, screenplay Graeme Manson); Bruce Sweeney's *Dirty*; and *My Father's Angel* (director Davor Marjanovic, screenplay Frank Borg).

Television

In 1958, CBC television in Vancouver began production of its first drama series, *Cariboo Country,* which was based on stories by Paul St. Pierre and set in the ranching country of the Chilcotin. Another CBC series, *The Beachcombers,* was set on the Sunshine Coast; it ran from 1971 to 1991 and won international popularity. *DaVinci's Inquest,* which explores social issues from the point of view of a Vancouver coroner, was broadcast by the CBC beginning in 1999.

Dancers

In the 1970s, Norbert Vesak choreographed a dance based on George Ryga's play about Native-White relations, *The Ecstasy of Rita Joe*; Anna Wyman created *Klee Wyck* to expore the spirituality of Emily Carr's paintings; and Paula Ross (who is part Native) created *Coming Together,* about the effects of imprisonment on Native men. In the 1980s, Renald Rabu produced *The Creation of Eve,* inspired by Tsimshian artist Roy Vickers's depiction of the Eden story in the Northwest Coast art style, with costumes by Vickers; and Kokoro Dance presented *Rage,* about the repercussions of the Japanese internment during the war. In the 1990s, Karen Jamieson collaborated with First Nations groups to create cross-cultural works such as *Meek Ax/Gawa Gyani* and *The River*; JumpStart made *Deep West,* on the theme of the brutality of nature in the rain forest; Mascall Dance presented a look at Emily Carr's life in *The Brutal Telling,* for which they commissioned music by Veda Hille; and Judith Marcuse at DanceWorks workshopped and presented the community-based multimedia *ICE* and *FIRE* for teenage audiences.

Composers

In the 1950s, Jean Coulthard began composing pieces to capture in music "the varied moods of the West Coast" as Emily Carr had in her paintings, particularly in *The Pines of Emily Carr* (1969); the third movement of her orchestral suite *Canada Mosaic* (1974) is derived from fragments of a Coast Salish song about a Native figure painted by Carr. Barbara Pentland began her career at about the same time and in particular wrote three pieces—including the opera *The Lake*—to the words of British Columbia poet Dorothy Livesay. Recently, Hildegard Westerkamp, who works only with environmental sounds, produced pieces such as *Voices for the Wilderness* (on the Stein Valley), *Harbour Symphony* (for over 100 boat horns in Vancouver harbour) and *At the Edge of Wilderness* (on ghost towns in the Interior); singer-songwriter Veda Hille released her album *Here Is a Picture,* inspired by Emily Carr's art and life; Bruce Ruddell scored Haida artist Bill Reid's words on his sculpture *The Spirit of Haida Gwai*; and Michael Conway Baker composed pieces inspired by place, including *Vancouver Variations* and *Through the Lions Gate.*

Architects

In the post-war building boom, established architects such as Ned Pratt and B. C. Binning were joined by Ron Thom; they were interested in creating modern designs suited to British Columbia's climate, setting and lifestyle. The firm of Thompson, Berwick, Pratt designed B.C. Hydro buildings in 1950s in Victoria and Vancouver, and more than two hundred schools in the province. The next decade saw the emergence of Arthur Erickson (Simon Fraser University, the Museum of Anthropology, Robson Square) and Frank Musson (Bentall Centres in Victoria and Vancouver, Canada Place and the Daon Building in Vancouver). The firm of Downs Archambault, whose goal is to relate human use to structure and to incorporate natural materials, also achieved prominence. In the 1970s, Blue Sky Architecture began designing homes for island and mountain settings, taking into account theories of ecology and topography; in the 1980s, Richard Henriquez made playful references to a site's history in projects like the Eugenia Place apartment building in Vancouver. More recently, John and Patricia Patkau have concentrated on "sustainable" architecture integrated with locale and culture.

Now, at the beginning of the twenty-first century, it is hard to believe that there was a time when theatre relied on imported plays, when artists and writers did not use the province as inspiration for themes and settings in their work, when British Columbians had not been interested in their own place, heritage and culture.

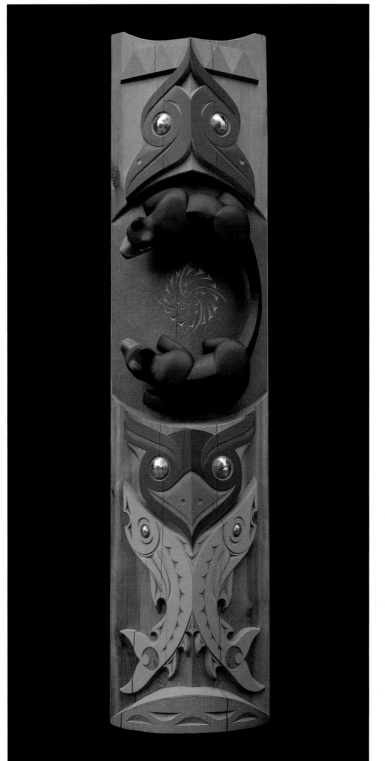

The River by Susan A. Point, Spirit Wrestler Gallery.

Originally valued at $6, BCRIC shares rose to $9 and then sank like a stone.

In November 1975, when Barrett surprised British Columbians by calling an election, his Socred opponent was Bill Bennett, son of the former premier. The campaign launched by the Socreds and the Conservatives against the NDP was among the most negative the province had ever seen. The Agricultural Land Reserve was interpreted as a communist plot to take over all privately held land. The sheriff's service, initiated to relieve police of the responsibility of guarding courtrooms and transferring prisoners, was described as "an armed secret police force."

Bill Bennett and the Social Credit Party won the election and began to unpick the socialist legislation. The Crown corporations that ran NDP-acquired resource companies were disbanded and their holdings rolled into the British Columbia Resources Investment Corporation (BCRIC). Every British Columbian was given five BCRIC ("brick") shares. That accounted for 10 million shares. The remaining 80 million were offered for sale at $6 each. The premier encouraged people to keep their free shares and to buy more, and many followed his advice, but after a giddy rise to $9, BCRIC shares sank like a stone.

Bennett emerged unscathed by the BCRIC debacle, more than ready to meet the problems of declining revenues and mounting costs. He instituted wage restrictions on government employees, and he cut funding for education and health, and the public rewarded him with a second term.

In 1983, shortly after the election that brought the Socreds a third term in power, Bill Bennett announced that British Columbians must practise restraint. To help them along, the government introduced legislation to limit collective agreement wage increases to a maximum of 5 per cent, to cancel the government's contract with the B.C. Government Employees Union, to reduce the number of public sector employees by 25 per cent, to abolish rent controls and to do away with the Human Rights Commission.

The government was not itself practising restraint, however. The premier decided to help Vancouver celebrate its hundredth birthday by hosting Expo 86, a world's fair with a transportation theme. To demonstrate that British

Tumbler Ridge was built in 1981 near Dawson Creek for the employees at two open-pit coal mines. Unlike the instant mining-boom towns that blossomed in the Cariboo in the 1860s and the Kootenays in the 1890s, Tumbler Ridge had the advantage of being well planned.

Columbia was up to date, he ordered a high-speed transportation system for the Lower Mainland and the construction of the Coquihalla Highway. The estimated cost of the Coquihalla was $375 million. By the time it was rushed to completion to coincide with Expo, the cost would reach $1 billion and British Columbians would be asked to take comfort from the fact that Expo had "put the province on the world map" and made of Vancouver a "world-class city."

The Coquihalla Highway, running from Hope to Merritt, operates as British Columbia's only toll highway.

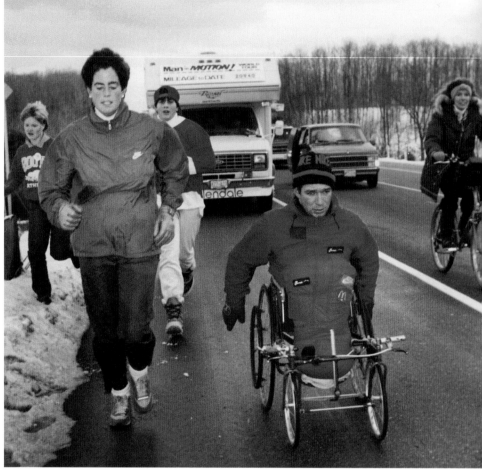

During the 1980s two young British Columbians became national heroes.

Left: In 1980, twenty-one-year-old Terry Fox, who had lost a leg to cancer, embarked on a cross-country run, a "Marathon of Hope," to raise funds for cancer research. He had run from St. John's, Newfoundland, to Thunder Bay, Ontario, when it was discovered that the disease had spread to his lungs. He was forced to abandon his marathon and died eight months later.

Right: In 1985, Rick Hansen, a paraplegic since an accident when he was fifteen, launched the "Man in Motion World Tour." He believed that if he propelled his wheelchair around the world, he would stimulate interest in spinal cord research and prove that people with disabilities were capable of great achievements. He succeeded on both counts.

Solidarity protesters march on 30 August 1983, holding home-made signs that draw attention to a number of issues.

Opposition to the restraint package was immediate. Trade unionists formed Operation Solidarity, adopting the name of the Polish opposition to Russian control. Other groups, from environmentalists to women's organizations to teachers, came together as the Solidarity Coalition. On 27 July, more than twenty thousand people gathered on the lawns of the legislative buildings to roar a protest. In August, a Solidarity rally packed Vancouver's Empire Stadium. In October, when Social Crediters gathered for their convention at the Hotel Vancouver, a parade of protesters, over sixty thousand strong, marched along the surrounding streets. On 1 November, thirty thousand government workers walked off the job. A week later, teachers and Crown corporation employees refused to report for work. Ferry workers were scheduled to go out next, followed by trade unionists.

For the first time in its history, British Columbia seemed to be on the brink of a general strike. But polls indicated that the majority of British Columbians stood solidly behind the premier. And the coalition was not so solid as it appeared: government employees were anxious to settle, teachers were beginning to return to work, ferry workers served notice that they would strike for only four hours. Labour leader Jack Munro met with Bill Bennett and hammered out the "Kelowna Accord," which changed very little but proved to be a face-saving exercise for both sides.

When Bill Bennett stepped down as leader of the Social Credit Party, William Vander Zalm astounded political observers by sweeping away more experienced contenders for the leadership. He served as premier from 1986 until 1991, and, during that time, people found reason to remember the

"Now that the effects of restraint are being widely felt, it is time to show compassion and introduce government-sponsored suicide clinics— where people who feel they cannot cope any longer could at least end their lives with some dignity."
—Rick Butcher

remarks made by leadership candidate Kim Campbell, who had warned Social Credit conventioneers: "Charisma without substance is a dangerous thing."

Premier Vander Zalm almost invited a general strike. His government introduced legislation to dissolve the province-wide teachers' union and replace it with smaller district unions, and to allow for the appointment of a premier's representative who would be empowered to end any labour dispute that threatened the "public interest." On 1 June 1987, a quarter of the province's labour force, an estimated three hundred thousand workers, staged a one-day strike. Schools and government offices remained closed, ferries did not leave their docks, buses did not leave their garages. No daily newspaper was printed. Mines, sawmills, pulp mills and canneries remained quiet.

The premier seemed unimpressed by this demonstration of muscle, and it was certainly not the power of the unions that brought him down. Rather, it was a series of scandals based on his inability to separate his role as a private businessman from his role as premier. His ultimate downfall involved the pending sale to an Asian billionaire of Fantasy Gardens, the theme park he had developed on the Fraser Delta. The conflict of interest commissioner suggested that, while there might not have been wrongdoing on the premier's part, there was certainly the appearance that he might be "beholden" to the potential purchaser. Forced to resign, Vander Zalm was replaced by Rita Johnston, the first woman to occupy the premier's chair. In the election of August 1991, Social Credit was swept from office and the NDP resumed power.

Whereas the first NDP government had pursued change with full-speed-ahead gusto, the one led by Mike Harcourt decided on a calm, cautious approach, calculated to smooth the divisiveness of the previous years. He was not overwhelmingly successful. In the summer of 1993, the government's

The 1993 protests to halt logging at Clayoquot Sound resulted in mass arrests and worldwide publicity for British Columbia's forest practices.

Tensions between loggers and environmentalists continued throughout the 1990s. At Squamish in 1997, loggers and their families and supporters formed a blockade to prevent environmentalists from entering the Squamish Valley.

new forest policy, designed to meet the goals of both loggers and environmentalists, came under attack. Attention was focussed on the old-growth forests of Vancouver Island's Clayoquot Sound. Thousands of people visited the sound that summer, and many joined the protesters who were attempting to block logging roads. Almost eight hundred people were arrested for disobeying the injunction secured by the logging company. As worldwide attention riveted on British Columbia and on the mass trials of protesters taking place in Victoria, a boycott of the province's forest products began to seem like a real possibility.

Premier Harcourt was determined to negotiate an equitable conclusion to Native land claims, and his NDP successors, Glen Clark in 1996 and Ujjal Dosanjh in 2000, followed the same course. The past was littered with lost opportunities, times when demands had been modest and the issue could have been settled. But now, the patience of the people, who had come to call themselves the province's First Nations, had worn thin. They approached the negotiating table with a new confidence, coupled with an edge of resentment produced by the abuses experienced by their people at residential schools.

When the system of residential boarding schools had been introduced by the federal government in 1890, the intentions were well-meaning. If Indians were to survive, the thinking at the time went, then they must be taught skills that would allow them to find a place in the wider world. At first, enrolment was voluntary. But in 1920, it was made compulsory, and efforts were redoubled to separate children from their parents and their culture. And that changed everything. Parents objected to the forcible removal

Top: In 1953, Premier W. A. C. Bennett had described the province's resources as "virtually limitless." During the 1970s, the public began to realize that that was not the case and by the 1990s, attention had focussed on the dwindling salmon stocks. At Prince Rupert in 1997, British Columbia fishboats blockaded the Alaska State Ferry *Malaspina* to protest American fishing of Canadian sockeye.

Bottom: Retiring Speaker of the House, Emery Barnes (left) with Premier Mike Harcourt (right) and Lieutenant-Governor David Lam. In 1972, American-born Barnes and Rosemary Brown became the first black people elected to the provincial legislature. A successful businessman and philanthropist, David Lam served as lieutenant-governor from 1988 to 1995, the first Chinese Canadian to hold the office.

of their children. Students grew up feeling cut off from their families. Their language and culture were made to seem worthless and foreign. And when some people in authority physically or sexually abused the isolated students, there was no one to whom the children could turn. Now, as Native leaders came to the negotiating table, many of them demanded that the federal government issue an official apology and provide compensation for its residential school policy.

On 16 July 1998, the federal and provincial governments signed a treaty with the Nisga'a nation, the terms of which gave fifty-five hundred Nisga'a sovereignty over 200,000 hectares of land and a cash payment of $200 million. Proponents lauded the treaty as a giant step toward First Nations' self-reliance and independence. Opponents insisted that the government was "giving away the farm" and that the treaty would produce "apartheid" and "entrench racism and inequality."

At New Aiyansh, elder Harry Moore led dancers celebrating the signing of the Nisga'a Treaty.

In December 2000, the Nuu-chah-nulth Tribal Council, representing about sixty-five hundred people, rejected the government's offer of $200 million and 34,000 hectares, and laid on the table their counter proposal: 333,600 hectares of land and $950 million in cash for the timber, fish and other resources already removed from their traditional territories. According to Nuu-chah-nulth negotiator George Watt, "This is probably the worst time in history for us to be negotiating a treaty."

But there he may be wrong. When the Nisga'a Treaty was signed, there were those who suspected that the past had weighed heavily on the negotiations and that the federal and provincial governments had acted out of "a profound sense of guilt" and had "made practical decisions for sentimental reasons." And perhaps that is true. But whatever happens, British Columbia's past will be sure to have a profound effect on its future.

"No longer beggars in our own lands, we now go forward with dignity."
—Chief Joseph Gosnell, Nisga'a Tribal Council

PHOTOGRAPH AND ILLUSTRATION CREDITS

SELECTED BIBLIOGRAPHY

c-07957 / 211: City of Trail Archives sp613 / 212: left, BCA D-05059 / 212-13: BCA PDP-02286.

CHAPTER 16

Page 214-15: BCA PDP-00931 / 216: Royal Victoria Yacht Club / 217: VPL 44965, The Province photo / 218: Maritime Museum of British Columbia 993.017.1959.02 / 219: BCA F-03697 / 221: BCA C-07293 / 222: VPL 1384, The Province photo / 223: top, NAC C-024452; bottom, BCA E-09913 / 225: BCA H-06875 / 226: Private Collection / 227: BCA F-09694 / 228: Penticton Museum and Archives / 229: Jack Lindsay photo 1048-1945P / 230: BCA PDP-03567.

CHAPTER 17

Page 231: Private Collection; 232: Private Collection / 233: BCA I-02030 / 234: BCA A-03925 / 235: BCA NA-09304 / 236: The Vancouver Sun / 237: BCA PDP-03239 / 238-39: Private Collection / 241: BCA G-01514 / 242: BCA H-03738 / 244: top, BCA H-01741; bottom, BCA C-08656 / 245: BCA I-27353 / 246: BCA I-27967 / 247: BCA D-01803.

CHAPTER 18

Pages 248-49: VPL 41563, The Province photo / 250: BCA I-51780 / 251: BCA C-01724 / 252: VPL 3042, The Province photo / 253: The Vancouver Sun, Ralph Bower photo / 254: The Vancouver Sun, Randy Thomas photo / 255: The Vancouver Sun, Steve Bosch photo / 256: Museum of Anthropology University of British Columbia, Bill McLennan photo / 257: courtesy Laing and Kathleen Brown Collection and Doris Shadbolt / 258: courtesy Robert Bateman and Mill Pond Press, Inc., Venice, Florida 34292-3500 / 259: courtesy Spirit Wrestler Gallery and Susan A. Point, Kenji Nagai photo / 260: top, The Vancouver Sun, Steve Bosch photo; bottom, The Vancouver Sun, Ian Smith photo / 261: The Vancouver Sun / 262: left, The Province, Colin Price photo; right, The Vancouver Sun, Rob Draper photo / 263: The Vancouver Sun, Brian Kent photo / 264: The Vancouver Sun, Brian Kent photo / 265: The Vancouver Sun, Rob Draper photo / 266: The Vancouver Sun, Mark van Manen photo / 267: The Vancouver Sun, Ian Smith photo / 268: top, The Vancouver Sun, Ian Smith photo; bottom, The Vancouver Sun, Ian Smith photo / 269: The Vancouver Sun, Ian Smith photo.

NEWSPAPERS

Bridge River–Lillooet News
Cariboo Sentinel
Enderby Commoner
Inland Sentinel
Nanaimo Free Press
New Westminster Columbian
Vancouver News-Advertiser
Vancouver Province
Vancouver Sun
Vancouver World
Vernon News
Victoria Colonist
Victoria Gazette
Victoria Times
Williams Lake Tribune

BOOKS AND ARTICLES

Adachi, Ken. *The Enemy That Never Was: A History of the Japanese Canadians.* Toronto: McClelland & Stewart, 1976.

Akrigg, G. P. V., and Helen B. Akrigg. *British Columbia Chronicle, 1778–1846.* Vancouver: Discovery Press, 1975.

———. *British Columbia Chronicle, 1847–1871.* Vancouver: Discovery Press, 1977.

Andrews, C. D. "Cominco and the Manhattan Project." In *British Columbia: Patterns in Economic, Political and Cultural Development,* edited by Dickson M. Falconer. Victoria: Camosun College, 1982.

Archer, Christon I. "Spanish Exploration and Settlement of the Northwest Coast in the 18th Century." In *Nu·tka·: Captain Cook and the Spanish Explorers on the Coast,* edited by Barbara S. Efrat and W. J. Langlois. Sound Heritage Series, vol. VII, no. 1. Victoria: Provincial Archives of British Columbia, 1978.

Arima, E. Y., Louis Clamhouse, Joshua Edgar, Charles Jones, John Thomas. "From Barkley Sound Southeast." In *Between Ports Alberni and Renfrew: Notes on West Coast Peoples.* Hull: Canadian Museum of Civilization, 1991.

B.C. Hydro Power Pioneers. *Gaslights to Gigawatts: A Human History of BC Hydro and Its Predecessors.* Vancouver: Hurricane Press, c. 1998.

Balf, Mary. *Kamloops: A History of the District up to 1914.* Kamloops: Kamloops Museum, 1989.

Balf, Ruth. *Kamloops 1914–1945.* Kamloops: Kamloops Museum, 1975.

Bancroft, Hubert Howe. *History of British Columbia.* San Francisco: The History Company, 1887.

Barman, Jean. *The West Beyond the West: A History of British Columbia.* Toronto: University of Toronto Press, 1991.

Barrett, Dave, and William Miller. *Barrett: A Passionate Political Life.* Vancouver/Toronto: Douglas & McIntyre, 1995.

Bayley, Charles. "Early Life on Vancouver Island." Typescript. British Columbia Archives, Victoria.

Belyk, Robert C. *John Tod: Rebel in the Ranks.* Victoria: Horsdal & Schubart, 1995.

Benson, Eugene, and William Toye, eds. *The Oxford Companion to Canadian Literature.* 2nd ed. Toronto: Oxford University Press Canada, 1997.

Berton, Pierre. *The Impossible Railway: The Building of the Canadian Pacific.* New York: Alfred A. Knopf, 1972.

Bolton, Herbert Eugene. *Fray Juan Crespi, Missionary Explorer of the Pacific Coast, 1769–1774.* 1927. Reprint, New York: AMS Press, 1971.

Boudreau, Jack. *Crazy Man's Creek.* Prince George: Caitlin Press, 1998.

Bowen, Lynne. *Boss Whistle: The Coal Miners of Vancouver Island Remember.* Lantzville: Oolichan, 1981.

Bowes, Gordon E., ed. *Peace River Chronicles.* Vancouver: Prescott Publishing, 1963.

British Columbia. Executive Council. Typescript of interview, 3 March 1911.

———. Papers relating to Censor of Motion Pictures.

———. Papers relating to Enemy Aliens.

———. *Papers Connected with the Indian Land Question, 1850–1875.* Victoria: Government Printer, 1875.

———. Papers Relating to Prohibition Act.

———. Report of the Superintendent of Indian Affairs, 1873.

Broadfoot, Barry. *Years of Sorrow, Years of Shame: The Story of the Japanese Canadians in World War II.* Toronto: Doubleday, 1977.

Brodie, Steve. *Bloody Sunday.* Vancouver: Young Communist League, 1974.

Browne, Colin. *Motion Picture Production in British Columbia: 1898–1940.* Victoria: British Columbia Provincial Museum, 1979.

Bulman, T. Alex. *Kamloops Cattlemen.* Victoria: Sono Nis Press, 1972, 1993.

Busch, Briton C., and Barry M. Gough, eds. *Fur Traders from New England: The Boston Men in the North Pacific, 1787–1800.* Spokane: Arthur H. Clark, 1997.

Cannings, Sydney, and Richard Cannings. *Geology of British Columbia: A Journey through Time.* Vancouver: Greystone, 1999.

Cash, Gwen. *A Million Miles from Ottawa.* Toronto: Macmillan of Canada, 1942.

Casoro, Victor. *Okanagan History.* 60th Report, Okanagan Historical Society, 1996.

Cheadle, Walter B. *Cheadle's Journal of a Trip Across Canada, 1862–1863.* 1931. Reprint, Edmonton: M. G. Hurtig, 1971.

Chittenden, Newton H. *Travels in British Columbia.* 1882. Reprint, Vancouver: Soules, 1984.

Dempsey, Hugh A., ed. *The CPR West: The Iron Road and the Making of a Nation.* Vancouver/Toronto: Douglas & McIntyre, 1984.

Doyle, James, ed. *Yankees in Canada: A Collection of Nineteenth-Century Travel Narratives.* Downsview: ECW Press, 1980.

Duthie, D. W., ed. *A Bishop in the Rough: Rev. J. Sheepshanks.* London: n.p., 1909.

Efrat, Barbara S., and W. J. Langlois, ed. "The Contact Period as Recorded by Indian Oral Traditions." In *Nu·tka·: Captain Cook and the Spanish Explorers on the Coast,* edited by Barbara

S. Efrat and W. J. Langlois. Sound Heritage Series, vol. VII, no. 1. Victoria: Provincial Archives of British Columbia, 1978.

Elliot, Marie. "The Japanese of Mayne Island." *B.C. Historical News* (fall 1990).

Falconer, Dickson M., ed. *British Columbia: Patterns in Economic, Political and Cultural Development.* Victoria: Camosun College, 1982.

Favrholdt, Ken. "Air Raid Precautions," 1 November 1981. Typescript. Kamloops Archives.

———. "Fur Trade Trails Through British Columbia." Typescript. Kamloops Archives.

Fedorak, Charles John. "The United States Consul in Victoria and the Political Destiny of the Colony of British Columbia, 1862–1870." *BC Studies* (fall 1988).

Finlayson, Roderick. "History of Vancouver Island and the Northwest Coast." Typescript. British Columbia Archives, Victoria.

Fish, Gordon, ed. *Dreams of Freedom: Bella Coola, Cape Scott, Sointula.* Sound Heritage Series, no. 36. Victoria: Provincial Archives of British Columbia, 1982.

Fisher, Robin. *Contact and Conflict: Indian-European Relations in British Columbia, 1774–1890.* Vancouver: University of British Columbia Press, 1977.

Gibson, James R. *The Lifeline of the Oregon Country: The Fraser-Columbia Brigade System, 1811–47.* Vancouver: University of British Columbia Press, 1997.

Goddard, Joan. "When Whales were Fair Game." *Frontier Days in British Columbia.* Langley: Sunfire, 1993.

Gough, Barry M. "Nootka Sound in James Cook's Pacific World." In *Nu·tka·: Captain Cook and The Spanish Explorers on the Coast*, edited by Barbara S. Efrat and W. J. Langlois. Sound Heritage Series, vol. VII, no. 1. Victoria: Provincial Archives of British Columbia, 1978.

———. *The Northwest Coast: British Navigation, Trade, and Discoveries to 1812.* Vancouver: University of British Columbia Press, 1992.

Grant, Rev. George M. *Ocean to Ocean: Sandford Fleming's Expedition through Canada in 1872.* Toronto: Radisson Society, 1925.

Greater Vernon Museum and Archives. *Valley of Dreams.* Vernon: Greater Vernon Museum and Archives, 1992.

Griffin, Geo. Butler, trans. and ed. *Diary of Fray Tomas de la Pena.* Documents from the Sutro Collection. Los Angeles: Historical Society of Southern California, 1891.

Haig-Brown, Roderick. *The Living Land.* Toronto: Macmillan of Canada, 1961.

Harris, Cole. *The Resettlement of British Columbia.* Vancouver: University of British Columbia Press, 1998.

Hayes, James H. "Kelowna in World War One." 61st Report, Okanagan Historical Society, 1997.

Henry, Tom. *Small City in a Big Valley: The Story of Duncan.* Madeira Park: Harbour, 1999.

Higgins, David. *The Mystic Spring.* Toronto: Briggs, 1904.

Holliday, Charles W. *The Valley of Youth.* Caldwell, Idaho: Caxton, 1948.

Hosie, John. "James Charles Stuart and His Expedition to the North-West Coast of America in 1786." In *Fourth Report and Proceedings.* N.p.: British Columbia Historical Association, 1929.

Howay, F. W. "Early Shipping in Burrard Inlet: 1863–1870." *British Columbia Historical Quarterly* (January 1937).

Hutcheson, Sydney. *Depression Stories.* Vancouver: New Star Books, 1976.

Hutchison, Bruce. *The Far Side of the Street.* Toronto: Macmillan of Canada, 1976.

Ireland, Willard E. "The Annexation Petition of 1869." *British Columbia Historical Quarterly* (October 1940).

Johns, Harold Percival. "British Columbia's Campaign for Better Terms, 1871–1907." Master's thesis, University of British Columbia, 1935.

Johnson, Barney Leitch. "Recollections." Typescript. City of Vancouver Archives.

Johnson, R. Byron. *Very Far West Indeed: A Few Rough Experiences on the North-West Pacific Coast.* 1872. Reprint, London: Samson Lowe, Marston, Lowe & Searle, 1985.

Jordan, Rosa, and Derek Choukalos. *Rossland: The First 100 Years.* Rossland: Rossland Historical Museum Association, 1995.

Keeble, Sheila Mary. "The Search for Settlers: Some Aspects of British Columbia's Immigration Policy, 1872–1914." Master's thesis, University of Victoria, 1981.

Keddell, Georgina. *Ma Murray and the Newspapering Murrays.* Toronto: McClelland & Stewart, 1967.

Kennedy, Dorothy I. D., and Randy Bouchard. *Lillooet Stories.* Sound Heritage Series, vol. VI, no. 1. Victoria: Provincial Archives of British Columbia, 1977.

———. *Sliammon Life, Sliammon Lands.* Vancouver: Talonbooks, 1983.

Kilian, Crawford. *Go Do Some Great Thing.* Vancouver/Toronto: Douglas & McIntyre, 1978.

Kloppenborg, Anne, Alice Niwinski, Eve Johnson, R. Gruetter, eds. *Vancouver's First Century: A City Album, 1860–1960.* Vancouver: J. J. Douglas, 1977.

Kluckner, Michael. *M. I. Rogers, 1869–1965.* Vancouver: privately printed, 1987.

Laforet, Andrea, and Annie York. *Spuzzum: Fraser Canyon Histories, 1808–1939.* Vancouver: University of British Columbia Press, 1998.

Lai, David Chuenyan. *Chinatowns: Towns within Cities in Canada.* Vancouver: University of British Columbia Press, 1988.

Lamb, W. Kaye. "Early Lumbering on Vancouver Island. Part I: 1844–1855." *British Columbia Historical Quarterly* (January 1938).

———. "Early Lumbering on Vancouver Island. Part II: 1855–1866." *British Columbia Historical Quarterly* (April 1938).

———. "The Governorship of Richard Blanshard." *British Columbia Historical Quarterly* (January–April 1950).

———, ed. *The Journals and Letters of Sir Alexander Mackenzie.* Toronto: Macmillan of Canada, 1970.

———, ed. *Simon Fraser: Letters and Journals, 1806–1808.* Toronto: Macmillan of Canada, 1960.

———, ed. *Sixteen Years in the Indian Country: The Journal of Daniel Williams Harmon.* Toronto: Macmillan of Canada, 1957.

Macdonald, Bruce. *Vancouver: A Visual History.* Vancouver: Talonbooks, 1992.

McDonald, Robert A. J. *Making Vancouver, 1863–1913.* Vancouver: University of British Columbia Press, 1996.

Mackie, Richard. *Trading Beyond the Mountains: The British Fur Trade on the Pacific, 1793–1843.* Vancouver: University of British Columbia Press, 1997.

Marlatt, Daphne, and Carole Itter, eds. *Opening Doors: Vancouver's East End.* Sound Heritage Series, vol. VIII, nos. 1 and 2. Victoria: Provincial Archives of British Columbia, 1979.

Mayne, R.C. *Four Years in British Columbia and Vancouver Island.* London: n.p., 1862.

Mayse, Susan. *Ginger: The Life and Death of Albert Goodwin.* Madeira Park: Harbour, 1990.

Melrose, Robert. "Diary of Robert Melrose." *British Columbia Historical Quarterly* (July-October 1943).

Mitchell, David. *W. A. C. Bennett and the Rise of British Columbia.* Vancouver/Toronto: Douglas & McIntyre, 1983.

Mitchell, David, and Dennis Duffy, eds. *Bright Sunshine and a Brand New Country: Recollections of the Okanagan Valley, 1890–1914.* Sound Heritage Series, vol. VIII, no. 3. Victoria: Provincial Archives of British Columbia, 1979.

Miyazaki, Dr. M. *My Sixty Years in Canada.* Lillooet: privately printed, 1973.

Morley, Alan. *Vancouver: From Milltown to Metropolis.* Vancouver: Mitchell Press, 1961.

Morton, James. *The Enterprising Mr. Moody, the Bumptious Captain Stamp: The Lives and Colourful Times of Vancouver's Lumber Pioneers.* Vancouver: J. J. Douglas, 1977.

———. *In the Sea of Sterile Mountains: The Chinese in British Columbia.* Vancouver: J. J. Douglas, 1974.

Muckle, Robert J. *The First Nations of British Columbia.* Vancouver: University of British Columbia Press, 1998.

Nakano, Takeo Ujo. *Within the Barbed Wire Fence: A Japanese Man's Account of his Internment in Canada.* Toronto: University of Toronto Press, 1980.

Nicol, Eric. *Vancouver.* Toronto: Doubleday, 1970.

Ormsby, Margaret. *British Columbia: A History.* Toronto: Macmillan of Canada, 1958.

———. *Coldstream—Nulli Secundus.* Vernon: Corp. of District of Coldstream, 1990.

———. "Frederick Seymour, the Forgotten Governor." *BC Studies* (summer 1974).

Patenude, Branwen C. *Trails to Gold.* Victoria: Horsdal & Schubart, 1995.

Pethick, Derek. *First Approaches to the Northwest Coast.* Vancouver: J. J. Douglas, 1976.

———. *The Nootka Connection: Europe and the Northwest Coast, 1790–1795.* Vancouver/Toronto: Douglas & McIntyre, 1980.

Pioneer reminiscences. Fort George Museum and Archives.

Popp, Carol. *The Gumboot Navy: Memories of the Fishermen's Reserve.* Lantzville: Oolichan Books, 1988.

Reimer, Derek, ed. *The Gulf Islanders*. Sound Heritage Series, vol. V, no. 4. Victoria: Provincial Archives of British Columbia, 1976.

Reksten, Terry. *A Century of Sailing: Royal Victoria Yacht Club, 1892–1992*. Victoria: Orca, 1992.

———. *The Dunsmuir Saga*. Vancouver/Toronto: Douglas & McIntyre, 1991.

———. *The Empress Hotel: In the Grand Style*. Vancouver/Toronto: Douglas & McIntyre, 1997.

———. *"More English than the English": A Very Social History of Victoria*. Victoria: Orca, 1986.

———. *Rattenbury*. Victoria: Sono Nis, 1978, 1998.

Roberts, John E. *A Discovery Journal of George Vancouver's First Survey Season on the Coasts of Washington and British Columbia, 1791*. Victoria: privately printed, 1998.

Roberts, Morley. *The Western Avernus*. London: J. M. Dent, 1887, 1924.

Ross, Charles. "Five Letters of Charles Ross." *British Columbia Historical Quarterly* (April 1943).

Rothenburger, Mel. *The Chilcotin War*. Langley: Mr. Paperback, 1978.

———. *The Wild McLeans*. Victoria: Orca, 1993.

Roy, Patricia. *Vancouver: An Illustrated History*. Toronto: Lorimer, 1980.

———. *A White Man's Province*. Vancouver: University of British Columbia Press, 1989.

Roy, Reginald H. "From the Darker Side of Canadian Military History: Mutiny in the Mountains—The Terrace Incident." 47th Report, Okanagan Historical Society, 1983.

Ruhmann, William. "Soldiers of the Soil: Recollections—the Activities of Vernon Boys, 1914–1919." 47th Report, Okanagan Historical Society, 1983.

Runnalls, Rev. F. E. *A History of Prince George*. Prince George: n.p., 1946.

Scott, Andrew. *The Promise of Paradise: Utopian Communities in B.C.* Vancouver: Whitecap Books, 1997.

Scott, David, and Edna H. Hanic. *East Kootenay Saga*. New Westminster: Nunaga Publishing, 1974.

Shelford, Cyril. *From Snowshoes to Politics*. Victoria: Orca, 1987.

Slater, G. Hollis. "Rev. Robert John Staines: Pioneer Priest, Pedagogue, and Political Agitator." *British Columbia Historical Quarterly* (October 1950).

Smith, Dorothy Blakey, ed. "Harry Guillod's Journal of a Trip to the Cariboo, 1862." *British Columbia Historical Quarterly* (1955).

———. *Lady Franklin Visits the Pacific Northwest*. Victoria: Provincial Archives of British Columbia, 1974.

———. *The Reminiscences of Doctor John Sebastian Helmcken*. Vancouver: University of British Columbia Press, 1975.

Stanley, G. F. G., ed. *Mapping the Frontier: Charles Wilson's Diary*. Toronto: Macmillan of Canada, 1970.

Steele, Col. S. B. *Forty Years in Canada: Reminiscences of the Great North-West*. 1915. Reprint, Toronto: Coles, 1973.

Stern, Netta. *Fraser Gold, 1858!* Pullman: Washington State University Press, 1998.

Stevenson, Henry. "Balloon Bombs: Japan to North America." *B.C. Historical News* (summer 1995).

Stewart, Hilary. *The Adventures and Sufferings of John R. Jewitt: Captive of Maquinna*. Vancouver/Toronto: Douglas & McIntyre, 1987.

Stewart, John. "Tranquille," 1983. Typescript. Kamloops Archives.

Stursberg, Peter. *Those Were the Days*. Toronto: Peter Martin, 1969.

Stursberg, Peter, ed. *Extra! When the Papers had the Only News*. Sound Heritage Series, no. 35. Victoria: Provincial Archives of British Columbia, 1982.

Suttles, Wayne, ed. *Northwest Coast*. Vol. 7 of *Handbook of North American Indians*. Washington, D.C.: Smithsonian Institution, 1990.

Swannell, F. C. "Mackenzie's Expedition to the Pacific Ocean." In *Fourth Report and Proceedings*. N.p.: British Columbia Historical Association, 1929.

Taylor, G. W. *Timber: History of the Forest Industry in B.C.* Vancouver: J. J. Douglas, 1975.

Teit, James. *Traditions of the Thompson River Indians of British Columbia*. New York: Houghton, Mifflin, 1898.

Thom, Ian M. *Art BC: Masterworks from British Columbia*. Vancouver/Toronto: Douglas & McIntyre, 2000.

Thomas, Phillip J. *Songs of the Pacific Northwest*. Saanichton: Hancock House, 1979.

Tippett, Maria. *Emily Carr: A Biography*. Toronto: Oxford University Press, 1979.

Turnbull, Elsie G. *Ghost Towns and Drowned Towns of West Kootenay*. Surrey: Heritage House, 1988.

Turner, Robert D. *Railroaders: Recollections from the Steam Era in British Columbia*. Sound Heritage Series, no. 31. Victoria: Provincial Archives of British Columbia, 1981.

United States. Deptartment of State. Letters from War Department, 18 November 1867 to 29 January 1868.

Wade, Mark S. *The Cariboo Road*. Victoria: Haunted Bookshop, 1979.

Walbran, Captain John T. *British Columbia Coast Names*. 1909. Reprint, Vancouver/Toronto: Douglas & McIntyre, 1971.

Walkem, W. Wymond. *Stories of Early British Columbia*. Vancouver: News-Advertiser, 1914.

Walker, Alexander. *An Account of a Voyage to the North West Coast of America in 1785 & 1786*, edited by Robin Fisher and J. M. Bumsted. Vancouver/Toronto: Douglas & McIntyre, 1982.

Webber, Bert. *Retaliation: Japanese Attacks and the Allied Countermeasures on the Pacific Coast in World War II*. Corvallis: Oregon State University Press, 1976.

Webber, Jean. *A Rich and Fruitful Land: The History of the Valleys of the Okanagan, Similkameen and Shuswap*. Madeira Park: Harbour, 1999.

Webster, Jack. *Webster! An Autobiography*. Vancouver/Toronto: Douglas & McIntyre, 1990.

Weir, Joan. *Walhachin: Catastrophe or Camelot?* Surrey: Hancock House, 1995.

Weir, Winnifred Ariel. "Two Wars Viewed from Windemere, B.C." *B.C. Historical News* (fall 1990).

Wejr, Patricia, and Howie Smith, eds. *Fighting For Labour: Four Decades of Work in British Columbia, 1910–1950*. Sound Heritage Series, vol. VII, no. 4. Victoria: Provincial Archives of British Columbia, 1978.

Williams, David Ricardo. *Call in Pinkerton's*. Toronto: Dundurn Press, 1998.

———. *"The Man For A New Country": Sir Matthew Baillie Begbie*. Sidney: Gray's Publishing, 1977.

Williams, Judith. *High Slack*. Vancouver: New Star, 1996.

Wilson, J. W. *People in the Way*. Toronto: University of Toronto Press, 1973.

Woods, John G. *Snow War: An Illustrated History of Rogers Pass, Glacier National Park, B.C.* N.p.: Canadian Parks and Wilderness Society, 1992.

Wright, Robert Thomas. *Barkerville*. Williams Lake: Winter Quarters Press, 1998.

MAPS

Bawlf, Samuel. "Secret Voyage to B.C." *Vancouver Sun*, 5 August 2000, sec. B.

Gentilcore, R. Louis, and Matthews, Geoffrey J. *Historical Atlas of Canada*. Vol. II, *The Land Transformed, 1801-1891*. Plate 19. Toronto: University of Toronto Press, 1993.

Harris, R. Cole. *The Resettlement of British Columbia*. Figs. 2.2, 6.2 and 6.4. Vancouver: University of British Columbia Press, 1997.

Harris, R. Cole, and Matthews, Geoffrey J. *Historical Atlas of Canada*. Vol. I, *From the Beginning to 1800*. Plate 67. Toronto: University of Toronto Press, 1987.

Mackie, Richard. Trading Beyond the Mountains. Map 14. Vancouver: University of British Columbia Press, 1997.

Manitoba. "Hudson's Bay Company Archives Post Map, British Columbia." <http://www.gov.mb.ca/chc/archives/hbca/resource/cart-rec/postmap/bcnmap.html> (12 Nov. 2000).

Museum of Anthropology, University of British Columbia. "Map of First Nations of B.C." <http://www.moa.ubc.ca/Collections/FNBCpom/map.html> (12 Nov. 2000).

Smith, James K. *Wilderness of Fortune*. Maps "Explorers' Routes and Fur-trade Routes" and "Railways and Highways." Vancouver/Toronto: Douglas & McIntyre, 1983.

Woodcock, George. *British Columbia: A History of the Province*. Map "Historic Roads and Railways to 1918." Vancouver/Toronto: Douglas & McIntyre, 1990.

INDEX

Page references to captions are in *italic type*.